PRAISE FOR CALVIN MILLE

All the way from Vernon, Texas, to the uttermost parts of the world, Calvin Miller gleans the fields of his life to produce an amazing crop of humor, insight, revelation, romance, and pathos. Not your typical biography, this memoir is a must-read of total delight.

—Gloria Gaither, best-selling author
and award-winning songwriter

Calvin Miller unwraps the gift of miracles and lays it exposed for all of us to see and understand. And he does it perfectly while celebrating the wonder and mystery of God.

—Karen Kingsbury, best-selling author

When I pick up a memoir, it is not because I am hungry to learn the details of another person's life (although that sometimes helps, especially if the person turns out to be as irregular as I am). I pick up a memoir because I want to learn how other people come to their senses, learning to live the lives they have been given instead of the lives they might have planned. If they happen to write truthfully, with generosity and humor, then I also hope those virtues will rub off on me. Calvin Miller's book fills my cup. You can read him for the great stories he tells or read him for the great soul he is. Either way, he will show you the art of brinkmanship, inviting you to join him at the unsafe edges of human life where true joy is found.

—Barbara Brown Taylor, author of
Leaving Church: A Memoir of Faith

The writings of Calvin Miller have consistently stirred joy in my heart and brought focus to my faith. For over three decades, I have turned to his penned reflection for guidance. This new book is a welcome addition!

—Max Lucado, minister and
best-selling author

Calvin Miller has for a long time been one of our Christian community's best story tellers. This is one of his best: the richly textured narrative of his becoming a Christian, becoming a pastor, becoming a professor. None of these "becomings" easy; all of them poignant, painful, and praise-filled

—Eugene H. Peterson, author of
The Message

Calvin Miller's great gift is to sing Jesus powerfully, to the blessing of our generation and those to come.

—Dallas Willard, author of *The Divine Conspiracy*

This is a rollicking account of a rollicking life. Calvin Miller is a master of our language and all its idioms; hw is a literary stylist, a rare phenomenon in whatever circles one reads.

—Bill Griffin, editor, writer, and playwright

Calvin Miller is the Poet Laureate of today's Evangelical World. He has something profound to say, and he says it beautifully.

—Michael Duduit, editor of
Preaching

Life is Mostly Edges

A Memoir

Life is Mostly Edges

A Memoir

CALVIN MILLER

THOMAS NELSON
Since 1798

NASHVILLE DALLAS MEXICO CITY RIO DE JANEIRO BEIJING

Published in Nashville, Tennessee, by Thomas Nelson. Thomas Nelson is a registered trademark of Thomas Nelson, Inc.

Page Design by Casey Hooper

Thomas Nelson, Inc., titles may be purchased in bulk for educational, business, fund-raising, or sales promotional use. For information, please e-mail SpecialMarkets@ThomasNelson.com.

Unless otherwise noted, Scripture quotations are from the HOLY BIBLE: NEW INTERNATIONAL VERSION® (NIV). © 1973, 1978, 1984 by International Bible Society. Used by permission of Zondervan Publishing House. All rights reserved.

Scripture quotations marked KJV are from the King James Version of the Bible.

Library of Congress Cataloging-in-Publication Data

Miller, Calvin.
  Life is mostly edges : a memoir / Calvin Miller.
    p. cm.
  ISBN 978-0-7852-9798-7
  1. Miller, Calvin. 2. Christian biography. I. Title.
  BR1725.M44625A3 2008
  277.3'082092—dc22
  [B]

2008013237

Printed in the United States of America

08 09 10 11 12 QW 5 4 3 2 1

To Barbara, fellow sojourner and lifelong companion,
whose courage has taught me confidence,
whose insight has been a light in life's dark passages,
whose love strengthened me for the journey,
and whose buoyant spirit gave me wings
to soar above despair and name it joy.

Contents

Contents

PART THREE
THE PROFESSOR WHO LIKED TEACHING
BUT LOVED LEARNING
1991–2007

A Backward Glance at Up-Front Things

At the age of seventy-two, I have grown honest about the best years of my life. I have lived those years—all of them—past threescore and ten, knowing all along that this life was never mine. It has belonged all the way through to another.

Given the size of the universe, the world I have lived in is quite small, and I have lived it out mostly along its edges.

This is not surprising, for life is mostly edges. It is small—like a postage stamp. So small that it all but disappears against the busy days it devours.

My own small stamp has retained just enough sticky on its backside to adhere to the strongest of my memories. It comes dated with my long ago birthplace, but as of yet has no final return address. The time of my passing lies out ahead shrouded in the mists of things undefined. So the following account is all a matter of memory. It is this that makes my story shaky.

Memory arrives sometime after we get here, and generally abandons us long before we leave here. So the umbilical trot that squirts us into the world is unremembered, and the EKG we need to keep it all going is likely to abandon us too suddenly to allow us to write it all down before our passing.

Like the rest of the human race, I grew slowly to self-awareness on the fuzzy front edge of the stamp, and am now approaching the fuzzy back edge. I can neither remember getting here nor what I did after I got here. So I can't remember how old I was when I learned that my mother's name was Ethel and I had no knowable father. I can't even remember enough about life in the middle of the stamp to get the story exactly right. But all that follows herein is an actual account of my years, as faithfully recounted as I can remember them.

I do remember enough to know I liked the middle of my stamp more than the edges. This is not unusual. We all like the middle. The middle is safe. You can't fall off the middle. Only the edges are dangerous. The great lessons, the deep tragedies, the storms of unbearable heart-quakes always happen along the edges. We don't cry much in the middle, but then we don't laugh much there either—at least with any belly-deep laughter. Still, every day, nine to five, we suit up for the only contest that can be played along the unsafe edges of our years.

Brinkmanship is the name of the game.

We are all rather like the Buddhist monk—or was it a Sufi healer?—who in running from a lion ran directly into a bear. Then running from them both and realizing that he was losing the race, he leapt into a well, falling, falling, falling to his death. But before he hit the bottom, he had the good fortune to snag himself on a tree root jutting out from the wall of the abyss. Below him yawned death. Above him in the circle of light growled a grizzly, roared a lion. But in this not-to-be-envied position, he spied an abandoned beehive and stuck his finger into the honeycomb. He put the honey to his lips and laughed at the sweetness.

But did that poor, trapped monk really laugh?

Can you laugh while you're staring infinity in the face?

Of course.

I once met with a circle of widows to do book reviews. What amazed me was their laughter. All of them had walked with heavy steps behind life's shiny hearses and watched as the shallow earth swallowed up what seemed their only reasons to live. Each of them had known the grim necessity of setting a table for one. All of them had wept over tasteless bread and wide, empty beds that nibbled at their security. But amazingly, in time, they learned a new laughter along the edges, and what wholesome laughter it was too. They had learned to play and survive the game of brinkmanship. They had finally accepted life's greatest truth: joy rarely erupts in the safe centers of our lives. Laughter may inhabit the middle, but not joy. Joy rises only along the edges.

I have just begun my eighth decade on the planet, and I don't have a lot of time left for innovations in living: but oh the perspective! It is good to be alive and to sense the final edge of things. The nights grow late so fast. I wake up, smile, and take my oatmeal and Vitorin. Then suddenly I realize the sun is up, and I'm still on the planet—still on the stamp. And I give thanks above the altar where yesterday's offering still burns. I walk over to the edge of the stamp and can see that I have had the good fortune to be born on a comfortable planet on the edge of the Milky Way galaxy. I can see it now so clearly from the edges of my life. So I have hope that even on my last morning here I will still exult that the milk is sweet and the bread is affordable.

I, like the best of my fellow pilgrims, am an edge dweller, and God is with me.

So this book, like every worthy book, is born *on* and written *from* the edges.

I am not sick at the moment, nor am I in any danger. But I am also not safe. Never have been. Don't wanna be.

My security has been compromised by the dangers I face daily. Each time I drive to the market I am only eighteen inches from being in the oncoming lane. I eat spinach from California, so who

---

knows? I trust my life at thirty thousand feet to a pilot I've never met. I was once pelted by rocks in Yemen, simply for looking so American. On another occasion, I strayed too near the geysers of New Zealand. But my footing was secure enough to save me. So I remain here. The tissues that comprise my physiology are all a little leaky, but they seem to be functioning. I wanted to write this tale while I am still a mere seven decades from my initial spank on my butt, because I am now at the age when the annual inspection of the same area seems mandatory.

Don't feel sorry for me. I am in no greater danger than you are.

The edge is a good address. It is a good place to remember our temporariness.

It teaches us to spend our time wisely.

So our last days can become our best days.

Life is good. So is God.

And life with God is full of glorious daybreaks. After all, it was God who gave me the courage to walk the edges of a life that was never mine!

Brinkmanship, anyone?

Calvin Miller

Birmingham, Alabama

PART ONE

The Early Years

1936–1955

ONE

Oz Is Where You Find It

WHEN THE UMBILICAL CORD IS CLIPPED AND WE CRY OUR FIRST hellos, the sun is not the center of our universe. We are. So when I was old enough to remember anything and took my first glimpse of the solar system, it was small enough for me to manage. Its center was not the sun. Enid, Oklahoma, was. It was not "helio-centric"; it was "Enid-centric." The planets that surrounded my dusty little hometown were such hamlets as Covington, which kept its orbit at twenty-six miles, and Garber at some twenty-one miles distant.

THE ENID-CENTRIC GLOBE

Everybody, or nearly everybody, in my very small galaxy went to church. The main menu on churchgoing—like the Trinity itself—was divided into three parts. The first denomination was the Christians or Disciples of Christ, who said you had to be baptized to be saved. The second was Baptists, who said it was nice to be baptized although grudgingly admitted you could be saved without it. Baptists used the good thief on the cross for their key argument of debate. This thief was saved without being baptized, thus proving their point. While this repentant thief could never have been a member of the Disciples of Christ church, he did go to heaven, said the Baptists. The third category was the Methodists, who "sprinkled" at their baptisms and, as Baptists saw it, were clearly not using enough water to do it right. Baptists believed they used enough water to symbolize the "washing away" of sins, while Methodists only dry-cleaned.

There was a very small Catholic church in Enid. It was called Saint Francis Xavier's. As Baptists saw things, it was full of idols, worshipped the pope, and had a preacher who didn't believe in sex . . .

for priests at least. He also liked the Virgin Mary whom he called Saint Mary. Baptists didn't like using the word *saint* and preferred calling Saint Mary, Mary, and Saint Paul, Paul. Neither Christians nor Methodists nor Baptists believed in worshipping Mary, even at Christmas. They grudgingly admitted that Mary may have been the mother of Jesus, but this did not cut her any slack with the Almighty. They also didn't believe in calling any preacher "father," reserving that word only for God.

All three of Enid's popular denominations held revivals and believed in being saved on the spot. They all also said Jesus was coming again, and it was hard for me to imagine him coming back anywhere on earth without showing up first at Enid. And it went without saying that if he came for more than two days, he and all his holy angels would be staying at the newly finished Youngblood Hotel on North Independence.

The most devout among us studied prophecy and looked for clues as to when Jesus would actually arrive. There was great interest in who the Antichrist might be. The title was passed around from movie producers to the pope to Moussolini and Hirohito. But by 1940, the Antichrist was most generally thought to be Hitler. The Great Whore of Revelation was believed to be the Axis countries.

There was great effort expended in all Oklahoma pulpits to try to figure out when Jesus would come and what would be the signs of his second coming. But five times in the Gospel of Matthew, Jesus made it clear that when he surprised the world with his second coming there would be "weeping and wailing and gnashing of teeth"! Sermons often grew fiery on the subject, except for a few preachers who were so liberal they often said nothing about it at all.

This was a clear sign that when Jesus came again they would be among those who wailed and gnashed their teeth. I was never sure how this "gnashing" was done, but it was frightening to imagine whole fields filled with our local friends crying "woe is me!" and gnashing and gnashing.

But for all our interest in the subject, Jesus never came. The circus came to Enid, the governor came once, but not Jesus. He never came . . . never. We prayed "even so, come quickly, Lord Jesus," but he never came. Some started the story that his mother showed up once and appeared to a startled farmer in a field near Bison, Oklahoma, twelve miles south of Enid. They put a little marker beside the Rock Island Railroad track to mark a shrine for our lady of Fatima. The shrine still remains in the small hamlet, but the bogus report of Mary's appearance has faded. Most Baptists didn't believe the farmer who said he saw her. Baptists didn't pay much attention to the Virgin Mary but wondered why on earth she would come to Bison and not Enid, which was the cultural center of Garfield County and a far better place to be seen by more people. Too bad it was all rumor. Bob Wills and the Texas Playboys were the the most important people who ever came to Garfield County.

That is, until Grandma came.

THE PRAIRIE WOMAN

When I first knew that I had a grandma, she was living in Vernon, Texas. Only occasionally did she leave Vernon and come up to Enid on the Frisco passenger train. Her name was Sadie Nebraska Kent, and I liked saying it over and over. It was a fun name to say, like Ida Lupino or Lawrence of Arabia. Grandma was a captivating character who wore a brown tweed coat with a fox fur collar. A necklace formed of six long loops of amber beads hung around her neck, and she looked very elegant. She was a stout woman who supported her ample legs and corseted torso atop a pair of Cuban heeled shoes. As she did not visit often, I was delighted when we got the word that she was coming to Enid. Grandpa worked for the railroad, so she could get free passes on any Frisco train anytime she wanted to come. She just didn't seem to want to come very often.

When the day of her arrival finally came, I was more excited than I can possibly describe. We had no car to meet her, so when she arrived, she walked from the Frisco depot down the railroad tracks to our house, some three-quarters of a mile distant. Mama and I sat on the steps, and I looked as far down those tracks as I could until my eyes teared up from the strain. And yet we stared and stared. For down those very rails soon would come Grandma and the birth of all joy.

"Mama," I asked, "how did Grandma come to be named 'Sadie Nebraska Kent'?"

"Well," Mama said, "she was born in a covered wagon in Nebraska on the Oregon trail in 1882. My grandparents and your great-grandparents and Grandma's mama were named Schetrompf. And the Schetrompfs [which almost rhymed with "tree-trunk" or "spelunk"] were headed for Oregon when she was born. She was born in a covered wagon on the rolling plains of Nebraska." Mama stopped. She could see that I was troubled that Grandma, too, had grandparents. She was right about that. Somehow, I just assumed that Grandma had dropped out of heaven and fallen on the earth somewhere around Vernon, Texas.

When the cloud moved from my face, my eyes brightened to some amount of understanding. Mama went on. "So, because she was born in Nebraska, they wrote that down squarely in the middle of her name. But after her birth, for some reason, unknown to all of us now, the Schetrompfs left the Oregon Trail, turned their wagon south, crossed Kansas, and finally settled in Oklahoma, which at that time was called Indian Territory."

In the middle of our discussion, I looked far down the railroad tracks and I saw her. Grandma! Hooray, Grandma! She walked with a brisk step and carried a large carpet-sided train case. Had I known that within the train case she brought a little paper sack filled with peppermint candies, my elation would have held no bounds. Even so, my anticipation of her coming was overwhelming. But the peppermints would add to her charm. My mother had nine children, and the youngest of us were delighted by sweets, which were never frequent in our house.

Grandma arrived.

We embraced her fanatically.

Each of us took turns sitting beside her at meals. When it was my turn, I enjoyed that treat more than the meager meals Mama provided. I loved to feel Grandma's warmth and mostly her mystique. She was a mighty foreigner from Vernon, Texas. She had peppermints and was born in a covered wagon. I wanted to know all about her and deluged her with questions, particularly about being born in a covered wagon. But she could not remember being born.

What a coincidence! Neither could I.

She lost her godlike status in her admission, but she gained an immense humanity, and if you can't be a goddess, being a real human being is a close second. She told me wonderful things about my grandpa, whom I had never met. She said he had once spiked steel rails to creosote ties all the way across Oklahoma. Later he had become a Frisco telegrapher. Then she told us how you could take Indian Head pennies and put them on the very rails that Grandpa had spiked into place, and when the trains ran over them, they would become huge pennies, as round as Liberty half dollars. We actually went with Grandma over to the Frisco tracks a block from our house, and we waited for trains and smashed pennies until we were delirious. But smashing pennies has a limited appeal. And a few smashed pennies are all you really need to prove you could smash them. Besides, pennies were expensive and their spending power held a Tootsie Roll appeal that caused a body not to want to waste them.

By her own admission, Grandma never went to church. This bothered me a lot because Sister Thompson, our pastor at the Highlawn Church, said that if you didn't go to church you would go to hell after you died. Further, Sister Thompson said that where you went after you died depended pretty much on where you went before you died. It was just that while you lived you had to make a choice between church and hell, and Grandma chose hell. Grandma was sure to go to hell, and while I didn't want her to go to hell, I knew it wouldn't be till after she died, and she looked like she was feeling pretty well at the time.

But even if Grandma preferred to go to hell rather than church, I could see the common sense in her decision. It seemed to me that sermons were a kind of hell all by themselves. And I could admire

Grandma's courage for wanting to go there when her time came. You could tell just by seeing Grandma's staunch resolve that she didn't relish facing the devil, but if it came to that, she wasn't the type who would whine about all the fire. She was the type who would endure the fry with fortitude. Besides, she had always said that the part of Texas south of Vernon was hotter than hell in July. It would be years before I learned she was speaking metaphorically, and so—for the moment—it helped me get a handle on where hell was located.

Our Pentecostal evangelists always said hell was down under the ground, but I never believed it. We didn't own many shoes in our house and sometimes went barefoot until December. My feet were cold all through November in Oklahoma, and hell couldn't possibly be under the ground or why would our feet be so cold? Grandma was wise: south of Vernon was the best place for hell.

Grandma didn't stay long—not near long enough to satisfy me. I cried when the magical woman left. Enid was just a lot less interesting without her. Vernon had all the luck. To my way of thinking, all of life in Vernon was lemonade and vanilla wafers. And Vernon was far enough north of hell to be safe. What a glorious place— Vernon, Texas, where everyone went around with railroad passes and peppermints in their pockets. There Grandma walked on streets of gold and was married to a man who had spiked rails all the way across Oklahoma. Everyone dressed in fox fur and wore jumpy-rope beads. If one had to choose between Vernon and heaven, it would be hard to pick. Grandma lived in one place and Jesus lived in the other. And you needed a railroad pass to get to one and a rocket to get to the other.

FINDING JOY AS BEST WE COULD
WHILE GRANDMA WAS AWAY

So we Millers just stayed home—Mama and all nine of us, in our one-room house, where there were never any secrets and yet the obvious naked truth was that the sexes were different. In those days sex was not something you did; it was something you were. It was how you were built—the knobs and handles that said whether you circled "M" or "F" on the U.S. census form. David and Dickie and I all had . . . well, never mind. The girls didn't have what we had, and that's the kind of thing you notice right off. It would be years before I would encounter Freud and wrestle with the ins and outs of gender envy. But gender pride was another matter, and the three boys in our small house were instantly aware of the pecking order in that matter.

There was no plumbing in our little house, and we had—as the rural cliché runs—three rooms (or the dream of three rooms, for the inside studs had been put up but never any plaster applied) and a path. Most all of us preferred a trip to the family outhouse rather than resorting to the family pot, which was circled about with a curtain, so we could have a little privacy when inclement weather forced us to honor our necessity in the midst of our very congested family life.

I liked the outhouse, because that's where people in rural Oklahoma who couldn't spell "Kimberly-Clark" kept their Sears and Roebuck catalogs. There, while your intestines were wrenching their fill into the pit below, you could shop the catalog. Not that you could actually buy anything in the hundreds of pages of pictures, but there were boats and electric trains. And wonder of wonders! There were bicycles, if only you had thirteen dollars. And the underwear pages! We voyeurs in the outhouse could look at the underwear models. It was fascinating! People standing around in their underwear, smiling as if they had just been saved down at the Pentecostal church. They all looked truly happy too. You could even lust, if you wanted to, and busy your mind with wickedness. But the fantasies never lasted long. The odor of the outhouse was a constant challenge to long-term lust.

What always amazed me about the catalogs was that they seemed to forge a kind of family agreement among all of us who used the outhouse. Concerning the issue of long-term catalog interest, the first pages to be used were the tool advertisements and the catalog sections on floor furnaces and prefabricated siding. The underwear, toys, and nice china sections endured the longest. I knew the china pages meant more to my sisters than to me, and as long as they used up the paint and tile sections of the big book, I would use the auto-part sections and honor their preferences as they honored mine.

But all of us left the ordering sheets in the center of the catalog to the very last. In all of my years, I cannot remember anyone ordering a single thing from these books; nevertheless, next to the King James Bible it was the most studied book in our world. Still, there were those moments of winter dysentery when the pages went faster than usual and even the beautiful things like china and chatty underwear models were called upon to yield up their lives and, like all the Millers, serve as best they could in their own humble way.

The outhouse catalog was the best part of my day-to-day humdrum once Grandma left. The Ringling Brothers Barnum & Bailey

Circus came to Enid every three or four years, but we couldn't go. Tickets were expensive, Mama said. I knew she was right. She said we children needed to realize that money didn't grow on trees. It was an odd expression Mama seemed to use any time we wanted to buy anything. I acquiesced. What did I think Enid was, Vernon, Texas?

But when—after the dull years—the circus train did come to town, it pulled off on the Rock Island Railroad spur. I had never cared much for the Rock Island Railroad, since it was the railroad Grandpa hadn't built. Its one redeeming feature was that it ran between Wichita, Kansas, and Dallas, and both were circus stops for Ringling Brothers. Mama said P. T. Barnum—whose name was in the circus name—bragged that there was a sucker born every moment. Mama said this to discredit both the circus and the notion that it was essential. Still, at least the idea of the circus I found immensely appealing. Looking at the circus train was as free as lusting over underwear advertisements, so we all went down to watch the circus unload. When they opened those slatted livestock cars, elephants walked the streets of Enid!

It was like being born again. It was glorious enough to cause us to talk in tongues like we did down at the Pentecostal church when we got the Holy Ghost. (Actually, I never could talk in tongues, which at first cost me my spiritual reputation in the church and finally my membership.) But even lowly Enid sometimes held wondrous things. A circus parade! Glory! How ever do you teach one elephant to hold another's tail in its trunk and walk along for miles? It all eluded me. And the clowns and pretty ladies in silver suits! It was all very heady stuff.

They also had Ernesto Pagalino and the Flying Faralinis.

The Flying Faralinis I never got to see, since they performed under the big top and I never got to go inside. But Ernesto—may God ever be blest—put an eighteen-inch circle of wood atop the First National building, one of the tallest buildings in Enid along with the fourteen-story Broadway Tower. There, a full six stories above Randolph and Grand streets, Ernesto did handstands and double somersaults above the streets. *With no net!* Clearly, he was an extraordinary soul from the Land of Extraordinary Souls— Vernon, Texas. I could not imagine the courage it took to do that. Nor could I imagine why life had to be so ordinary in Enid. The circus left Enid all too soon and moved to Ardmore, Oklahoma, where the buildings were shorter and Ernesto could hardly make the impression he had managed in Enid. There were barely any buildings in Ardmore tall enough to fall off and really hurt yourself.

GRANDMA'S SECOND COMING

Somewhere between circuses, we got a letter from a doctor in Vernon. The letter informed us that Grandma was losing her mind. I asked Mama what that meant, and Mama said it meant that she was losing her ability to think and act in a rational manner. It seemed to me that most people I knew in Enid were in that category, and so, at first, I didn't worry too much about it. In fact, Enid seemed the perfect place for Grandma.

Other letters came. Other months went by. "Children," said Mother one day, "Grandma is coming back to Enid to live with us.

Grandpa is dead and Grandma has no money and nowhere to go, so she's coming here."

I was so happy.

"Calvin," Mama said, "you must prepare yourself. Grandma is terribly altered."

What could Mama mean? I couldn't think of how anything could alter Grandma. She was completely unalterable, and I said so.

Since finding a place for her seemed more important than how altered Grandma was or what it was that had altered her, I asked, "Where will Grandma sleep?"

"In the bedroom," said Mama disconsolately. It wasn't really a bedroom. It was only stud walls that could be draped with sheets to make it seem kind of like a bedroom. It was only after Grandma got there that I began to pick up the reasons for Mama's dour mood. Grandma had lost her fur collar and her elegant beads, and she would sit drooling and staring for hours at a time.

"Grandma," I asked, "how's everybody in Vernon, Texas?"

"Vernon?" she asked.

I knew she was altered. I might as well have said New Delhi. She had brought no peppermints, and her lovely Cuban heels were scuffed and worn.

There was hardly room for Grandma in our already crowded house, and she brought with her a huge trunk that held her things: a few dresses, some beige hosiery full of runs and snags, and a couple of foundation garments. Her foundation garments were as stiff as whalebone could make them, and though her sane moments were fleeting, she never went out in public without them. Because there was no plaster on the wall, we hung some sheets on the inside walls of the bedroom area so she could get into her foundation garments without being observed. Still, I had the greatest urge to watch her put one of them on, for they were so much smaller than Grandma that I could only imagine the stress she put on a girdle in the courageous act of getting dressed. I always wondered that her eyes didn't bug out more.

People who lose their minds never mind it much, but they put a whole lot of stress on those who still have theirs. So it was with Grandma. She kept the key to her trunk on a string around her neck, so she was the only one who could get into it. This would not have been bad except that as she lost her mind, she developed the art of kleptomania. She would steal our things and put them in her trunk, and it was impossible for us to get them out. We had to wait until she went to sleep, and then Mama could get the string off her neck and open the trunk and get back whatever Grandma had stolen.

I had an El Producto cigar box filled with various trinkets, including my six-bladed pocket knife, a half box of Smith Brothers Cough Drops, and, above all, my glow-in-the-dark *Sky King* ring. For my *Sky King* ring, I had saved six Kellogg's box tops and a whole quarter that I sent to Battle Creek, Michigan, to get the ring. When these treasures disappeared, I knew at once Grandma had stolen them and put them in her trunk! Naturally, I was anxious to get them back. I was angry. What possible use could an old woman have with a *Sky King* ring? But I had to wait to get them back until Grandma was asleep and Mama got the key out from between Grandma's ample breasts. I did, of course, get them back, and in the process of protecting my El Producto box, I developed the art of hiding it where Grandma couldn't possibly find it.

In the summer of '47, I attended the Wesleyan Methodist vacation Bible school. This was after I had attended the Davis Park Christian vacation Bible school, and the Olivet Baptist vacation Bible school. Mama always liked her children to go to as many VBSs as we could. She had her hands full taking care of Grandma. It was good to get us children out of the house, if only to help her with the whole issue of time management. But it was okay with me. I liked vacation Bible school, where we learned the books of the Old Testament and saluted the Bible and the American and Christian flags. Plus we got Kool-Aid and Oreos for snacks, something we never got at home. But best of all, we got to make things out of plywood and alphabet macaroni. Once, we made the headdress of Ramses—who was so mean to Moses—out of tongue depressors, and we also made caterpillars out of egg cartons.

But at craft time in the Wesleyan Methodist church we made flannelgraphs; that is, storyboards that were covered with sky blue flannel on the top and brown ground-colored flannel on the bottom. Onto these flannel boards we fastened little characters we had colored and cut out with scissors. When we put a tab of flannel on the back of each of the paper figures—like, say, Jesus and the woman at the well—the flannel tab on the back of the paper figures would adhere to the board. So you could stop passersby and have them sit and watch as you put Jesus and the woman at the well and tell their story.

The whole point was that you were supposed to use the flannelgraph as an evangelistic tool to win your friends to Christ. All you had to do was tell your friends the same story you had learned in vacation Bible school. I was never able to win any of my friends in this manner, but I loved my witnessing flannelgraph. In truth, most of my friends were hopelessly sliding into the pit of hell from watching too many Gene Autry movies. So they were not interested in Jesus or the woman at the well, no matter how enchantingly I positioned them on my flannelgraph.

When Bible school was over, I took my flannel graph home and laid it on the table. After dinner on Friday night, I couldn't find it. I knew instinctively where it was. It was in Grandma's hellish trunk! But it was getting harder to get things back once Grandma had swiped them. She had shortened the length of her neck string, and the string was now too tight to slip over her head without waking her up. She was very strong, and when awakened she would arise as furious in her rage as the Great Whore of Babylon.

Not every story has a happy ending, and this is one of those. I never got back my flannel graph Jesus, so I never got to witness to all my friends. Grandma didn't have any friends, so the witnessing value of my flannel graph Jesus was forever lost.

It was this single event that most caused me to abandon my fascination with Grandma. To lose both your *Sky King* ring and your flannel graph Jesus in the same summer was too much to forgive. And so when Mama said we were going to have to take Grandma to Fort Supply, Oklahoma's final stopping place for the insane, I was glad. The day they came to take her away we went through her trunk for the last time, but alas, the flannelgraph Jesus was gone. The woman at the well, too, was lost to me, and my evangelism career fell into decay.

The Funeral Grandma Never Knew She Went To

Over the next two years, we got periodic letters from the director of the asylum informing us that Grandma's physical state was degenerating along with her mental health. And in the spring of 1951, she passed away. We Millers had no car but managed to ride with other relatives who did, to make the long, long drive from Enid to Fort Supply.

The funeral was austere. A plain service, a cheap casket, paid for by the state. I was going on fifteen years of age at Grandma's passing and was struck by the reading of her obituary. Her life story was so much simpler than I thought it would be.

Those in our family who had predeceased Grandma were her son, Calvin, whose name I wore and whom my older siblings simply called Uncle Cal. I never knew him. He died of diphtheria in the winter of 1933, two and a half years before I was born. Grandpa had died in the years just prior to World War II, and there was a grandson who died in 1940, my brother. Mother's brother, Carl, a veteran of the wars, didn't attend. I had two uncles—Short and Fred, as they were known—who did.

I don't remember my mother weeping at the memorial service. Perhaps too many heavy and wearing events had tumbled down over all our need to feel sorry for Grandma, or guilty either, for that matter. I remember thinking about Grandma's views of hell, and wondering whether in death she had found out its precise location. Maybe the Good Lord had looked down on her and pitied her for her own struggles, and so let her pass on into heaven. Maybe there was a special corner of heaven for old, lost women with absentee minds and locked trunks.

It is not to my credit that I thanked the Lord there would now be more room in our house because Grandma had found a way to sleep off her eternity in a dry-baked cemetery in Northwest Oklahoma. But the oddest of all moods came over me. It was a sense that some gallantry ends in a kind of madness that not even the noblest escape.

Sadie Nebraska, a prairie woman, had lasted some sixty-nine years. For one brief, shining moment—believing or not believing in hell—she had made a bit of magic come to pass on the prairie. And the yellow brick road for me was little more than a couple of steel rails Grandpa had driven into the prairie to help build the Frisco railroad. I was content with all things. Oz in the mind of a child looks a lot like Vernon, Texas.

TWO

The Five Good Gifts
of a Scoundrel

I NEVER MET ANYONE WHO SPOKE WELL OF DAVID FRANK MILLER. He was my father, arriving at the title in August of 1936. He was thirty-eight that month and I was, of course, zero. He was himself zero in the year 1898.

PAPA, A SOUL IN SEARCH OF REPUTATION

He was a rogue—never wealthy enough to afford his habits. He purchased brief seasons of camaraderie in such places as Charlie's Beer Garden and the Independence Street Bar. Like Shakespeare's Falstaff, he set the bar for many a free-drinker. He was not a great reader, nor a great thinker. He was handsome, warm, reasonably funny, and, I am only guessing, very insecure. He liked himself best at the end of an evening of drinking, when alcohol had made him mighty in his own eyes. Only then was he bleary enough of soul to see himself as one funny man. My older sisters told me he could be mean as a snake when he was drunk at home. But his "friends" said he was a warm, spontaneous, and generous soul and the best of the local comedians with a beer mug in his hand.

Since I was only four when he left home, I remember none of his frailties that my older siblings learned by observation. What I know, I learned by listening to my sisters talk in later years. I, like them, had noticed the wistful silence of my mother whenever his name came up. She loved him. There was no doubt of that. But her own longsuffering with his drunkenness and sullen temper taught her that love does not conquer all heels, neither is every drunken frog a sober prince waiting to be kissed into a man of character.

Because of her love for him, my mother rarely allowed anyone to criticize him. His flaws were as numerous as his critics, but in good conscience she had chosen him as a lifelong love that kept her somewhat blind to his faults. She could see his flaws, but rehearsing them, or demonizing him for having them, served neither to correct them nor make her wish she had chosen a better man. A matter once decided finds little betterment in being fondled. "What might have been" leads only to a dour rehearsal of "what ifs?" It consumes our good judgment. It negates reality with years of frivolous fictions.

So I will try to be positive in saying that between 1921 and 1942 I know of five good things that my father did, and the mention of these would, I think, please my mother, who since 1977 has slept out a well-deserved rest. Her body still awaits the coming of the New Jerusalem in a cemetery just outside of Enid. Her good, sturdy soul is now gathered with the angels, and the angels are mighty lucky to have her.

THE FIRST GOOD THING MY FATHER DID

The first wonderful thing my father did was to sire a family who surrounded my mother with pride. In a time when there was little to rejoice about, Frank Miller furnished her with a sense of wealth. It is amazing how *poverty* was not a word my mother used or knew. How could anyone be poor with such devoted children? And if all that my father did was to enable her to make babies, he had served her well. It is not bad to have a lot of children if they are good children. And for more than fifty years, her children were all she lived for.

Of course, when Mother first met Frank, he was handsome and well liked and, like most eighteen-year-olds, would have considered himself "a good catch." No good woman ever falls in love with a man simply because she can see that in time he will be the father of very nice children. All real love is love at first sight, they say, and at such first sight there is no hint that your Prince Charming will someday be an alcoholic guilty of bruise and abuse. He was, in 1918, good-looking, charming, and in charge.

In 1918, he was twenty and on the way back from France, where he had served as a mule skinner in the U.S. Army. Mule skinners drove the mules that pulled the cannons and other heavy war equipment for an army that was just barely motorized at that time. My mother was eighteen when he returned, and their correspondence had furthered their relationship while he was overseas. Within a year after Frank's return, they were married, and little more than a year after that my eldest sister, Izetta, was born, in 1921. By 1926, I had four older sisters, and within the next ten years, three boys were born, of which I was the third. The first of the boys was named Richard; the second was named David Frank, after our father. Then I was born and named after Uncle Cal (and perhaps after John Calvin, the sixteenth-century reformer). In 1939 and 1940, my younger sisters were born. With their births David Frank Miller had sired his two final children to complete Mama's brood of nine.

Mother used to read to us Louisa May Alcott's *Little Women*, and it was not hard for us to believe that Ms. Alcott's Marmie was real, and so were Meg, Jo, Amy, and Beth March. I saw the March children—newly named Miller—gathered about Mrs. Frank Miller. Fortunately, the bad times are never as memorable the good times, and the best memories live longest. And so my eight brothers and sisters were my father's finest gift to my mother. I cannot believe

---

that my father saw it that way. For him, each conception was likely the pursuit of some fiery, inner need. But for my mother, each conception was a building block in her fortress of survival.

FRANK MILLER'S SECOND GIFT

I know not where the Millers lived when my older sisters were little. But in 1931, Frank Miller gave my mother his second gift. My grandfather Miller, whom I have already confessed that I never knew, gave Papa a building lot, which he parceled off the end of his own small acreage. Grandpa said Papa could have the lot if he would build a house for his family of five (my oldest brother had been born by this time). And Papa actually did build a house . . . of sorts. It was prefaced by a porch the exact width of the house and was deep enough for two old lawn chairs. This porch greatly widened the home. When so many people must live inside such a small house, everyone lives on the porch a lot. Without the porch, the house was eighteen by twenty-four feet, with six windows and two doors. There were two windows on the front of the house and two on each side. A front door. A back door. And a chimney built squarely in the middle of the house. It had two flue openings so that the draft would service both a wood-burning, potbellied, heating stove in the living room and a four-burner wood stove in the kitchen area.

There would have been three rooms, had Papa ever finished them as rooms. But as I have explained, the rooms were rather three "areas" of the house, one a nine-by-twelve bedroom to be divided between seven people at the time it was built. A nine-by-twelve kitchen held a table that seated four and could double for a dish-washing cabinet. Orange crates were the cupboards and larders for such meager things as onions, potatoes, and a few items of canned goods. The kitchen and the bedroom were back-to-back. There was no wall between them. There was only a framework of studs, screened here and there with a few plaster lathes that would never, at any time in the house's history, know plaster. Under the front room stove and dilapidated furniture there was a linoleum floor.

The house was never painted. But it was shingled.

If Papa had ever brought home a real paycheck, the house might at least have been painted. But alas, Frank Miller was the prodigal father. By the time he was in his thirties, Papa's lifestyle was so wasted that he never brought any money home. His living was spent on booze, and while the house was never properly finished, I cannot imagine how we would ever have done without it. It had a roof and was tightly shingled, and we slept dry. It could be heated when we could afford the wood or coal, and most of the time we managed a bit of both.

What the neighbors saw in the winter of '34 led them to harsh judgment of my father and caused most of them forever after to call him that "no-good Frank Miller!" It was during the Thanksgiving of '34 when my mother got a certificate for a ham from county welfare. Her elation was beyond words! She made the mistake of giving the coupon to Papa to redeem at the courthouse, where the hams were to be doled out to the needy. On the way to get the ham, my father stopped at a bar and traded the certificate for a pint of whiskey. He spent Thanksgiving in an alcoholic stupor while we, of course, went hungry.

I do not pretend that Mother could not see what Papa was doing to his family. I simply mean that there was no use belaboring his sins as though there was anything redemptive in the rehearsal of his failures. Life had to go on, and Mama alone among the eleven of us knew how to keep it going.

And the place where life went on was the house that Papa built. It never occurred to us it might have been better.

It was good. Good enough.

There was no natural gas.

There was no electricity and wouldn't be for years.

And generally there was coal and wood.

But there was one thing more essential than any of those things: Water!

This was the great blessing the old house offered. Water—city water. This my father had also managed. There was no plumbing in the house, but there was a hydrant beside it. Papa, in a spasm of meager cash, had the city install a water pipe and a meter. In our underdeveloped corner of the world, we had this one important vestige of civilization: running, chlorinated water. There was no curb, no paved street, but on the edge of our dustbowl lawn there *was* a water meter. It was something of a novelty that we would have it. Others who lived around us had yard pumps and cisterns. It wasn't much of a bragging point, but when the weather was dry and the neighbor's pumps were sluggish, we offered them drinking water, free from our tap.

We had a water bucket and a dipper that made good, fresh, chlorinated water available all through the year. In the winter we learned that we could let the water drip slowly on cold nights and it would not freeze. So on any December morning, the water flowed as abundantly as it had in July.

I suppose that what we called a house was really a shanty. It was a squatter's shack. It was little more than a cardboard barrio dwelling. But this I tell you: the house was a gift from my father. And Mother cherished the gift. So bright were the passing of our days that I must confess I had not the slightest idea we were poor. I can remember no Christmas when we had meat to eat, but when Mother read to us *A Christmas Carol*, with never a goose of our own, we all felt sorry for the Cratchitts. It is a rare woman who is so rich in her glorious poverty that she gives such a wonderful gift to her children. And lest I tread too heavily on the substance of the next chapter, I must at least say that I never felt insecure in her presence. Whatever had to be faced in the post-Depression years, we knew no real dragons. My mother brought the water of life from the hydrant outside to the drinking pail with its glorious dipper, a communion cup that provided us a common worship of survival.

Life was a feast, and Frank Miller was the founder of that feast. And if he looked like a ne'er-do-well drunkard to the community, it was merely because they simply didn't have eyes to see the truth.

THE THIRD GOOD THING MY FATHER DID

But his third and best gift was the manliest sort of gift a man can give to a woman: support in the hard times. This was his 1939 gift to my mother. It was in that year that my oldest brother, Dickie, went with a group of his peers to swim in a farm pond three miles north of our house. When his playmates returned from the outing, they were out of breath and all speaking at once. Dickie was not with them, and their mutual alarm set my mother on edge. Here was born a mighty coincidence: Papa was not only home, he was sober. This great double gift was one that called the black day blessed.

Papa took charge. We had no car, and yet the absolute urgency of getting to the pond where Dickie had been swimming led him to sprint to the site in an amazing thirty minutes or so. It was he who searched the muddy waters of the pond and retrieved my lost brother.

The day was the darkest my mother had ever experienced. In all her years she outlived two of her children: Dickie, who died in her fortieth year, and Ruth, who died of cancer in her sixty-fifth year.

Dickie's death affected us all. Papa stayed sober during the three days that lapsed between Dickie's drowning and burial. And during those three days, I learned the glory of the word *Father*. He, who never had time for any of us, suddenly had time for all of us.

And I can remember that at Dickie's burial, Papa lifted me up over the edge of the little casket and I saw my brother for the last time. There has been some disagreement between my sisters and me about how he was dressed. I say he was in his overalls and barefooted. They say he was in a little pair of brown trousers, dressed in a pale but starched dress shirt with shoes. They are perhaps right, but even if they are, I will always remember him as he customarily dressed, in a little pair of overalls and without any shoes.

I was three then, and it is possible I am mistaken, for this is among the very earliest of my memories. But this much I am sure of: Papa lifted me up over the edge of the casket to have a final look. It was Papa's hands I remember, how big they were and how strong. And if little boys with little hands remember anything, it would be that—hands so large they could move the stolid world when the world needed moving. You don't forget that. That was the last time, really the only time, I can remember being touched in any way by my father.

I don't remember that there was any exchange between my mother and my father, but I feel sure there was. I think he must have held Mama when she cried. They say that one of her children tried to console Mama by saying to her, "But, Mama, you still have seven other children" (Baby Bonnie had not yet been born). And Mama answered this attempt at consolation by saying, "I want them all!" Daddy, if he knew anything, must have known this. And if a man has only one moment in which to claim he had a reason to be upon the earth, this must have been Papa's red-letter day. He lifted his youngest son to see his silent brother, and held his children's mother. He did these two things with the same great hands that were part of the reason that God made hands.

The Fourth Great Gift My Father Gave

If Dickie's passing had brought Papa to his senses, he did not long live in his newfound sanity. Soon after the funeral, his public drunkenness landed him in jail. His public drunkenness caused him to be thrown in jail any number of times. This kept him from holding a steady job. Mama was not able to scrape together enough money to feed us most of the time. When Papa actually got paid for any of the odd jobs he held, he spent the money before he got home. It was in final desperation that Mama, poor woman that she was, put on her best print dress and called on the county attorney. They agreed together that the next time Frank Miller was in jail, the police would keep him behind bars until divorce papers could be served. Mama and the attorney would then go together to the jail to begin the process of divorce. Before Frank was released from custody, they would make him "deed the house over" to her and her eight remaining children.

When that time actually came, my mother and the county attorney entered his jail cell. Frank, embarrassed by his behavior, which he generally was during his moments of sobriety, took the pen and signed the documents. Then Frank Miller left town, moving to Oklahoma City, where he spent the next ten years. The prospect mother faced was instantly better. She didn't have much money, but what she was able to scrape together was hers, and she herself could control and plan its spending.

Her children could see that their prospects instantly improved. In later years, as a preacher, I was often asked how I felt about divorce. It was always a tough question, and I never answered it hurriedly. But generally I could see a woman trapped between the possibility of having the county take her children away from her and getting a divorce would choose the lesser of evils. I know Mama did the right thing. There was no residual bitterness, no tears that I caught her shedding. She never hated Frank Miller. In fact, she never allowed others to speak slightingly of him in her presence. But the first day of her divorce was the best day of our lives.

The divorce was Frank's gift to all of us. I've wondered if he understood how much a gift it was. I think he did. I think his sober moments had taught him what a rotten father looks like. I think he accepted his failures and knew there was a kind of nobility in getting his fatherhood out of the quicksand before he took us all under. I am sure he wept over the loss, for in his best moments he was capable of weeping.

MY FATHER'S FIFTH GREAT GIFT

His last gift was to me. He gave me a cheese sandwich and a bowl of Campbell's cream of tomato soup.

By my fifteenth year, I had the awfullest urge to see my father, something I could not remember having since that odd moment at Dickie's funeral. I told Mother about my desire to visit Papa just to see what he looked like. My mother did not try to talk me out of these urges. In fact, she seemed to abet my feelings on the matter.

"I have his address, or at least his last known address," she said. "He's living with another woman, possibly your stepmother." I had heard the term *stepmother*, and yet it seemed odd that I might have one. I remembered that Cinderella had one, as well as a couple of stepsisters who were homely and cross and made Cinderella sleep on the cinders.

"Do I have stepsisters?" I asked.

"Perhaps, or a stepbrother," she said.

"You're not upset that I want to see him?"

"Of course not," she said. "What boy wouldn't want to see his father, especially if it had been ten years since he last saw him? There's a Continental Trailways bus that goes down to Oklahoma City every morning at six, and another that returns every night at seven. It costs two dollars and eighty cents round-trip for a ticket."

"Do we have that much?" I asked.

"We will when you're ready to go," she promised.

So we saved and scrimped, and in a couple of weeks we had the extra money. I could tell that even though Papa was married or living common law, Mama was interested in his welfare, and even though she tried to conceal it from me, she was clearly concerned as to how he might be doing.

On the appointed morning, I walked to the bus stop. Mama kissed me good-bye, though to my way of thinking I was far too grown up to be kissed in public. Still, it was six in the morning and nobody seemed to pay much attention to the smaltz. And, of course, it made Mama feel good. The trip took just over three hours. It was only eighty miles straight down U.S. Highway 81, but we had to stop at Waukomis, Hennessey, Kingfisher, Dover, and El Reno on the way. Once I got to the city, I took out a map Mama had encouraged me to carry, and I walked down a route I had pencil traced for about three and a half miles.

If it seems that there is a great deal of walking in this book, it must be remembered that we had no car. Walking was how we got about. We never had a car in our immediate family, and neither Mama nor Papa ever held a driver's license. We walked and thought nothing of it. I was sixteen before I managed enough money to buy a jalopy of my own, a 1939 Ford coupe that I purchased for thirty-five dollars. That was our first family car, and we drove it sparingly because gas was eleven cents a gallon, not to be frivoled away on unnecessary trips. It's funny that we never saw walking as an impediment to life. It was slower than driving might have been, but for where we wanted to go, "shanks horses" was a certain way to get there.

In some ways my search for my father created a most exotic day filled with insight. When I got to the address on the map, it was a small but inviting house, with a well-manicured lawn. Standing upright in the lawn was a sign picturing an open hand with the words underneath, "Madame Regine knows all!" At first I thought I must have the wrong address, for no one had told me that my stepmother was a fortune-teller. Could it be that I had the wrong house? I must confess that I had strange feelings of fear. But that was the address on the paper.

I rang the doorbell. It was the very first time in my life I could ever remember seeing or ringing one. I held it down a long time, and the ringing sounded like how a telephone sounded in the movies. (That was my only key to explaining the sound of the doorbell, for it was years before we would have a telephone of our own, and we never had a doorbell.)

I was fascinated by the bell. I was lost in the wonder of the technology of the whole thing, and when the door opened abruptly, there was a woman standing there. *It must be Regine*, I thought.

"My name is Miller," I said.

"So?" she replied. She clearly had no idea who I was, so the sign in the yard was a lie. Madame Regine did not know all, or she would have had some idea who I was.

"Madame," I stammered tentatively, not knowing whether I should call her Madame or Miss Regine, or possibly Mrs. Frank Miller. Mrs. Frank Miller was clearly not my first choice, since it didn't sound very mysterious. Further, the very notion that my stepmother could be a fortune-teller was a bit of an aversion.

"Madame," I repeated, "could this possibly be where Frank Miller lives?"

"Frank!" she yelled, not very mystically. "The door's for you."

Ye gods! I was about to see my father, and my stepmother was a witch!

In a moment Frank was at the door. I knew him instantly. He had lost an eye in a wood-cutting accident in his middle thirties and had ever since worn a black patch over his left eye.

"What can I do for you, son?" he asked.

"I'm your son," I said.

"Davy!" He blurted out the name of my elder brother.

"Calvy!" I said.

I instantly felt he was disappointed that I was not Davy. And there followed an awkward silence. It seemed forever until he climbed out of his stupor and said, "Come in, son." He didn't hug me. So it was less romantic than I wanted it to be. I wanted him to break into tears and sob how good it was to see me, and that I had grown up to be quite a man, and that sort of thing.

"Billie Lou, this is my son, Calvin!" he said. "Calvin, this is your stepmother, Billie Lou."

Billie Lou turned to me and said, "Welcome, son! Frank has told me a lot about you." This was clearly not so; she didn't even know who I was.

I was baffled by all these low-class monikers. "Where is Regine?" I asked.

"Why Calvy I'm Regine, when people come to me for consulta-

36

tion, but most of the time I'm Frank's little Billie Lou. Nobody would come to Billie Lou to have their fortunes read. That's why I put Regine on the yard sign."

Needless to say, I was a bit put off, and the stalemate wouldn't untangle itself in my mind. I looked around the room. There were purple drapes and a small round table with a deck of cards and a crystal ball.

"Can you really tell the future? Do you know all? I mean neither one of you had a blue-eyed idea who I was."

They both laughed.

"Billie Lou makes a living at this sort of thing, Calvy."

"Calvin is what I like to be called," I insisted.

"Calvin it is," Papa said. "Anyway, people pay five dollars for Billie Lou to tell their futures. I can see more with my one eye than she can see with both of hers. She doesn't even know what time the mailman's coming today, do you, Billie Lou?"

"Nope, but I know a good man, Frank," she said to him in a kind of open compliment. She was playful, almost kittenish, and for a moment the both of them seemed to be like a couple of lovebirds. Their playfulness seemed to ignore the fact that I was actually in the room. Finally Papa said, "Will you fix this boy a bit of lunch?"

"You bet!" said Billie Lou.

Lunch was a bowl of canned soup and a grilled cheese sandwich. But it was tasty, and not being used to any better cuisine, I suppose it was among the top-ten cheese sandwiches I had ever eaten. But best of all was my stepmother. It was the only time I ever saw her, but she was the most congenial witch I had ever met.

She and my father laughed and talked and asked me questions

about my brother and all my sisters, which I answered as best I could. It was genuinely fun. But the moment was not perfect. My dad's eye patch gave him a piratey appearance, and all things didn't seem quite right. Billie Lou, congenial or not, was still a witch. This left me disarmed. But Papa was insistent that Billie Lou had made a new man out of him. He had not "touched a drop," he said, since they had begun to live together. And this made me not like Papa for managing personal reform right after he abandoned my mother with her eight remaining children.

I also resented the fact that Papa was having it so easy with Billie Lou, while his whole family was still living in a house without any indoor plumbing or electricity. Papa had a real cushy life with his "swamette." There was no getting around my resentment. He and Billie Lou were enjoying the good life while we, his abandoned family, were living on an unpaved street in a shanty that he had barely provided.

There was one bright spot to my mood. Every once in a while, Papa would say, "And how's Ethel?" Amid all the merriment, the question came to me a half-dozen times. I wasn't savvy enough as a teenager to catch the significance of it all. I was so loyal to my mother that I felt a twinge of guilt that I liked the witch Billie Lou as much as I did. When I left they asked me to come again, and in a way I was sure they meant it. After all, I was a three-hour bus ride away at a cost of $2.80 in hard cash that wasn't to be picked up just everywhere.

A million things went through my mind on the way home. First, I wondered how Mama would feel knowing she had been replaced by the capricious and giggly Billie Lou. And if Billie Lou truly had reformed my father's drinking habits, how was my mother to take to his reformation when his profligate life had dealt her so much largely uncorrectable misery?

Not a dime of support money had ever come from Papa to help us. Mama picked up such welfare money as she could from being an unsupported woman with a family. And to Mama's good credit, she worked at whatever menial jobs she could find. As the war loomed, my older sisters made what money they could. Not one of the Miller children was lazy. But now the four older ones were married, we were earning money doing such work as we could find.

After the long bus journey, I was back in Enid, and I walked back to our home.

"How's Frank?" Mama asked.

"I think he's fine, Mama . . . I think he's quit drinking."

"And how was your new stepmother?" Mama asked.

"She's a witch. She has a sign in the yard that says so." I went on to tell Mother that they seemed happy together. "They seem to have a lot of money, Mama. I think they're rich. Maybe Papa will send you some child support."

"Maybe he will," said Mama.

But he never did.

A Twenty-One Gun Salute

In the spring of 1956, when I was nineteen years of age and my third year of college (I'll explain how I got there later), two of my older sisters called and said Papa had suffered a heart attack and was in the VFW hospital in Leavenworth, Kansas. I had bought a used car to get back and forth between Oklahoma Baptist University in Shawnee, Oklahoma, and Hunter, Oklahoma, where I was a student pastor at the First Baptist Church. I drove my car to pick up my older sisters, and then the three of us drove to Leavenworth.

Frank Miller looked very old to me through the plastic walls of the oxygen tent. But he could speak. "Calvy," he said through his labored breathing—I allowed him to call me Calvy, but only because he was in coronary care—"I'm divorced from Billie Lou. I want to come back to Enid if I live through this. All I have is a bit of Social Security, and I want you to help me find a cheap sleeping room so I can be near the family, which I too long have ignored."

"All right, Papa," I said.

"I haven't had a drink in years," he said.

"That's good, Papa," I replied.

"How's Ethel?" he asked.

"She's fine," I said. "She wanted us to come and be with you. She wants you to get well, Papa."

"She's a good woman. What I have done to her was wrong. But I intend to make it right. I'm coming home. I'm sick and I'm not sure I have the strength to atone for all the bad things I have done. I have no money. But somehow I'm going to make it right. You're a preacher now?"

"Well," I said, "not much of one. I'm a student pastor. I have a little church I serve on weekends."

"When I'm home, son, I want to come and hear you preach."

"Okay, but you'll get nauseated like everybody else who sits through my sermons."

"Nonetheless, I'm proud of you, boy."

I prayed for Papa to get well, and when I finished, he looked through the plastic oxygen tent and smiled. I somehow knew he would get well.

He did.

When he was dismissed from the hospital, he came back to Enid. As surely as old Ebenezer had seen Marley in his doorknocker, Papa was a new man. He came to see his children and grandchildren virtually every day. He rode with me to my student parish and listened to me preach. He visited with my mother, and I think would have welcomed a reunion, but there was too much in the way. Too many memories, too much unsupported poverty, too much Billie Lou. Mama was always nice to him and they visited for hours upon end, but Mama was clearly not interested in trying to reassemble an old puzzle of which so many of the pieces were now missing. The gallant Frank Miller had aged a hundred years in the forty since they were married. He had aged fifty in the nearly twenty years since he had abandoned his family.

In his sixtieth year in 1958, he was struck by a second heart attack, which he did not survive. No one was there at his funeral except his eight living children and Ethel Miller, a woman who I think would never stop loving him. I can only guess that Billie Lou outlived Daddy, but if she knew he had died, she made no attempt to come to the funeral. Neither did she write any letters of condolence at his passing.

His was a wistful passing, though not a teary one. Our weeping had all come earlier, and the biggest pain had come during the Depression and in the immediate years thereafter, when we struggled on without him. We cried more than Frank did during those years. And it may have been that we were all cried out by the time he actually died. Mama, too, had spent all the tears she had, no doubt. Her heart and hopes had been broken so often that she looked at Papa lying in the coffin as soberly as a stranger might. And when she leaned over his coffin for the last time, she perhaps wished that all they once hoped for might have come to pass. But lost were the days of 1918, when this rogue of a man's man had come home from the war and promised her the world.

She had gained the world, but Frank hadn't given it to her. She had conquered it by sheer resolution. She had won out over wounds that would stagger a lesser woman to her knees. But it was not my father, but my mother who owned the family. It was Mother who held the respect of the children. It was Mother who was the dowager empress of all her needy empire. It was she alone who had given her children enough hope to live.

Papa was buried with a military honor guard who fired their rifles, played taps, and folded the flag. He was laid to rest in a military cemetery. The chaplain said he had served his country well back in 1918. Had he served his family as well as he served his country, perhaps the life he tried so hard to recapture would never have been lost. It seemed odd that he could ever have been such a patriot, when he was such a poor parent.

With white-gloved folderol, the honor guard folded the flag above his coffin and gave it to my mother. What's a widow to do but accept it and take it home? Mama took the flag back to the home that was still unpainted and existed without indoor plumbing. And Mrs. Miller, who had been forced to live as a divorcée for so long, could now legitimately lay claim to being a widow. There was more honor in that somehow.

I think she walked a little straighter than she ever had before. And in her stately stride she always walked with purpose. "Who," said King Solomon, "can find a virtuous woman? for her price is far above rubies." Ethel Miller would outlive Frank Miller, her only love, by more than twenty years, and her children were the wealthiest children the world has ever known. Neither I nor any of the other children have ever visited Frank's grave. But Mother's grave, from holiday to holiday through thirty winters and springtimes, never wants for flowers.

THREE

The Woman Who Was Richer Than She Knew

ONE OF THE MOST THOUGHTFUL THINGS THAT MOTHER EVER DID was to be born in the year 1900. Falling on the planet in such a thoughtful moment made it so easy to remember how old she was. In 1941, she was 41. In 1945 she was 45. And in 1958, when I graduated from college she was 58. She was born October 24, 1900, which she abbreviated 10-24-00, having only zeroes at the end of the encryption, where everybody else had numbers. Conveniently locating her descent upon the planet in that year must have been calculated. Mother was so intentional in all that she did, it seems to me she must have gotten all the angels together and planned this timely feat down to the very day and century.

Uncles I Had but Never Knew

Mama was born to the aforementioned Sadie Nebraska Kent, who before her long sojourn in Vernon, Texas, had spent a bit of time in Indian Territory. Mama was the eldest girl in a family of boys: Carl, Short, and Fred. I'm fairly sure Short had another name, but I have no idea what it was, and no one in my family can provide a clue. Short and Carl were my uncles who were married to my aunts who were of even less consequence to me than my uncles, for I never met either of them a single time. (I hoped that Short married someone even shorter than he was if only to boost his self-esteem.)

I do know that Fred married a "stocky" girl . . . no—let's be honest—he married a heavy girl. She was also a nice girl, whom I very much liked, but she was—to put it bluntly—fat. Joy was her name. We used to sing a song at the Pentecostal church that went:

Joy, Joy, my heart is full of joy,
Joy, Joy, my ears are full of joy,
Since Jesus Christ came in
And saved my soul from sin,
Everything I have is full of Joy.

After Fred married, I never sang the song without thinking of his wonderful, warm but obese wife. Literally everything Uncle Fred had was full of "Joy"—his entire existence.

Where were all Mama's siblings born? I have no idea, but Mama was born in Guthrie, Indian Territory, seven years before Oklahoma became a state. Only seven years before her birth the great land run known as the Cherokee Strip Run (1893) had occurred. Many had made the mad dash across the Kansas line to stake out 160 acres of free property in northern Oklahoma. The rush changed those who in many cases had "rushed" out of poverty to become quarter-section land barons. They staked their claims in and around Enid, where I would be born forty years later. My wife's grandfather, Lucian Young, was actually carried into Oklahoma as a four-year-old boy. His parents, managing to keep the baby with them, had staked out a claim that after statehood would come to be known as northeast Garfield County. Mama's folks were not "strippers," as those who made the Cherokee Strip homestead run were called.

Following her marriage to Frank, Mama lived for the first years in an unknown address—at least unknown to me—where the first five children were born. Then with Papa's building of the Miller house, she spent the rest of her married years there. David, myself,

Shirley, and Bonnie were all born in the front room of that little house.

There was a threadbare couch in that room that, I suppose, served as the delivery bed. The whole notion of using the family settee as a birthing stool never seemed very sanitary to me, but it became a unique way to brag about the versatility of our décor, if not its posh status. I'm sure it was not a new piece of furniture when it first came to inhabit the front room of the house. But as none of the four Miller children who first drew breath on the couch were unhealthy, it must have been somewhat germ free enough to permit the antiseptic deliveries of Mrs. Miller's last four children.

The idea of being born on a sofa really appealed to me. I liked bringing my little friends home from school to show them the sofa. It gave me, somehow, a feeling of historical significance. The old couch was like the Church of the Nativity in Bethlehem. I wasn't as important as Jesus, but my place of birth was just as certain.

Mama's Three Values: Music, Literature, and Poetry

Nobility is never born of the moment, and my mother—whose character was, it seemed to me, flawless—had lived through an amazing time of suffrage that must have fashioned her quiet, take-charge mystique with massive doses of insecurity. But by the time she entered my awareness in 1940, her divorce would soon be final, and she became for me the basis of security that is so imperative in a child's development. I can see looking back that we grew up poor, but as I have said, it is a wonderful thing when children who are poor never think about it. Mother, of course, must have known it, but it takes a great deal of time to feel sorry for oneself and Mother just never set aside much time for the mopes.

My earliest memories of my mother are hidden in three values I have kept in the widely separate pockets of my life. First, she sang. Not professionally, nor even publicly, but in the daily chores of keeping house and making a home. She had a husky voice, not raspy, but low and gentle. As Lear said of his Cordelia, "Her voice was ever soft, gentle and low, an excellent thing in woman" (*King Lear* V, iii, 274). So it was with Mama.

Yet there is something about a melody, however softly it is sung, that says that life is good, or at least bearable. Of course, I do not remember any lullaby she sang to me, but when I was six or eight, I can remember her singing to my younger sisters. Two of her lullabies were unforgettable. First, she sang, "Toora, loora, loora" . . . that's an Irish lullaby. And I also recall her singing, "How are things in Glocca Mora?" It would be years before I knew the tune was from *Brigadoon*, and for the life of me I don't know how she learned it. We had no radio, nor electricity, nor any means I can think of, by which the melody might have first come to her and become part of her everyday repertoire.

Why did she sing? I think singing keeps terror at a distance. Fear and music never keep to the same side of a dark road.

I've heard that whales sing in the heart of the sea to communicate with each other, and especially with their little ones. Maybe the Creator sets a tune loose in the best of nature's families, so no one need be afraid. Mama's opinion was that music was the exorcism that ordered the demons of fear back to hell.

As for hymns, Mama loved "Beulah Land" and "Abide with Me." She also loved Christmas carols. And she loved Christmas. It was not always a time for gift giving, but she believed that God had given the greatest gift of all, the Christ child. Christ was just something to sing about even when you'd run out of all other reasons for a song. Mama seemed to trust others who sang. Singing people don't hurt others; they are not abusive. Traitors and despots can't play kazoos. In fact, it is hard to imagine Hitler or Hirohito or Genghis Kahn ever whistling a happy tune.

The second value I so esteemed in Mama was that she read to us. She loved to read to her children. I still have in my possession a small, well-marked copy of *A Christmas Carol*, which Grandma had purchased from a drugstore in Guthrie, Indian Territory, in 1906. I have no doubt that Grandma Kent read it to Mother as she was growing up, which is doubtless where Mama got the idea to read it to us. Next to the King James Bible it was the book that probably got the most attention on Mama's reading program.

Mama brought a huge liberation to my life in helping me get a library card. The books I could never have afforded to buy were free for the reading at the Enid Public Library. I never wanted to steal anything but books. I still love books. If I am ever caught shoplifting, it will be in a Barnes & Noble bookstore. Further, I have always had a problem giving back anybody's book that I really liked. And many times when I really enjoyed a book from the library, I had the most awful urge to stick it under my coat and slink out of the library past Enid's more honest readers.

Because I had no radio, reading became my primary pursuit. By the time I was in the sixth grade, I was reading Dumas, Hugo, and all of Dickens I could. I tended to feel sorry for the kids across the street who had electricity that enabled them to listen to radio serials after school. Sometimes I would go home with these friends after school and listen to an episode of *Jack Armstrong: The All-American Boy*, or *The Lone Ranger*, or *Challenge of the Yukon*. But I pitied them. They wasted so much electricity on *The Green Hornet*. This was the first time I actually ever noticed that the ignorant are strangely unaware that they were. When I tried to tell them about the *Last of the Mohicans*, they looked at me like I was the last of the schmucks. Still, once you've read *The Man in the Iron Mask*, it's hard to take *Sky King* seriously.

But the third value that Mama gave me was a love of poetry, good poetry. We had a book of Mother Goose, but from the first I never liked it. I think even as a child I thought it was shallow and connoted no great themes. I don't mean to seem high-hat in considering it shallow, but even as a child I could see through it. Would anyone who had a nice bowl of anything to eat be frightened off her tuffet by a spider? Miss Muffet should have swatted the spider and gone on eating. I would have. Why—on Christmas Day—did Jack Horner eat his pie in a corner? Was he being punished and yet allowed his dessert? Mother Hubbard should not have complained; at least she had a cupboard. We had orange crates.

Mama loved poetry. Mama loved the freer verse of Longfellow, and I learned much of "Evangeline" and *The Song of Hiawatha* out of her love for the poems. I can still recite much of them, and all of "The Wreck of the Hesperus." It is not a talent I'm called upon to exercise often, but if I'm ever on a quiz show, I might fare better than most of the contestants.

Mother would try to sound as masculine and patriotic and basso as she possibly could when she read, "Listen my children and you shall hear of the midnight ride of Paul Revere." She could sound as spooky as a Transylvania scientist when she read Mary Shelley. I also liked to have her read "The Raven" with only a single lamp burning, as near midnight as possible. I was so influenced by Mama's readings of "The Raven" that I wrote my first poem in a Poe-esque style. Edgar Allan Poe's poem, as you may recall, began:

Once upon a midnight dreary as I pondered weak and weary
Over many a quaint and curious volume of forgotten lore,
Suddenly there came a tapping as if someone gently rapping,
Rapping at my chamber door.

But my poem, "The Lark," went:

Once upon a bleak September,
    or 'twas maybe late December,
'Tis quite hard when to remember,
    that I watched each dying ember
Of a brilliant flame grow dark.
A greater love was never known,
    than for this lady I had shown,
Who left me sad and all alone,
    bewitched and ever anon to moan,
The last faint glimmer of a dying spark.

Well, of course, mine was amateurish mimicry. And frankly, a lark is hardly as spooky as a raven, and I had to accede that Poe had chosen the better bird. But it helped me feel better about my bird when I remembered a raven was really a crow. And would anybody have ever read his poem if he had called his poem "The Crow"?

THE STRAW SPINNER

My mother owned Rumpelstiltskin's talent for spinning straw into gold. All through the Great Depression and the "dirty thirties" that followed it, we Millers felt well fed. As I look back on the few family photos we have, I see that like our mother before us, we were all thin and willowy (a condition I wish I had been able to hang on to). But we ate as well as we could. Never did we have to be told to clean our plates. We ate. The hungry never count calories, fat grams, or cholesterol. Indeed, it would be decades before we even learned the terms. Mama cooked everything with lard, which we bought in huge wax boxes. I am sure the nutritionists are right—lard clogs arteries—but our problem was that too much of the time there was not much clogging our esophagi, so artery clogging was a bridge we would cross when we came to it. And lard, well, just let me say, I don't think I've had a good biscuit or a great pie crust since the world gave it up.

Mama cooked. We ate. Still, even back then we couldn't help but notice that some meals are not rich with their variety and are mostly absent of protein. I learned early in life that potatoes were frequent but not beef. Pasta is both cheap and versatile. It is as tasty with tomatoes as it is with milk if you have no tomatoes. It's great with butter if you have no milk. It is not bad with simple salt, if you have nothing but salt. The key to making it taste good is not so much what you ladle over it, but how long you boil it. To make it taste good, you must keep it al dente enough to have substance and even after washing it well enough to keep it from clumping. It gets the *paste* out of the *pasta*—which is where the word *paste* comes from, or vice versa. Limpness and mushyness are the only real sins spaghetti knows.

Lots of good food is free. Dandelion greens are as spinach-like as greens can be. They have the double advantage of being plentiful in the spring and a lot of fun for the children to help gather. Cooking fat was once given away by butchers to anyone who asked for it just before they threw it away. Berries—both black and raspberries—are wonderful, and in some seasons plentiful. Sand plums and elderberries were the number one source of jellies and jams in our home. They were plentiful everywhere outside of town. The bar ditches were thicketed by them. There were enough apple trees around for apples to be had for free, to be canned or kept cool in a box for pies clear through Christmas. Wild pecans were thick-shelled and hard to crack, but always good. We had three black walnut trees. The walnuts were horrible to crack, but once they were broken open, they became the stuff of cakes and goodies. The point was that what was free needn't be bought.

There were many other simple ways my mother had learned to monitor her thrift. Checking is most valuable for income-tax records, but since we had no income, we had neither checks nor tax. Our purchases were totally cash-and-carry. All of our finances were kept in an old Pond's Cold Cream jar that was hidden, for security reasons, at various places in the house.

All of Mama's children knew where she kept the jar, but none of us would ever have considered stealing from the jar. Not ever! First of all, it would be a sin against the Holy Ghost to steal from the jar, punishable by a hundred years in hell for each theft. But there was a more practical reason we never stole from the jar. Mama kept a close count on the contents. Some of my siblings believed that God had blessed her with such sensitive ears she could hear the unscrewing of the cap, even during thunder at midnight. The family fortune was as safe in that cold cream jar as if it had been kept in the vaults at Lloyds of London. Every dollar was always to be accounted for.

Once Mama sent me to Chapman's Grocery Store to buy a few slices of bologna and a loaf of bread. On the way to the store, I lost the dollar, which would be like losing twenty dollars now. When I returned home in tears with no groceries, Mama knew instantly I had lost the money. She went with me to retrace every step of the five-block trip, searching the bar ditches and ruts of the unpaved roads to try and locate the bill. Alas, it was not possible. I wondered if she would whip me, but she didn't. I wanted her to. I deserved it. It would be my way of atoning for my sin of carelessness. Still, there was no second dollar to replace the lost one, and therefore there were no meals until our economy found a way to replenish itself.

Mama had one other hedge against such unsure times. I know not what to call this hedge except "cans under the bed." The bed— we only had one—was an iron bed whose slats kept the bed springs and mattress far enough off the floor to allow us to store things underneath. We had no cupboards or root cellar, and the house was quite small. The larder for our rather large family was the space under our only bed. That's where we stored the cans of edibles designed to get us through the long seasons that stretched between summers.

The cans were of two types. There were the home-canned jars of green beans, tomatoes, and such vegetables as we grew in our hand-spaded garden. The jars were treasured and used year after year. Even the rings that screwed down the seals were reusable. Only the rubber-sealed caps had to be purchased brand new with each canning season.

But my favorite cans were not the things that Mother put up in her pressure cooker, but the "real food" in tin cans, like rich people bought in the grocery stores. Our most dependable source of these canned foods was church Christmas baskets. Every year we Millers got church baskets. We weren't churchgoing people during the early forties after Mother's divorce. Widows were more welcome in church than divorcées, and Mama was in the latter category. It was just easier to stay at home and believe in God rather than go to church and try to believe in churchgoers.

MAMA'S GOD

Mama loved God. Not like the theologians did, austerely or as a career. Mama loved God for free, with no real study of the theologians to back it up. I don't think she loved the God of denominations, who seemed to be shut up in different congregations, each claiming that they knew God best.

She loved God as the Lord of the free life, who couldn't be

bought and never charged a pin's fee for his harvest moon or a sunflower. She loved him as he was, the God of sunrise, the God of first snow, the God who a desperate mother might call on when she was out of ideas on how to hold her world together.

Mother generally liked church. She would have gone without missing if they had been nicer to her, I think. But she didn't complain of their treatment. She tried to avoid Baptist sermons because they were usually severe on divorce. So it took Mama awhile to get up the nerve to walk into church. It was in the late forties when she began to go regularly. When she did return, she volunteered to work in the church nursery. She had a lot of experience in taking care of babies, who never seemed to mind that she was a divorcée. It was only their parents who were prone to criticize her.

Working in the church did not stop the flow of Christmas baskets from the church. In fact, I think it increased the flow. I went to church with Mama, and what I learned during those years was that I never felt particularly poor until the rich came by in December to leave us a Christmas basket. Each time they stopped they "tried to win us to the Lord." They meant well. They were just trying to keep us out of hell till the next holiday, I think. And since we were the benefactors of their annual attacks of piety, we didn't mind being "won to the Lord" several times each Christmas, as long as the rich people kept us shoving the canned goods back under the bed.

Needless to say, we children didn't want to go to those churches that brought us the baskets. The last place you want to go worship is the place where the people need you to be poor so they themselves can feel rich in the dispensation of their charity. There is something grandiose about giving a beggar a dime, but there is nothing grandiose in receiving it. Beggars don't ask for money so they can think well of themselves, but because feeling bad about themselves is usually less painful than starvation.

I think it was in this spirit that Mama received gifts from the church. She knew that church members usually gave two ways. To their own well-heeled members, they baked casseroles and dropped them off at elegant addresses, with a sprig of parsley and a Hallmark card. But to the poor, they dropped off a basket and a can opener. Of course, Mama never refused their baskets, for the shame of it was less than the joy she derived out of being sure her little ones were fed.

There was one other difference in how church members gave food to their own peers. They never asked if they'd been born again when they dropped off a casserole. But it was mandatory that they win as many of us poor people as they could. They would have said they were giving a cup of cold water in Jesus' name. But it was demeaning to have to confess Christ every time they dropped off a basket. Lucky "their own kind," who got casseroles and cards.

For most of my young years, I thought Mama would be an agnostic like Grandma. But by the time I was six or eight, I had changed my mind. Mama was a believer, and it seemed to me she liked Jesus. It was mostly Christians who made her feel bad about who she was, or, more exactly, who her family was. While Grandma had been certain that hell was in Texas, Mama didn't know where it was. But she seemed to feel that those who went there, went because of pretentiousness.

MAMA'S POLITICS

Mama was a Democrat, and while my father was often too plowed under to vote, Mama always went to vote. She saw her vote as altogether important. It was up to her to keep the Democrats in power as best she could. She believed the Republicans were plutocrats who didn't understand the common person.

MAMA'S VILLAGE

Poor or not, everybody has social needs, including Mama. They say it takes a village to raise a child, and Mama was a woman in need of a village. She particularly liked two women who came to touch my own life. They were Mrs. Duerksen, my principal, and Miss Thompson, a self-ordained preacher who opened a little mission church within three blocks of our home.

Mrs. Duerksen was the principal of Woodrow Wilson Grade School. She was a Mennonite with a wonderful sense of largesse about her. She could see that most of her first graders were from very poor families, but she seemed committed to the notion that no child deserved to live in poverty. One family was so poor the children had no shoes to wear to school even in the severest months of winter. I know this bothered Mrs. Duerksen. She managed to get coats for all of us, and she managed to find shoes for one of those boys. Once he was shod against mud and frostbite, Mrs. Duerksen asked me why I never wore galoshes when it was raining. I told her I had never had galoshes and that if my mother thought them necessary, she would see to it that I got a pair.

The next day Mrs. Duerksen asked me to stay after school, and when all the children were gone, she asked me to sit down in one of the little front desks, and she brought me a pair of galoshes. They were shiny black and each of them was equipped with four metal snap hooks. They were beautiful. I started to take off my shoes so I could try them on, and she said, "No, no, child! You can keep your shoes on. These are made to slip right over your shoes." I was amazed that you could actually wear two pair of footwear at a time. I put them both on, and smiled and stood and walked around in them.

"How much do they cost?" I asked.

"They're free for everybody in the Woodrow Wilson first grade whose initials are 'C.M.'" I was flabbergasted! Those were my initials! "You wear them home," said Mrs. Duerksen. "It looks like rain to me."

I hung around for a minute or two.

"What is it, child?" she asked.

"Well," I hesitated, "don't you want me to be born again or something? I never got anything free without being born again."

"Well, now you have. I'm sure if you need to get born again, the Baptists can help you with that. But the galoshes are yours. You run along now!"

It was bright and sunny outside and it didn't look like rain at all, but I thought I better keep them on just in case it came a gully-washer.

"Son," asked Mama, "where did you get those beautiful galoshes?"

"Mrs. Duerksen gave them to me, and I didn't even have to be born again!"

"Then it was truly a gift," said Mama.

From that moment on Mrs. Duerksen was a part of Mama's village.

MISS THOMPSON

Another person in Mama's village was Miss Thompson.

With a house full of little ones, Mama felt she should take us children to church. So it came to pass that in 1946 a woman named simply Miss Thompson opened a little church in a reclaimed barracks building over on Davis Street. There was an abundance of old army barracks available after the war was over, and they could be bought cheap and moved around on flatbeds. Miss Thompson apparently had bought one, along with a small lot to put it on. She opened a church that she called Highland Church. There were no other adjectives on the sign. Being single herself, Miss Thompson didn't seem to mind the fact that Mama was a divorcée.

At Highland Church we had a church anthem written by Miss Thompson. It was a spinoff of the old hymn "The Church in the Wildwood." Miss Thompson often played it on the piano as we sang:

> Oh come to the church out at Highland
> [rather than *in the Wildwood*]
> Oh come to the church in the dale
> [which was really on the prairie],
> No church is so dear to my childhood,
> As the little brown church [the church was really white]
> in the dale.

Miss Thompson encouraged all the boys and men (of which there weren't many) to sing the countermelody on the hymn. So we boys would sing, "Oh, come, come, come, come, come, come, come, come . . ." while Miss Thompson and our mothers and sisters sang the main chorus. It was all heady stuff, and we had a wonderful time singing in that little church.

We also sang "Marching to Zion," which my little sister Bonnie could never get. She asked where Zion was, but no one seemed to know. Further, the chorus ended with "and *thus* surround the throne," which she sang, "and *dust* around the throne." It did no good to try to explain to her that "thus" was an old adverb that people didn't generally use anymore but it was proper to use it when singing "Marching to Zion." She never got it, however, and to the final time we ever sang the hymn together, she believed that our main activity in heaven would be to dust around the throne.

Miss Thompson preached short sermons. This made Jesus look attractive to all of us. She had some hang-ups—don't all preachers? She believed movies were "of the devil." I was not a moviegoer, for they were very expensive. Still, I was sorry to hear they were of the devil because I really wanted to go to one. I'd heard of Rhett Butler, but I was resigned to the fact that, like the apostles, he lived in another day. While Rhett came and went at the Aztec Theater on Randolph Street, he was rich and out of reach for our economy. I had a desperate urge to see Judy Garland in *The Wizard of Oz*, mostly because it all happened in Kansas, which was only sixty miles from Enid. But Miss Thompson felt that movies were addictive and you could start out with Toto and end up with Lon Chaney Jr., the Wolf Man.

Along with preaching against movies, Miss Thompson also preached against wearing shorts. She said women in shorts could cause men to lead a life of lust. I liked to hear her preach that doctrine, 'cause Oklahoma men didn't wear shorts much in 1940 as they were generally thought of as sissified. In fact, I didn't even own any shorts. For that matter, I didn't own many shirts either, so often in the summer months I would go to church only in my overalls, sans shirt or shoes. Nobody as far as I knew ever lusted after me.

Miss Thompson—and she went right along with the Baptists in preaching this—said Jesus was coming back again and that we should all get ready. I wasn't sure how to get ready with such a limited wardrobe. Miss Thompson said it wasn't what you were wearing that got you ready. It was the state of your heart. "You should not think wicked thoughts," she said.

Darn it! I thought wicked thoughts all the time. I sinned constantly in my heart! I wanted to go to see Judy Garland. I wanted to play cards. I even thought it might be fun to smoke Lucky Strikes, once I got enough money to make such wickedness possible.

Miss Thompson really felt that cigarettes were sinful and "you surely wouldn't want to be smoking them when Jesus came again." We shouldn't do anything that Jesus wouldn't do. "Can you imagine Jesus hanging on the cross with a cigarette in his mouth?" she challenged rather forcefully from the pulpit. I couldn't imagine Jesus up there puffing away while he was trying to save mankind, so I knew she was right.

"Girls, be cleaner than a nicotiner!" she preached, quoting a church sign I had seen out on U.S. Highway 81. Once she said, "If

God wanted you to smoke he would have put a chimney on your head." This seemed to be going a bit too far.

But Miss Thompson loved divorcées, and she made Mama feel right at home. Mama loved the church, where she picked up quite a few other divorcées for her friends. There were many ex-Baptist, ultra-wicked divorcées who attended there.

Miss Thompson's origin was unknown; she just showed up on Davis Street with an old barracks and started being nice. The Baptists said women could not be called to preach. There were verses in the Bible that prohibited it. I don't know if Miss Thompson knew about those verses, but we didn't. And when you find some-one who's nice, you don't start looking through the Bible to try and hunt them down.

Maybe Miss Thompson was disobeying the Bible for being a woman preacher; I don't know. Miss Thompson might have been the Antichrist, but she didn't seem like it. All I know is she didn't look down on us Millers and Mama liked her for that.

Miss Thompson must have spent all her own money to make the Highland Church happen. Just her Oreo and Kool-Aid fund must have been stressing. It's funny for children who were unaccustomed to having sweets, how one little dangerous sally into doctrine can wreck things. She gave us oranges and hard candy at Christmas in little brown sacks, and I liked her for that.

Her sermons were generally kind, and if she didn't like movies and shorts and cigarettes, she must have had her reasons. Miss Thompson also did not like dancing. "You will never find a praying knee and a dancing foot on the same leg," she said. In the midforties, Mama belonged to the Townsend Club. It was not an elite place. It was just a place where the middle-aged played records and danced to folk melodies, like polkas and schottisches. Most of those who frequented the Townsend Club were married and everyone— whether married, or not—brought their children. Mama took the three youngest of us (Bonnie and Shirley, my younger siblings, were four and six, consecutively. I was eight). I rather enjoyed seeing Mother have a good time with women and men in their early forties. And two such men from the club took a fancy to Mother.

The first man had a harelip that made him talk funny, and his lack of good clear consonants caused us children to refer to him as "Motna Motna." We did this with no disrespect. It's just that everything he said came out "motna, motna," and thus his conversation was largely unintelligible. Mother apparently could understand him. She also understood that he was visiting our poor little house in an effort to strike up an alliance of sorts. We children prayed earnestly that Mother would not fall in love with Motna Motna, and the gracious Lord answered our prayers. Mother had enough problems to handle without adding Motna Motna to her to-do list. Furthermore, he, like us, had no car, and I believed that if Mother should ever marry again, she should at least have the good judgment to marry someone with a car.

In this respect the second man was a better choice for Mama than Motna, Motna had been: he owned a 1939 Hudson coupe. We children all realized his "one-seater" would be an impediment to us all going on a family outing together, since the car only held two people. He was quite heavy, and his dancing at the Townsend Club was ponderous and slow. Still, he huffed and puffed his way around the dance floor as best he could.

When he came to our house to see Mama, he didn't really seem to walk as much as he puttered about. It is perhaps because he puttered around that we children began to call him "Potterby," the kind of name you come up with when you cross a "putterer" with a potbellied Romeo.

We never called him Potterby to his face, which seemed to us to be as Christian as we needed to be. We didn't really mind Mama "dating" Potterby; after all it is nice to ride in a car sometimes. This was a treat we children would never really get to experience. Once, Potterby drove me around the block, and just the feel of riding with the windows open and going fast was exhilarating. But once the ride was over, Potterby had used up his only possible way of causing me to think well of him.

Miss Thompson didn't approve of my mother going to dances. And while she never said so out loud in any private conversation, she was a little more prone to denounce dancing in her sermons if my mother was present in the preaching service. Miss Thompson thought dancing could lead to sex and raw lust. Obviously she had never met Motna, Motna and Potterby.

SENSIBLE THRIFT

Mother's sense of thrift amazed me even as a child. For seven cents apiece you could buy a new-hatched chick, if you purchased them in hundred-chick lots. So in mid-February every year, as the coldest of Oklahoma weather was winding down, Mother always came home from the hatchery with a box of one hundred little chickens. I cannot describe the excitement the day brought. To open the box in the front room floor was to release a storm of yellow-fuzzed fury. I could never resist the urge to play with them as long as Mother would allow. But the playtime never lasted long. The little chicks had a destiny that would not be realized until June and July, when they were encouraged to give up their lives for a place in Mama's cast-iron skillet.

In the meantime, these little chicks flew about the house and scattered so explosively about the room it was hard to get them all rounded up again to take out to the brooder house.

The term *brooder house* suggests a well-planned structure, built by thoughtful, rural carpenters. In reality it was a crudely constructed coop made of scrap lumber, weathered two-by-fours, and warped pieces of plywood. Nonetheless, it was relatively snake proof and entirely cat proof. Cats could worry the chickens, but creating a fidgety neurosis was about all they could manage.

Gradually, as the weather warmed, these growing pullets and young roosters could go in and out of their coop at will and play in the small, fenced-in area that surrounded the brooder house. Then came June. By this time they looked less like playful pets and more like drumsticks and thighs. When it was time for our first chicken dinner of the season, Mama would advance into the chicken pen, corner a bird, and grab the startled fowl by its neck.

She had two ways of slaughtering a chicken. The first was the use of a small hand axe, by which she merely guillotined the bird. The second way she dispatched a chicken was a method known as "wringing the chicken." It was done by grasping the chicken's head in the hand and beginning a circular movement of the body around the axis of her very strong wrist. Then, when the rotation of the chicken's body was straining to keep its continued attachment to the neck, Mama would snap her wrist in a kind of lethal whip-crack that separated the edible part of the chicken from its more useless, thinking part.

What happened next was what was amazing. The flurry of activity by the headless fowl was a spastic and exaggerated rolling and jumping about. They did things—acrobatic things—they had never done in a better state of health. I would have thought the whole business cruel, had I not known how necessary it all was to provide our chicken dinner. And however inhumane it first appeared, it was just another step toward a meal, like peeling a potato or mixing up a batch of biscuits.

When the birds ceased their dying, they were plunged headlong into a scalding bath, and then their feathers were easily pulled out. Sometimes reluctant pinfeathers had to be dealt with in a more tedious fashion. Following this, a bird could be held over the flame until the fuzz had been singed away, and then it was only a matter of gutting the bird, throwing away all the entrails (except the hearts, livers, and gizzards), dismembering the bird, dipping its various parts in egg and flour, and throwing them all in the sizzling lard of the cast-iron skillet. The key to doing it well was to be sure the kindling in your wood stove was providing a good bed of glowing embers that would keep the grease hot enough to bring the chicken to a golden brown in a matter of thirty minutes or so.

These were robust days. People were robust, and the chickens were, in a sense, robust. I remember years later seeing the pale blue chickens huddled under cellophane at the Safeway store. They looked not like they had been slaughtered for human consumption but that they had died of a lingering illness that left them covered with yellow pimples and a leprously opaque skin. Life is too purchased now, but back then it was created by people who began their chicken dinners with real live chickens, not barcoded, rubber replicas of something that looks edible only after it has been cooked.

Mama Fought the Welfare System

Mama fought vigorously to hold our family together in the hard times. Once, the richest woman in our neighborhood, being married to a prosperous fireman, turned Mama in to the county welfare for not taking better care of her children. She said there were five to ten people living in what was essentially a one-room house (during the war years some of the older girls were back in the house, creating what seemed an unbelievably crowded situation), and all were well below the poverty line and did not have enough to eat. The county welfare officer came to talk to Mama about putting her children in a foster home until she could get on her feet financially.

I didn't know exactly what a foster home was, but it was clearly somewhere the state forced you to go. The "foster mama" was not your real mama, whom you would never get to see again. I was terrified by the concept. So the hardest moments of my life were when I saw my mother crying, as I did after that woman turned us in to the authorities.

Mama fought the case like a wildcat and was very stern with the various authorities who visited our house. Mama did all she could to make the house presentable and clean. She could, of course, not make it opulent. But she did manage to get her young sons-in-law to put up more sheetrock on the bare studs to divide the house a little better into a semblance of having three rooms. It was not enough, the authorities said. And again Mama cried.

When Mama cried, we all did. She argued and resisted, and finally the welfare officers began to retreat from their suit. I was absolutely broken as a child as I thought of losing Mama as our mother. When children are afraid, their fear destroys their hope. There is nothing sadder than to see children torn from their parents.

Mama never liked our neighbor after that. None of us did. I wanted to burn her house down, but was dissuaded by my mother, who told me how poor she really was. "She has no cans under the bed, and she doesn't even know how to put up tomatoes. She doesn't own a single Ball Mason jar," said Mama. Only after I heard of our neighbor's poverty did I feel charitable enough toward her to keep from becoming an arsonist.

My mother was a miracle worker. Wood ranges were supposed to yield hot berry pies and overflow with yeasty loaves of bread. Life was an economy. Mama gave dignity to thrift. There were wonderful things all about us that were free and left us with no need to frequent pretentious shops. Department stores were for people with limited ingenuity.

I realize now after all these years what a wizard Mama was. She was an engineer of sorts, a specialist who had learned home economics from her mother who had eaten meals by a covered wagon. And if there were boysenberries, we had a pie crusted with flour and lard, golden and delicious. Flour was almost always there, yeast was cheap, and light rolls were her specialty.

MAMA'S MANNA

Mother taught us that it was God who supplied the bread, while we were but the "managers of heaven's gifts." God's care of us was like manna. It lay on the ground to be taken up fresh every morning.

Our house backed up to "the tracks." The tracks were the steel footprints of these mammoth dragons that stalked the land in which we lived. I often sat by the rails and waved at the engineers who rode the iron dragons like powerful warlords on armored beasts. These "puffer-bellies" drew strings of namby-pamby boxcars along the silver strands. Some said the railroad went all the way to St. Louis in the east and ended in Los Angeles in the west. I could only sit and dream.

But these tracks were not dreaming places to my mother. While I celebrated their intrigue, she celebrated their gravel beds that held more than the rails. The old boxcars that held the grain jolted and banged their way around the tracks during harvest. When they banged, they leaked, and their spillage became our manna—our daily bread.

So Mama took a broom and burlap bags and went and swept up the piles of spilled grain. She often took me with her to help carry the grain back to our house. I hated doing it, because it was heavy and we had to carry it a long way, or it seemed to me.

She was cheerful, however, that there was so much to be gathered for free. There was a picture in our Bible of Ruth the Moabitess. (I always liked saying *Moabitess*, and even in my adult years I maintained a fondness for saying it just that way and rarely thought of Ruth in any other way.) Ruth was a gleaner, gleaning in the fields of Bethlehem. In the pictures, she was standing tall with her small scythe, looking out over the fields of sheathed grain. Mama was tall, and I couldn't help wondering if she had posed for the artist who painted the Bible picture. Her whole deportment seemed to say, "We are the gleaners," though she never once said it out loud.

Despising the drudgery of the work, I often complained. "Mama, these fields are so wide. It's such a long way to carry the wheat back home."

She would stop and rest and pat me on the head and say, "The fields only seem large because you're so small. When you are bigger, you will see the fields won't seem so big at all."

Thirty years later, Mama died and was buried only a few miles from those very tracks where I learned the nature of her thrift. After the funeral, I went back to the old house and walked alone down those very tracks, where I once had complained about the size of the fields. Mama was right. They were not all that wide. Everything shrinks—the globe itself—when your perspective is right. And while it took me years to see this, the vision was clearer after Mama herself lay sleeping beneath those very fields I once felt were unmanageable. After her funeral I wrote:

Three decades past I skipped along beside
Her. Soul tired—I carried grain and grumbled.
How tall she looked! How large the fields! Her stride

Was smooth. Attempting to keep pace, I stumbled.
She sat the grain where all the grass looked dead,
And ran her fingers through my tangled thatch.
"Someday the fields will seem so small," she said.
"When you've grown large the fields will be no match."
"The fields are very wide," I said. "You'll see!"
She grinned and kissed my immaturity.
Our shadows were El Greco-esque as we
Trudged on across the endless earthen sea.
She sleeps beneath those fields where she stood tall,
And I, at last, can see the fields are small.[1]

FOUR

The War the Pentecostals Ended

"Ive never gotten so tired of any one word in my life as war,'" said Scarlett O'Hara in *Gone with the Wind*. The year Margaret Mitchell wrote those words, 1936, was the year I was born.

The Prophecy

Somewhere around 1940, a Ouija board came into our home and became a favorite plaything of my sister Patsy Ruth. One day, as she was playing with the board and asking it questions, she asked the little brown and yellow planchette when the war would come to an end. And the planchette moved erratically but steadily to August of 1945. So like Cassandra on the walls of Troy, she made a prophecy. She believed the war would last four years and would be associated with great heartache. She didn't say the heartache would affect the Miller family, but her words I think hung over my mother's heart with a force of soul that would not leave Mama for the next four years. It was not that Mama thought Patsy Ruth had the gift of witchery; it was just that Mama felt she had so much to lose if her third eldest daughter turned out to be right.

Here and there in life, though I cannot account for the gift, there seem to be souls who are gifted with a kind of second sight. I seek no accord for what I believe or doubt about the matter. While I will not write it into law, it was Patsy Ruth who early on made an accurate prediction about the war that to this day I am unable to shake, and find both fascinating and macabre.

During the war I watched Mama read the newspapers—which were not all that frequent in our house. She lived through a gut-wrenching four-year era of prayer. During those years newspaper headlines were heavily inked, large and intense. The battles were bloody. Behind all this, adding its ache to the days, was Patsy Ruth's prophecy. I hated the war simply because of what it was doing to my mother, four of whose children were married to soldiers or sailors by the middle years of the conflict.

THE MARRYING YEARS

The four eldest Miller children were girls born between 1921 and 1926. Izetta, Frankie, Patsy Ruth, and Nettie Helen were their names. And between the years of 1940 and 1943, at the rate of one a year, all four girls married. Their husbands were not all military men at the time of their marriages, but before reaching their second anniversaries, every husband answered the draft. One by one, the married girls left the house on Poplar Street. Patsy Ruth, having no prospects of a husband, decided to join the navy, and within a year of that decision had met and married a sailor herself. But before they got married, they dated, and it was their dates that most intrigued me.

While the two oldest, Izetta and Frankie, dated young men with no cars, their younger sisters lucked out. What I found most fascinating was that Patsy Ruth and Nettie Helen, when they began to date, lured boys who did have cars. First, Nettie Helen, when she was only fourteen, began seeing Jesse Dillon, a handsome young man who was himself one of seven children from a family in Pond Creek, Oklahoma. He worked on the "killing floor" of Bandfield's slaughterhouse in the industrial north end of Enid. This slaughterhouse was only a little ways from our home. He had a high school diploma, and this made him look like a collegian to most of our neighbors. But best of all, he had a brand-new 1939 Chevrolet—not a coupe either.

Nettie Helen was coquettish and a flirt—in the most honorable sense of the word—and had managed to catch his eye at the Rollarena, Enid's premier roller-skating rink. From that moment on, his Chevy could be seen parked in our unpaved driveway, on our dusty lane called Poplar Street.

I don't mean to be playing on your conscience by talking so much about unpaved streets. Before World War II, much of America was unpaved. In fact, the first transcontinental highway, the Lincoln Highway, which was to driving what the Union Pacific was to railroading, was only finished in 1936, and the beginning of the interstate program was still more than fifteen years away. Even at the end of the war, America had only 119 million citizens, and most of them did not own cars. But Jesse Dillon did. I never got to ride in Jesse's shiny car, but I loved to gaze at my reflection in its door panels.

Jesse and Nettie Helen's romance was furious and wild. When Helen was fifteen—Jesse was twenty—they married, and before Helen was sixteen they were living at Fort Bragg, North Carolina, where Jesse was in training for the U.S. Army. They recently celebrated their sixty-sixth year of marriage.

Patsy Ruth, being a Wave (Women's Navy), married a navy petty officer, Jimmy Boggs, in 1942, and as soon as they could, they came home to see us. He had a green 1939 Lincoln Zephyr. I was dumbfounded. I never got to ride in it either, but it also was really a nice car for looking at my reflection. They were stationed in Pensacola,

Florida, where Jimmy worked on an aircraft carrier—a new concept in battle fleet—and Patsy Ruth Miller Boggs worked in the naval offices on shore.

THE MILLER END OF THE WAR EFFORT

Everyone talked about the war, and Patsy Ruth's prophecy had settled on us like a heavy weight. Prophecy is a hard thing to bear. If you try to tell others about it, they think you are crazy. If you ignore it, you feel that you are unwise. So you carry it with you all the time without talking about it.

But there were two places we all talked about the war.

The first place was the church. Except for my brief summer experiences of vacation Bible school, I didn't go to church much. But everyone I met at vacation Bible school was pretty much convinced that Hitler was the Antichrist. I certainly believed it, as did all the Baptists, Wesleyans, and Pentecostals. And it was easy to pick up the chit-chat from the VBS Kool-Aid and Oreo line that Hitler was the Antichrist and would soon be crossing the Euphrates with a great army from the east. We all believed in Hitler's coming world domination even though it was hardly logical. Why was it illogical? Well, for one thing, crossing the Euphrates would not be Hitler's most direct route to Jerusalem from Berlin. Still, the Bible was clear: Armageddon would be fought by an army from the east, so Hitler would have to comply. Adolf Hitler and the entire German army would simply go into Iran, swim across the Euphrates, cross the Arabian Desert, pontoon the Jordan, and send the Panzer tanks into Jerusalem from the Middle East. Hitler would just have to learn that while it is not always easy to fulfill prophecy, it had to be done the Bible way. He would just have to learn that even if you really enjoyed being the Antichrist you still had to obey the Scriptures and do things right.

School was the other place we talked about the war. There were only three blocks of concrete sidewalks between Woodrow Wilson Grade School and our house, so we had to walk through the last four blocks of dust or mud, depending on the weather, to get home. But all along the first three blocks of sidewalk we chanted with fervor, "Step on a crack and you break Hitler's back." We stepped on every crack we could. It was our contribution to the war effort. The practice became so customary that the monotonous rhyme engendered inner pictures of the chancellor of Germany laid up as a quadriplegic and directing the German side of the war from an iron lung.

We also contributed to the war effort by holding our hands over our hearts as we pledged allegiance to the flag to begin every day's activities at school. We then sang "My Country 'Tis of Thee" with our hands remaining over our hearts. We prayed for the troops every day. Every child had someone in their family serving in the military, and most of them had fathers in uniform. No one thought of being unpatriotic. It would be years before any one of us would hear of the ACLU. We just supposed that God was on our side, and it never occurred to us that Germany was also considered a Christian nation. Why would we ever have considered that? After all, Germany had the Antichrist for its president.

At school we bought war-bond stamps. They cost ten cents apiece, and when you bought the first one, you were given a booklet into which you could stick the stamps. When you collected 175 of them, you would have $17.50 in your booklet, and then you could take it to a post office or bank and trade it in for a twenty-five dollars savings bond, or "war bond" as it was often called. Because we only bought one stamp a week, and we only went to school forty or so weeks per year, it took me a little over four years to fill up my war-stamp book. Nonetheless, we were enthusiastic about supporting our troops.

This, as Studs Terkel would later call it, was the "good war." It was a good war because all America believed it was the right course of action. None of Mama's four son-in-law soldiers objected to the military draft when they were called to go to war. They all served honorably and willingly. My sisters supported their husbands in the effort. My eldest sister, Izetta, like Rosie the Riveter, took her place working at Pillsbury Mill, because all the men in Enid—including her husband—were off to war. She worked in the mill for the entire length of the war. Mama couldn't afford to buy war bonds, but she encouraged us children to buy savings stamps. The war was for all of us a crusade we jointly owned. It wasn't the president's war or the congress's war. We owned the cause—this American cause. And the war was for us a holy war.

Before the war was over, each of Mama's four eldest daughters had a baby—most of them two. And one of those daughters, Patsy Ruth, came with her baby to live with us through most of the war years while her husband was overseas. Each time anyone lived with us for any length of time they always got to sleep in the only bedroom area the house had, crowding the rest of us into the remaining floor areas of the little house. Still, at the time it was a situation that had to be managed. All housing was tight during the war. No new houses were being built, and what already existed had to be redesigned to accommodate the transient, ever-moving families of a nation at war.

Nettie Helen and Jesse had their first child in 1943, while they were stationed at Fort Bragg. Helen was still only seventeen and was most anxious that Mama be with her when her first baby was born. So Mama packed up all three of her young ones, and we took the Continental Trailways bus from Enid to Fort Bragg. No one thought it unusual that a woman would travel by bus with her three children so far across the nation. Everyone was going somewhere. All buses were full.

I will never forget the trip. What I remember most was that the bus was filled to capacity with soldiers. And what I remember about them was that they were attendant to my mother at every turn, sometimes giving up their seats so she could care for her little ones. I was seven at the time, Shirley was four years old, and Bonnie two. In every crowded bus terminal the soldiers were as kind to us as if we were war orphans, and in a way I suppose we were. I was sick for the entire trip with travel nausea. I had never taken a trip anywhere by bus and had only been in a car a few times in my life. The diesel odor of the bus, the close air, the big crowds, the whining of the engine, and constant rolling and curving and churning and stopping left me desperately ill the whole way. Reaching North Carolina was a great gift to me. My nausea left me. I will never forget the joy of just being somewhere with no need to ride anything to go anywhere else.

Patricia Gail Dillon, Nettie Helen's first child, arrived on schedule, and Mama was overjoyed to have the grandbaby, who was only a couple years younger than the youngest of her own babies. And because the little one arrived in October of '43, we children were back in Oklahoma for Thanksgiving. It was a good one.

The following Christmas came and went, and then another. Mama read the headlines and prayed. I brought home news to Mama after listening to the radio at a friend's home. None of Mama's children, so far, had suffered any harm. Theron, Izetta's husband, served in the Pacific but had not fought on the terrible beachheads of Guadalcanal or Iwo Jima. Nonetheless, it was he who was ever in the most danger.

THE COURIER

I was able to be of some help to Mama, because I had made friends with two little school chums. They were identical twins whose house was nearly as small and as ill furnished as our own. There was one difference. They had electricity and a radio. Because the Oklahoma summers were so hot, we three boys would often play underneath their house where it was cooler. Their house sat high on foundation blocks, because our neighborhood was flat and low and subject to flash flooding. On any day during the war years we could be found playing there for hours, while I joined the twins as they listened to the radio serials of *Sky King*, *The Lone Ranger*, *The Green Hornet*, and *Challenge of the Yukon* (although, as I have already confessed, they appealed less to me than to most children).

I never left their house until after the six o'clock news, when the Walter Winchell newscast came on. I listened fervently to the war news and remembered all I could. As soon as the news was over, I ran home as fast as I could and reported to my mother all that Walter Winchell had said.

I was the only one of the three Miller boys at home long enough to serve as such a courier. Dickie's death and David's rebellious youth divided the family into two families, really. Mama had four girls, three boys, and two girls, in that order. David and Dickie, the oldest of the boys, dropped out of the family scene. Dickie died young and David began running around and staying out nights as early as twelve years of age. While his lifestyle bothered Mother, never knowing where he was drove her up the wall. His frequent absence at least freed some space in our house, but, along with Dickie's death, it did one other thing: it set a cleavage of years in the family, for without David and Dickie between the four oldest children and the three youngest there was now a gap of an entire decade. The oldest four were old enough to get married and go to war. As the oldest of the three younger ones, I was free to remember the war, to some degree, but certainly not old enough for the military draft. So during these turbulent years I was the courier.

In the spring of 1945, it became clear that the war was turning in our favor, and no one expected it to last much longer. Three short weeks before it was over, Roosevelt died, never living to feel the strong surge of victory that would have been his, a victory he had dreamed of since the declaration of war in 1941. The day he died, I was playing under the porch with my chums when the news came over the radio. The announcement filled me with fear. I didn't know how I was going to break this news to my mother. My mother was a Democrat—a yellow-dog Democrat—who very much admired Roosevelt, even to the point of idolization. She believed he had done so much to help the poor, especially in the post-Depression years. She even believed that her coming to a better state of financial affairs had been in some sense the direct result of a president whose programs had befriended people like the Millers. She also admired how he waged his own private war with polio.

Her esteem for the president was strong. Being the first to learn of the president's death, I felt afraid that merely to announce the fact would threaten my own life somehow. Mother had long reminded me in other circumstances that Shakespeare had said, "The bearer of unwelcome news hath a losing office." I was sure I held such an office. She might whip me just for the unwelcome report, true or false. So when I had run home, I hesitantly began to tell her the day's news that had come over the radio.

"Mama," I ventured cautiously, feeling my way, "I hate to tell you this, but President Roosevelt died today."

"Son, if you're lying to me, I'll beat you to death," she said sternly.

Suddenly I had cold feet. Had I heard the radio right? Maybe the commentator said he was just very sick. I could be the one who was going to be dead. I breathed a silent prayer, *Lord, please help President Roosevelt to be dead. At this point it looks like it is going to be either him or me!*

Lucky for me, the commentator had told the truth, and I had faithfully reported what the radio had announced. So I lived on, though Mama seemed less chipper for a few days. Just a few weeks later, Mrs. Duerksen called us all into the Woodrow Wilson auditorium and told us that Germany had surrendered and the war was genuinely over. It was a great day, and it was accompanied by military music and fireworks, even in Enid.

THE LAST YEARS OF THE CONFLICT

May gave way to more reports of heavy fighting in the Pacific. Then came the worst headlines of all: the August headlines. It was the horrible tale of bombs on Japanese cities, of multiplied thousands of souls all being instantly cremated. There were further tales of thousands of others suffering radiation poisoning, blindness, and burns. It was more than I could really stand. The newspaper pictures of the Japanese bombings were enough to make even the most secure child afraid. I trembled before the terrifying photos that dominated the *Enid Daily Eagle*.

Shortly after Nagasaki I went to Gore Park in Enid with a nine-year-old friend to watch a softball game. This friend was entranced by the sermons of various Pentecostal preachers who came to the church I had begun to attend. Their fiery sermons were lit by the charred remains of Japanese cities. I was appalled at how freely my young friend seemed to relish talking about the Japanese bombings. I didn't see how he could manage to be so blatantly cold about the whole subject of human suffering.

We were eating strawberry snow cones as we half-heartedly watched the ballgame. I leaned back against the backstop, thinking of the pictures in the paper. He told me about a verse of Scripture in Revelation that spoke of Armageddon. He said when the last battle was fought, there would be blood up to the horses' bridles.

He asked me if I knew about the Great Whore of Babylon and the mark of the Beast.

I was terrified by all that he told me about the end of the world. "We'd all be lucky," he said, "if we asked Jesus to be our Savior, 'cause you never know when Jesus will be coming back. It could happen just about any time, and it will be very secretive. Only those who know Jesus will be taken up into heaven, and those who don't will be burned up just like those poor people in Nagasaki, who probably didn't know Jesus because they are Japanese and not Christians like we are."

He also felt for sure that his uncle was probably going to be left behind and he would be burned up just like the Japanese. But his aunt would be taken up. One morning the uncle would wake up and his aunt would be gone, and he would know she'd been whooshed away, and that he would probably start whining—he was always a whiner—because of all the fire that he was gonna get for worshipping the Beast. "All unbelievers will be burned up, and there would be blood up to the horses' bridles," my friend repeated a second time.

I gazed down at my strawberry snow cone, and I burst into tears.

I cried all the way home.

That same month, my oldest sister received word that her husband, Theron, was killed by a Japanese sniper in the very first days of the occupation of Tokyo and the very last season of the war. All that Mama had prayed for seemed lost. Only one of her sons-in-law had died in the war, but just the idea of it caused a pall to settle down upon our little family.

It was a time of national hope, but the headlines and the pictures in the paper and Theron's death were more than I personally could stand. Mama noticed my moroseness and said, "The war is over now. Your sister's men will soon be coming home—all but one of them."

"But, Mama, the pictures in the paper."

"You will forget about them in time," she said. "The world will be better the pictures will fade."

But I couldn't get the newspapers to leave my mind. "But Mama, the pictures! Did the big bombs really float down on parachutes?"

"They say they did, but don't think about it now," she said.

I watched the maple seeds that summer twist in the dry wind and sail and spin like the propellers of P-38s and Flying Tigers. I knew all of the planes from their pictures in the papers. As I watched the maple "propeller" seeds spin their way to the ground, I thought of that great canopy of white silk that settled over the children of Japan until finally, like a lotus blossom, it erupted into fire that seared Nagasaki and its children forever into silence.

THE PENTECOSTAL CONCLUSION OF WORLD WAR II

It seemed like the future was no longer there in any real way. But my perceptions were soon to dissolve in an event that was as beautiful as Armageddon was horrendous. I found a new geography of joy that reigned over plains of peace. And as the song went, there really could be "peace in the valley."

Later in that same August, near the first day of school, some men were putting up a tent in an empty field near our home. I was excited at first, for I felt it was a circus coming to town. I was a bit disappointed when on the second day of raising their big tent they put up a sign out in front of it that said "Revival." I did agree so with Tom Sawyer who said that church "ain't shucks to a circus," and might not have gone to the revival at all except for a neighborhood chum who not only went to the revival but came home after the service telling me that he had been saved.

"Who saved you?" I asked. He had never been a model child and generally had a brattish reputation around the neighborhood.

"God," he said simply.

I was puzzled by God's good judgment. Why on earth would God want to save him when his folks had been looking for reasons to drown him over the years?

"Come with me tomorrow night," he said.

It was a simple invitation and I accepted it. The very next night I was there in the service with him. I sat on a plank supported by concrete blocks. I shuffled my naked feet through the wood shavings that served as a floor for the tabernacle. The aroma of the newly sawn wood fibers that filtered through the tattered canvas of the revival tent brought an exhilaration of spirit.

It was still years before I would visit the cathedrals of Europe, so in my provincial view, the tent was really a great church. The hymns were as happy as the brotherhood was exhibitionist. Here I found a reprieve from the heaviness of Nagasaki and ballpark prophecy. The sawdust seemed sweet and safe. It felt warm to my bare feet. The tent was a haven where they sang of heaven.

"When We All Get to Heaven," they sang . . . perhaps the hymn was escapist. Maybe it kept those who sang it from seeing the troubled world at hand. But its lyrics offered me a kind of hope. Could heaven's pearly gates and golden streets be any sweeter than fresh sawdust and amber canvas? The electric lights inside the tent shined out through the coarse canvas, making the tabernacle look like a huge, happy jack-o-lantern. Then they sang the "Haven of Rest," and I knew I had found a Pentecostal stopover in my parched Armageddon.

They sang "Just as I Am."

They begged me to come forward, but they really didn't need to. I hurried top speed into the arms of Jesus. I fell on my knees among much weeping and much joy and wash of emotion.

Two great ladies in flour sack dresses, as rotund as they were earnest, prayed me through to the throne of Jesus, and there in the rich smell of sawdust, I met Christ.

In he came!

My hefty weeping friends told me Christ had saved my soul, but I knew it was far better than that. I was new! I was free. The newspapers could no longer extinguish hope. The dark years met sunrise. Christ was there and he was mine.

I had changed worlds.

Years later in reflecting on both my mother's love and the love of Christ, I wrote:

> She gave me life and he extended it.
> She saved me from the cold and he from sin.
> She taught me hope and he defended it.
> From her I once was born . . . from him again.
> She let me skip in fields that he had made.
> He bid me bless the loaves she baked for me.
> She ordered me to gaze where he once lay.

He bid me knee in her Gethsemane.
I owe them both the treasures of my art
And am myself so saddled with my debt
I cannot fail in paying every part
Lest I should leave this prayer with one regret.
An humble woman made me love a King.
In both of them was hidden everything.[2]

FIVE

Weird People, Wrong People, Weak People, Strong People

"EVERYBODY HAS FIVE FRIENDS," SAYS AN OLD PROVERB. BUT between my tenth and twelfth years I could only count three. I had gathered a hodgepodge of fellow travelers, but had only three real friends.

THE ELDER BROTHER

I lived those years in the shadow of an older brother who was nothing like the role model I needed. David smoked from the time he was ten. I don't remember when he started drinking; I only know I can't remember a time when he didn't. When I was in the third grade, he was in the sixth, and under ordinary circumstances we would never have attended the same school. But in 1948, Enid High School burned to the ground. It was the only high school in the area, so the three senior high classes that would have attended there were pushed downward into the two existing junior high schools. This compressed the junior high school student loads back down into the grade schools, which meant that Woodrow Wilson Grade School took back the seventh and eighth grade students it had previously sent to Longfellow Junior High School. Therefore the fire at the high school was directly responsible for keeping my brother and me in the same school at the same time for several years.

Being in the same school with him was terribly debilitating. He didn't like acknowledging me to any of his ruffian friends in public. When I tried to speak to him in the hall, he completely ignored me. All of this continued to erode my self-confidence. Finally it just seemed best for the two of us to ignore each other completely at school. He didn't speak to me and I didn't speak to him. We would see each other across the crowd without making any acknowledgement that we were related. Only one event brought us together in those horrible years.

We actually ended up in the principal's office on the same day, and it was all because of Gloria. I was a good friend of Gloria's, who lived only two blocks from our home. Gloria was an artist of sorts. To me she was a glorious artist and her specialty was painting horses. She never had a horse, and never saw one, as far as I know, except in Johnny Mac Brown movies. Nonetheless, she could paint them fairly well. On one occasion, a neighbor asked her to paint one of her horses on the mirror that hung in their parlor (the family was rich enough to call their living room a "parlor," while most of us simply called our parlors "the front room"). Well, needless to say, Gloria, equine artist that she was, painted a glorious horse on the mirror, and it created quite a stir. Our well-to-do neighbor took great delight in admitting people into her living room to see Gloria's painting.

Until much later, when Enid people began buying velvet toreador paintings in Nuevo Laredo, Gloria was locally renowned as the best of artists. I think I even envied her a bit. She gained such acclaim that I thought for a while I would try my hand at horse art. But when I tried to emulate her, my horses always arrived on paper stiff, leggy, and a bit necky. That first commission helped Gloria start a minor business painting horses on mirrors for many. Her horses were usually so large that nothing else had room to get reflected in her mirrors. In fact, Gloria's business left many a man trying to shave while staring around a Palomino or a Clydesdale.

Still for all the inconvenience of her art, it was well accorded that Gloria's horse mirrors were objects d'arte to have and cherish.

It was my respect for her mirror art that led to one of the great conflicts of my school years. Out on the playground at Woodrow Wilson, Gloria angered my brother for telling him he shouldn't be smoking and that she had a mind to report him to the principal, Mrs. Duerksen. David took a puff from his cigarette, blew the smoke back in her face, and said, "Go ahead, you little whore!"

Gloria was stunned and began crying. I didn't really know what a whore was, but I felt very sorry for Gloria. To my way of thinking, my nicotine-driven sibling had been excessively rude to Enid's premiere equine artist. Gloria said she was going into the office and telling Mrs. Duerksen about the horrible name David Miller had called her. At the word *whore*, Mrs. Duerksen's body grew stiff with rage. Seeing everyone's reaction to the word, I had to ask, "Mrs. Duerksen, what is a whore?"

"Calvin, don't you ever say that horrible word again!" she said. I made a note of her advice, and I don't think I've ever used the word out loud since that day. Mrs. Duerksen sent for David. By the time he arrived in the office, he had doused his cigarette, although he still reeked of smoke.

"David Miller, have you been smoking?" asked Mrs. Duerksen.

"Who me?" asked David, as though the whole notion was impossible, like asking Ghandi if he listened to honky-tonk music.

"Did you or did you not call Gloria Pace a whore?"

"No, I did not" David lied. "I called her a horse face!"

There was a long silence.

"Well, that's not so bad, Gloria," said Mrs. Duerksen.

Gloria cried a little and we all left the office.

After it was all over, I took a long walk to the big dictionary to find out why merely being a "horse face" was so much better than being a whore.

Within a year or two, David was in the army—having lied about his age. He was in the Korean War, which left me feeling very sorry for the Koreans. I must admit the only duplicity I ever saw in my mother was that she signed the papers saying he was eighteen. Maybe she was just tired of David. Maybe she was just trying to get her wayward child into the army where he might become some sort of responsible man. Maybe she was afraid that if David stayed in Enid, I would take up his rebellious lifestyle. But for whatever reason, he was gone—at least for four years—from our home and our lives.

THE TENT PEOPLE

That same year, another family moved onto Poplar Street, just one block east of our house. They were really poor and had lots of children. The father's name was George and the mother's name was Roberta. They had several children, but notably two older boys who were just my age. They had managed to buy an unmodernized lot, and then with finances I can't imagine, managed to have a water meter and a tap put in their yard just as we once did. They had no house. They pitched an eighteen-by-twenty tent. It was an olive green army surplus tent, which were in great supply after the war and very cheap. Our wealthier neighbors believed you shouldn't be allowed to put a tent up in a neighborhood, just as though it was a house, and they were embarrassed to have these "Johnny-jump-up squatters" just down the street.

I rather liked having them move in, for living in a tent seemed rather exotic to me. Best of all, with their entrance into Poplar Street, the Millers were no longer the poorest people in the neighborhood. And it was nice to feel middle class, even if we weren't.

The oldest two boys were my peers. They were named Orbie and Eddie. Eddie was a year older than I and Orbie a year younger. Their father, George, was an amputee, having lost his right leg in the war. His leg was off at the upper mid-thigh. I never entered his tent without noticing that his wooden leg, the first detachable leg I had ever seen, was leaning against the tent pole that held the highest canvas gable of the home. The grass where the tent sat did not last long with all the traffic it received, and it finally turned into bare ground covered with bits of carpet remnants, fringed with dry dust in July and cold mud in February. The family didn't go to church at all, and their family life was a base kind of conversation filled with profanity and crudities.

The whole family slept in one room, for all tents I suspect are one-room tents. George and Roberta had managed to hang a limp curtain of sorts over one area where their mattress lay on the floor. Orbie said that they needed the curtain to keep them from being seen as they indulged themselves from time to time with sex. Knowing generally how sex was to be done, I still couldn't easily visualize tent sex. And it amazed me that having only one leg, sex would be all that important. But Orbie assured me that it was, and when the curtain began twitching at midnight, all the kids knew their one-legged father was at it again.

Of more fascination to me than George's amorous ways was just how George got out of bed. He had a chrome chair—of the kind that became quite popular in the fifties—which afforded him a plausible stronghold. With his very strong arms he would swing himself up and onto the gray plastic seat of the chair. His arms were strong as any I had ever seen on a Charles Atlas poster. His artful and muscular swinging up out of bed was a kind grace not to be found among most tent families. But he would grasp the chair, and then up he'd come in a swift resurrection from the floor to the chair. It was an act that was worthy of being placed alongside anything Ringling Brothers had to offer.

Having been raised without a father, I had never seen a couple argue. But George and Roberta had the kind of arguments that were fascinating to watch . . . and hear! She would call him "a one-legged old fool," and he would retaliate by calling her "a fat broad." It was exotic, and I loved hanging around their tent flap in case they happened to get into a fight. One day they began to fight outside right in front of their tent. "George," said Roberta, "let's go inside and quarrel, where the neighbors can't hear us."

"Get real, Roberta! There're more neighbors inside our house than there are out here."

George was right about that.

Theirs was the best tent I ever frequented. The Pentecostals had tents, as did Ringling Brothers, but their tent was the most fascinating. George, apart from not having the usual number of legs, was fairly congenial, and given his poverty, was fairly generous. Between his stump and the prosthesis that fit it, he had to place a woolen protector that looked like a stocking cap. This woolen sock kept the harsh edges of his wooden leg from cutting or hurting his thigh. This woolen artifice he called a "stump sock."

The Veterans Administration was generous in furnishing him with these socks. They were just the size of stocking caps, and he had so many of them that he supplied the children of the entire neighborhood with stocking caps. These were wonderfully warm all winter. I can't remember any child being able to afford a woolen, store-bought cap, but from December to March, we were all protected from flu and earache by George's stump socks.

George was enterprising in his own way, and it was scarcely six months before the bottom part of the tent was replaced with wooden sidewalls and only the top of the tent was canvas. In another year, George made roof trusses and put a roof on the sidewalls. This made the neighbors happier. For at last the residence didn't look like a white-trash shack. But I wasn't quite so content. Solid wood walls made it awfully hard to hear George and Roberta fight and I missed that. Within the next year George and Roberta had a real bedroom, and their once semi-private sex was now as walled in as the holy of holies in Solomon's temple.

I had heard that the Presbyterians believed in predestination. I didn't really believe much in the doctrine before I met this family. But Orbie changed my mind. Once I really understood things, I knew the Presbyterians were right: Orbie was destined for the penitentiary. He had a thousand ideas on how to make money, and none of them were legal. I never participated in stealing hubcaps with him, but I was amazed at his dexterity in using a single, narrow-bladed screwdriver to get the firmest hubcaps off a car. He then sold the hubcaps for pennies on the dollar to the local salvage yards, where often their real owners came to buy them back at a much higher price. Everybody made a little money on the deal except the person who had lost them to Orbie's screwdriver in the first place.

The only scheme of his that I ever got involved in seemed to me to be less dangerous. He came up with an ingenious idea of stealing wheat from government-sealed boxcars. All the boxcars that came to giant elevators in Enid were sealed with a thin, numeric tin strip. The only way the doors to the sealed cars could be opened was to snip the strip. Once the doors of a boxcar were opened, there were huge wooden grain doors that stretched across the lower four-fifths of the door, leaving only a two-foot opening at the top, where an athletic child might crawl through and enter the boxcar. During the months of harvest, it was beastly hot inside the cars, in that narrow space between the roof of the car and the top of the grain. But we children were small and could manage to enter the doors without much of a strain.

Orbie had stolen a lot of gunnysacks, which cut down on the expense having to buy them. Several of us in Orbie's preadolescent crime ring snipped the rings, climbed up the grain doors, and entered the cars. Then we set to filling the chubby burlap bags and handing them out to another part of the crime ring that carted the sacks away and hid them in the tall grasses beside the railroad tracks. I was on the upper crew that actually worked inside the boxcars. I am amazed, given the inner temperature of those cars, that we did not suffocate in the extreme summer heat. But we survived.

When we had filled many, many sacks, we left the boxcars, closed the doors, and replaced the snipped strip as best we could. Then over the next few days we would take the wheat to the elevator and sell it at sixty-one cents a bushel to the storage elevator. Amazingly, we got away with this. We took some of the wheat around the neighborhood and sold it to those who kept chickens. My mother bought four bushels for $2.04 and thanked us for bringing her the wheat. Like most of our neighborhood clientele, Mama assumed we had swept the wheat off the tracks.

"But this wheat is so clean," said Mama on looking inside the sacks. "Are you sure you boys didn't take this out of a full boxcar?"

"Oh no, Mrs. Miller," said Orbie. "We just swept it up off the tracks."

"Well how did you get it so clean?" asked Mama.

"We were just real careful," said Orbie. "We swept it really carefully so as not to get any rocks in it."

I was amazed at how sincerely Orbie could lie.

"Well, I sure hope you are telling the truth, Orbie. You know what would happen to you if you were caught stealing wheat?"

"Yes, ma'am," said Orbie. "We'd be sent straight to reform school."

"Or prison," said Mama.

"No, ma'am, you can't be sent to prison till you're of age, and we're too young to be sent to prison just yet."

I was stunned that Orbie was so schooled in criminal law. I knew it was wrong to break into boxcars, but I didn't know you could be sent to prison for it. I was so mad at Orbie for not telling us that we could be sent to prison for becoming partners in his creative thievery. I never gave back the money I made stealing stuff with him, but I was glad when I had spent it all up. After Mama's dynamite revelation, I quit being friends with Orbie. I always thought he had a stupid name anyway, and I really didn't want to end up in prison.

George died not too long after that—probably from complications of his old war wounds. The influence of that family was now on the wane. Nobody wore his stump socks for stocking caps after that. Even Orbie's slick ways were not to be trusted. Nobody much admired him, and at age eighteen, he was caught stealing cars and was sent to prison. Roberta came down and cried to Mama the day he was taken away. She cried and she cried. Mama tried to console her, but Orbie was in and out of McAllister—Oklahoma's version of Alcatraz—for as long as I could remember.

A LIFELONG FRIEND

At the end of the fifth grade, when Orbie had lost his influence over my life, a wonderful thing happened. The Roelses moved into the last house north on Eleventh Street. Art Roelse had been a farmer—on a sharecropper basis—in Covington, Oklahoma, but in the hard years found the income too scant to support his family of four. So he sold what he had and moved twenty-three miles west to Enid. He had two children: a daughter named Margaret and a son named Alvin. He was a pious man, in the best sense of the word, and took a job at Champlin Refinery in Enid. The influence of this family on my life was the greatest of all influences ever exerted on my development. Alvin and I became friends, a friendship which to this day, sixty years later, remains in force.

We met in 1948 in a chance meeting on our bicycles. I had a new Shelby, which I had bought at John B. Dykes Sporting Goods on time. He had a Schwinn, which I would have died to own, for it was the elite conveyance of every discriminating cyclist.

We both went to Woodrow Wilson Grade School and were prohibited from going on to Longfellow Junior High because of the aforementioned fire that had destroyed the high school. But Alvin took me home to meet his parents, and I was immediately taken with the charm of what might—in these days—be called a nuclear family.

Mr. Roelse, almost as soon as we met, began lumping me into a category of friendship with Alvin. The category was called *you boys,* a term which he applied to both Alvin and me. "*You boys,* wash your hands, it's time for dinner!" he would say.

"Ruth, you take *the boys* to church tonight, I don't feel well." Or even, "*You boys,* pipe down, you're making too much noise." Arthur Roelse would never understand what he meant to me just lumping me into this odd, simple category of *you boys.*

He seemed to want me in the house with Alvin or working on our bikes together, to tighten the chains or oil the sprockets, or tighten the bearings to keep the wheel from wobbling. But the most meaningful of all his statements was, "*You boys,* get your Bibles, it's time for church." And I would get my Bible and ride to church with them in their family car. They had selected the Washington Avenue Church of Christ to attend, and I sat with them in church. My mother had begun to attend the Olivet Baptist Church, from which the Christmas baskets continued to arrive for the next several Christmases. I hated not going to church with her, but I think deep in her heart, she had prayed that someday there would come a man like Arthur Roelse, who would be for me a snapshot of what a man ought to be. I believe she knew how badly I needed this primary role model to develop with any kind of hope. Jesse, my brother-in-law, was the arch picture of what a man should be, but not necessarily what a father should be. And for all his kindnesses, he was never really a father figure in my life. It would be years before I would really appreciate a man who could widen his family structure to include me—a child who struggled to define the word *family*.

Alvin seemed upper middle class to me. He had his own bedroom. What a triumph! And his dad built him a little shed where he could work on his bicycle or build racers out of two-by-eights and axles and wheels. Alvin was destined to become an engineer, and while NASA would wait a couple of decades to be born, by the time it came to be, Alvin was at Moon Central working on space shots, a job he held till his retirement. If it is possible to watch a child working on his bicycle and deduce that he would become a rocket scientist, I think I somehow knew it. It had happened to Wilbur and Orville Wright in their Dayton shop. It would happen also to Alvin Roelse in his Enid shop.

I could have wished my friend's name was anything but Alvin, but it was what it was. "Calvin and Alvin" was somehow too poetic and called too much attention to itself. Even before there were singing chipmunks, it sounded like we were singing chipmunks. Nonetheless, that was a part of the bonding, and when our names were mentioned around school, they were mentioned with this particular poetic slur.

We were not much alike, so maybe that was the attraction. I was wiry, even strong enough to work in the hay fields around Pond

Creek and put in a good day's work. But Alvin had a good Dutch, muscular physique. He was definitely the better looking, and in any matter of science or mathematics was my superior. But he was challenged by Latin and literature. He was as left-brain as a cerebrum could be, and I was as right-brain. It took both of us to have a really balanced worldview. But we were never far apart: David and Jonathan, Gilgamesh and Enkidu, the Hardy boys, the Brothers Roelse, all of these things were us.

We went to church, at Art Roelse's insistence, and read our Bibles perhaps more than we wanted to. By the time we reached high school, we were avid supporters of Youth for Christ, a high school spiritual movement. We were encouraged to carry our pocket New Testaments to high school and try to win everybody to Christ we could. Alvin loved metal shop, where he learned machine fabrication. I liked Latin and typing, and while most of the boys looked down on me for my preferences, Alvin never did. He seemed to understand when the Latin club wore togas that this was normative to all high school life. He was tolerant in his views and believed the world was large enough that a man could wear a toga if he wanted to.

And we both appreciated Mrs. Moore, our geometry teacher. She prayed every day before each of her classes, and she was tough in her discipline. But the day that she most endeared herself to both Alvin and me was when one of the boys in the back of the class began passing around some pornographic booklets. They were all over Enid High School, but these were being brazenly passed around in her class. Mrs. Moore noticed what we were doing, and came back and took the booklets from us. I thought we would go to reform school just for looking at the books. But Mrs.

Moore threw the books in the trash can and smiled. I don't think she smiled because she approved. I think she smiled at our immaturity. It was the encounter of a real Christian woman, who must have agreed with Jacques Barzun, who said that all adolescent boys are pornographers. I suspect Mrs. Moore could wait till God put us all back together in better ways, when we had a more mature light and could see a little better.

Our junior year, Alvin and I began to go with girls a lot, if it could be called that. We double-dated, mostly in my car or his dad's. Our cars were really little more than jalopies: his, a 1939 Ford coupe that prohibited double-dating, and mine, a roomier 1937 Chevrolet sedan. The girls who went to our church were more faithful than they were attractive, so we often tried to date more secular girls. It was easier for Alvin to get a date than it was for me. He was stocky and rugged; I was willowy and insecure. I was shy, none-too-handsome, and poor: the triple threat in getting dates. And so I would often envy the quality of his women. He dated frivolous prairie nymphs while I dated good girls who had taken open stands for Jesus. I didn't do this because I enjoyed good religious girls, but because the frivolous nymphs found me not to their liking. Still, Alvin, good friend that he was, never looked down on me for dating solid souls rather than vixens. A good girl who loves Jesus is, after all, a treasure of sorts even if she doesn't stir a man's libido.

Then came the most magic summer I could remember. It all began at the Tristate Band Festival in May of '53. The band from Ponca City was one of the more than one hundred bands competing for various awards at the music festival in Enid. This was always a magic time for the local boys. Broadway Street in front of the Garfield County Courthouse was closed off, and a carnival was set in the middle of the city. All these beautiful young fillies came to town, the prettiest of which were generally twirlers. The twirlers— dear Lord—the twirlers! Most of the Christians I knew could never have been twirlers. That took talent. To be a twirler, you had to lay down your Bible and pick up a baton. And they pranced in front of the band with their gold and silver batons glistening in the air. They appeared as erotic as mayflies, which are born, mate, and die all in the same glorious day. Still, it was their "vulgar" prancing about that had given them such a bad reputation in the church. Girls who were most respected were always clarinetists.

Alvin and I had a mutual friend who was a Mennonite and had graduated four years ahead of us (we were still to graduate). After his graduation our friend had taken a job working for the city sewer department. It was not the most elite of jobs perhaps, but he made $1.75 an hour. Like most Mennonites, he was frugal and had in a short time managed to buy a brand-new '53 Ford Sedan that cost him $475. He was no better looking than I was, but he did have an income and a brand-new car.

It was sheer fate that brought us three friends to the Tilt-A-Whirl ticket booth on May 9, 1953. In but a moment we eyed three beautiful girls in their bright Ponca City band uniforms. Dear God, two of them were twirlers! The other was wearing slacks, clearly a clarinetist. I remember praying, "Lord, let these women be ours, and give me the one with tasseled boots, and let my Mennonite friend get the clarinetist in slacks. So let it be written! So let it be done!"

The Tilt-A-Whirl had been responsible for the death of a couple of kids who had come to the band festival the previous year and had tried to get out of the fearsome thing while it was in motion. They had been thrown into the machinery of the ride and been minced by steel structures until they were beyond all healing. Their untimely deaths had made many a twirler afraid to ride the beast the next year. So the ride seemed the perfect place to offer timid twirlers our security. This ride cost us one U.S. quarter per twirler to enjoy. Alvin and I hung around the Tilt-A-Whirl looking for twirlers who might want to ride the death contraption but had lingering fears that we could allay. We were proof Tilt-A-Whirl phobias can be conquered by real men with the bravado they furnished. So we offered our courage to the three beautiful girls from Ponca City.

They took us up on our offer of a free ride on the Tilt-A-Whirl. We paired off easily for the ride. Darn it all! I got the clarinetist. But we were soon astride the iron beast, and the centrifugal force of the contraption threw us into heaving bodily contact. Our torsos were welded into oneness. Our faces came naturally together, then our mouths. Then we kissed. It was the first time I had ever kissed a girl! So what if she wasn't a twirler. At first the kiss didn't impress me. It seemed a lot like kissing my mother until . . . she had the smoothest tongue. Likely a smoothness begat from licking clarinet reeds since the fifth grade. Don't ask me how I knew that. I was a Christian and I suddenly realized that Ponca City girls kissed in a way that good Christian boys from Enid had not discovered.

All too soon, the ride was over!

But I had more quarters.

So we did it again . . . maybe four times.

Alvin and our friend confessed they had not had my luck on the Tilt-A-Whirl.

I felt rather smug. There were times when it was good to give up on the lusty fascination of white tasseled boots, and pick a girl who wears pants and looks more like a Christian, but behaves like a demoniac when the G-force is right.

All of this led to our getting the names and addresses of the Ponca City sirens and beginning a summer of driving to Ponca City. We took those same three girls out every Saturday night until September of our senior year. Ultimately, our friend's twirler seemed less fascinated with his slow career advancements at the Enid Sewer District. Even though he did have a nice ride, she seemed to feel that it was not enough to lure her to continue in the relationship.

Alvin's twirler seemed to grow increasingly more distant. I think it was Alvin's developing interest in engineering that seemed too prosaic to offer him any hope of a longstanding relationship.

It was only my clarinetist who seemed to want to hang on till they at least brought the Tilt-A-Whirl back to Enid the next year. But I had been feeling a little guilty about encouraging my aggressive clarinetist. She was anything but Christian, and her romantic aggression was not so much "come hither" as it was "let's get it on." I was a Baptist after all. She actually frightened me. She was so easy to turn on and so hard to turn off. Her open-mouthed kisses seemed to issue from a deep pit of mononucleosis, and frankly she was a whole lot of woman.

The rest of our senior year, Alvin and I continued dating girls from church a bit, but in truth everything was downhill from our lost wilderness of Ponca City hussies.

It was clear that our worlds would soon part. Alvin would in a few months be going to Oklahoma Agricultural and Mechanical College at Stillwater, Oklahoma, while I wanted to go to a private college in Shawnee, Oklahoma, called Oklahoma Baptist University, or OBU as it was popularly known. OBU was the Harvard of Oklahoma Baptists, and I must confess it was to my way of thinking the finest of all universities. I was vaguely aware of the Ivy League, but it held little fascination in Garfield County. Alvin's dreams were reachable, because Arthur Roelse had systematically saved to make his dreams come true. Mine was not so reachable, but was perhaps more ardent. All in all, a kind of morose fear of the future settled upon me.

Refocusing on the Future

I have always had a bit of terror connected with my periodic swings into the depths of Christian faith. This was one of those times. I felt like I had been frivolously going to movies and dating aggressive clarinetists too long. It was time that I "came back to the Lord," and so I left Washington Avenue Church of Christ and began going to Olivet Baptist Church. Alvin and I were always friends and kept on attending the Youth for Christ meetings and carrying our New Testaments in our book straps, but we attended separate churches our final year in school. Going to Olivet was a comedownance in dating. The women at Olivet all looked like clarinetists with terminal acne. So I was at last able to abandon the lustful spirit I'd sometimes felt at Washington Avenue Church of Christ.

At Olivet, a "simple" girl got quite a crush on me. And it was only with great effort over six months that I managed to convince her I was not the man for her. It was hard work, for, being once again very dedicated to the Lord, I didn't want to hurt her feelings, but I also didn't want to marry a woman who thought Dinah Shore was a beach resort. Gradually, I was able to elude her clutches and give myself fully to Jesus. This girl helped me do this. She was a strong argument for chastity and maybe even celibacy.

I began to read the Bible night and day. Hosea replaced Hemmingway. The Psalms replaced Wordsworth. Esther took over for Emily Dickinson. I just wanted to know where my life was going once Enid High School was past. Then, presto! Into my life came Brother Daley! He was the pastor of Olivet Baptist Church. He was a solid soul, with a fringe of hair around this bald pate. He was a monkish-looking Baptist preacher, and in a sack-cloth robe he would have looked Franciscan. Maybe this was why I was so attracted to him.

He told me that if I wanted to know God's will for my life, I must give up movies and card-playing, and above all I must not go to the high school prom, for dancing inevitably led to sex. This last requirement seemed more like a promise than a threat, but I believed him and I decided to renounce the value system that I had so lately embraced and try to find a more cardless, promless will of God for my life.

Brother Daley became my spiritual advisor. It was not hard to give up poker and the tango, since neither of them were a big part of my life. As Miss Thompson had taught me, praying knees and dancing feet rarely occupied the same leg. It was not hard to give up drinking; I was already a teetotaler. As a matter of fact, almost all of the things Brother Daley asked me to give up I had never taken up, so by his definition, I was already quite a saint. I did, however, go to movies.

This I knew I must quit. Never having indulged in sex, I didn't have to give it up. What I did have to give up was thinking about it all the time. Movies only contributed to this shortcoming.

I had seen Ava Gardner act—or maybe act up—in *The Barefoot Contessa*, and it spoiled my conscience for a whole week. I really didn't see much of Ava's body, but just her feet were sensuous. I knew I had a problem. A simple carrot would release a week's worth of unsavory thinking. What was I to do?

Brother Daley said that I should keep away from movies—all movies, even movies that were recommended for children. Who knew what Lassie was really thinking? What were Roy and Dale up to once things got quiet in the bunkhouse? Brother Daley reminded me that trying to choose between a good movie and a bad one was like trying to make a selection about one's favorite kind of garbage. "Suppose I would go into the garbage can and get out a lot of garbage and put it on your plate," said Brother Daley, "would you eat it?"

"Of course not," I said.

"Well, what if I took only the best garbage, the prettiest garbage with the least amount of maggots on it, would you eat it?"

I felt his metaphor was a little over-the-top, but I replied, "No."

"What if I took only the best garbage out of the can and put it on your plate and arranged it like Betty Crocker, and put a dollop of whipped cream on top and a maraschino cherry, would you . . ."

"Okay," I said, "I'm sorry I went to see *The Barefoot Contessa*. I'm sorry I lusted. I now reject Ava Gardner's feet, corns, callouses, and fungus."

I gave up movies and got deeper into Jesus until just before graduation. I went to an afternoon matinee, and it was dangerous because it was so sunny and I would be so visible coming out of the theater. Even in a pair of cheap sunglasses and a high collar, I might be seen by some fellow Baptist and lose my whole testimony. I was tempted to go and see *Shane*, which was playing at the Aztec Theater on West Randolph. I felt guilty as all get-out, watching Alan Ladd, but at least he never took off his boots, so there were no lusty bare-foot scenes. I sat there for the whole two hours and never lusted once and was feeling pretty good about my triumph over "my old thought life." But as luck would have it, Brother Daley, who had been having a cup of coffee at Dan & Bakes Diner just a few yards from the theater, saw me coming out of the movie.

He ditched his coffee and ran up to me and said, "How was the movie?"

"It was garbage," I said.

"Good boy!" he said "You know you've got to win out over this thing. Did you lust?"

"No, the horses were chaste."

I will never forget the humiliation I felt in getting caught that day.

I must not paint Brother Daley as a religious prude, however. I know for a fact that he loved me. And while I had not yet declared my intention to go into the ministry, I believe that somehow he knew it was going to happen.

"Are you going to go on to OBU?" he asked me after Sunday services one day in April of 1954.

"Well, I want to," I said, "but money . . . I don't know."

"Maybe the Lord will provide," he said.

"Even if I went to see Ava Gardner and Alan Ladd?"

"Well, the Lord forgives everything," he said. "You want to go to OBU or not?"

"Well, I'll be driving wheat trucks all the way to South Dakota this summer. I should come back with three or four hundred dollars, but the school costs nine hundred dollars a year, you know. Where in the world would I ever get nine hundred dollars?" I just reminded him how impossible the whole thing looked from where I was.

"You know, son," said Brother Daley, "the Lord owns the cattle on a thousand hills. A year of tuition is just not a problem for him."

"Well, it looks like a huge problem for me," I said.

I got my high school diploma and went north with the wheat harvest. By August I was back in Enid with almost four hundred dollars in my pocket. Brother Daley led the church to give me a scholarship of two hundred and fifty dollars for my first year of school. And I won another scholarship of two hundred and fifty dollars. When I reached the campus, I had exactly nine hundred dollars, and I laid it down before the university bursar for my whole first year.

College on a Shoestring

Just before I left home in August 1954, Brother Daley threw a kind of shower for me, and I received an offering of brand-new clothes. Slacks, jackets, new—all new. Lots of them. Underwear, outerwear, upper wear, shoes, and well . . . I saw that the Lord who owned the cattle on a thousand hills also had a lot of friends who shopped at Sears and Roebuck.

And I knew that a poor boy who loved Jesus and tried his best to give up Ava and Alan could still register a few marks in heaven.

In the next week, when I found myself on a bus, with two new suitcases crammed full of new clothes, I knew why I loved and will always love the church. To be sure, there is a great deal of struggle in the church, and there is a whole lot of naiveté in the organization. But there is also something there that energizes the human spirit, precisely because it is more than human.

What is it about Christians that produces such a yearning to make the world a better place—such a need to make perfect the imperfections of a corrupt world? What made Mrs. Duerksen so interested in poor boys' naked feet one December? She had her own shoes, so why should she care? And those wonderful black galoshes she gave me, what caused that? Or, take Mrs. Moore, who smiled at our youthful hang-ups, when she could just as easily have hauled us down to the principal's office. And what made Arthur Roelse refer to both me and Alvin as "you boys"? It wasn't just Jesus that appealed to me. It was what Jesus did through people, who could for brief shining moments stop thinking about themselves and turn their minds to someone else. To give up selfish concerns and think of others is a small miracle in a selfish world. This is the grand narcotic—self-denial! How addictive it is in the life of anyone with the courage to put it into practice. I think the self-denial of the great Christians I had known in adolescence was the megaphone God used to finally call me into the ministry. But that's the stuff of a later chapter.

In the meantime, I've just got one question: who was Brother Daley after all?

A common man, I think.

A man who saw a poor kid and wondered what God might do with him. He didn't go to movies, though I suspect he wanted to from time to time. Maybe that's why he found the flaw so forgivable in me. He was a Franciscan-looking Baptist, who I suspect lusted from time to time, though he was never free to say so without losing his spiritual reputation in the flock. For that matter, Saint Francis probably lusted. A sackcloth robe covers a multitude of sins. But what is the human condition if not an admission that we need each other, flawed or not?

How sad it was for me that Brother Daley resigned in the middle of a terrific church quarrel to take another parish in eastern Oklahoma during my first year in college. The quarrel would in time split the church, and the incoming pastor who took the Reverend Daley's place informed me by mail that the church, having lost a lot of members and a whole lot of income, would not be able to continue my scholarship during my sophomore year.

In August of 1955, when I again arrived back home from a summer driving combines and wheat trucks, I once again had four hundred dollars, plus another two hundred and fifty dollars I had received from an academic scholarship. I knew I was two hundred and fifty dollars short, and the university would not admit me without having all my financial ducks in a row for the whole year. Whether or not God owned a lot of cattle on a lot of hills, it was clear that I didn't have all my tuition money. It was with a great uneasiness that I approached the bursar's office that year two hundred and fifty dollars short. I apologized to him as he looked up my tuition page in his great university ledger.

"Now, I remember you," he said. "You received two hundred and fifty dollars as a special gift from someone. With this money you brought in, your tuition is paid for the year."

Tears came to my eyes.

"Who gave the money?" I asked, thinking it could only be Brother Daley.

"Uh, uh, uh," he said, "can't tell you. The donor wishes to remain anonymous. It could be anybody."

I had always disliked anonymous gifts. They force you to be nice to everyone, because you just never know.

I just thought it was my old Franciscan look-alike, Brother Daley. But I was wrong about it being him. For two decades I pondered over the anonymous offering, without which I might not ever have finished college and my entire future would have been altered. Twenty years later at my mother's funeral, while I stood at her graveside grieving my loss, an old man I barely knew approached me. Claude Simons is his name if ever you should want to celebrate his presence in heaven. The old man had always been an old man. He lived alone and he had never been anything more than a floor-sweep at the Pillsbury Mill. Still, had every soul been as noble as he, the gates of Eden would never have clanged shut. He walked up to me even as I wept, put his arms around my heaving shoulders, and patted me on the chest with his frail old hand. "Dr. Miller," he said softly, but with a twinkle in his eye, "did you ever wonder where that two hundred and fifty dollars came from on your second year at OBU?"

"I've wondered all my life," I told him.

"I gave it," he said. "And by the way, you were worth every penny of it . . . and then some." In such moments I forgive the church for sometimes being so unlike its Founder, and remember that here and there Jesus is right: the meek still inherit the earth.

SIX

Ethel's Axioms

Nineteen forty-five was a wonderful year. We got a wonderful new appliance—an icebox. Actually it wasn't new, it was used, but it was still an icebox. The iceman came every third day. We, like all our neighbors, got a card with four numbers on it: 100, 75, 50, and 25. To order ice, you had but to put the card in your front window, where the iceman could see it as he drove by. If you turned up the big number that read "100," the iceman would then leave a hundred pounds of ice. He would lug it up to the house in a leather carrier and then use his tongs to hoist it into the top chamber of the icebox. Our icebox was small, so we always left our number "50" up, or maybe even "25," because if the weather wasn't real hot, twenty-five pounds would last us for three days.

We had ice in our tea in July! It was wonderful!

After Esmerelda Died

That same year, the local peddler had a death in his family that blessed us all. Old Esmerelda, his horse, "went home to be with the Lord," and was replaced by a '37 Ford, which pulled his four-wheeled trailer at a much faster gait down the streets on our side of Enid. His fruit was somewhat better—and always a lot fresher—after his horse died. And all his veggies did better on ice, once we put them in our new icebox. Even the water in the drip pan was somewhat sweeter. Our sisters fought over the ice drip water, insisting it was better to wash their hair in. I can't say whether it was or wasn't. I just know that with a good iceman and a good peddler, all of life was somehow better.

But an even more wonderful thing happened when I was fourteen.

We got electricity. Ever since I could remember, we had read by lamplight. But I will never forget the exotic glare of a single incandescent bulb, hanging out of a hole in the ceiling, and oh the light! I could read till midnight, and I did. Every night! Homework was a cinch when I could actually see my textbooks.

Something nearly as wonderful as a new icebox happened to me in junior high school. We began buying packets of art cards so the teacher could tell us about the paintings and statues that hung in the great galleries of the nations. I loved those cards and kept them from year to year and tried to find out all I could about what caused the artists to paint and poets to write. I spent all the time I could at the library, and I determined that if ever I could travel widely in the world I would see those same paintings and admire those very statues.

I knew then what Ayn Rand meant when she said, "Art is man defining himself." Artists and sculptors created their masterpieces to tell others who they were. And they hoped their art would, in some way, define themselves and their world. I couldn't articulate it all at age fourteen, but I could feel the truth of it. And after living through World War II, I wondered why people ever went to war. Why didn't they quit trying to control each other. They simply show each other their pictures and statues and talk about the meaning of life.

Two stabilizing events occurred in my life in 1946 and 1948, respectively. Without these two "happenstances" I would never have been ready for adolescence. The first of these events was the return of Jesse and Helen Dillon to Oklahoma after the war. They moved to Pond Creek, a community twenty-two miles north of Enid where they had purchased a farm.

Our own small house, which for the past five years had been home to so many, suddenly was down to four of us: Mama, me, and my two younger sisters. There was so much room. My two sisters took over the big bed, and Mama took over a new little bed we had moved into the same small bedroom. I moved to the couch where I had been born nine years earlier.

But the years following the war were to be more formative than fun for me.

There is no way to get from age twelve to age twenty except by spending eight years as a teenager. Oscar Wilde was wrong; the pitiful thing about youth is not that it is wasted on the young so much as it imprisons them. These eight long years were the most wretched years of my life. In spite of the friendship and support I found in the Roelses, my school life was miserable. I managed to live through it, but the living was costly. This belittling decade fell between 1946 and 1954, my tenth and eighteenth years. My life fell equally into two roles: half of it on my sister's farm in Pond Creek, and the other half in Enid in the house where I was born. These two homes were both sanctuaries from a world I found so unfriendly. I spent an equal amount of time in both houses, but it was not as though I spent the time in large blocks, separated by long absences from either place. I tended to spend weekends, summers, and school holidays at my sister's farm. Weekdays and the school terms in general were spent at home in Enid, where I attended the city's public school systems through my seventeenth year.

I can hardly make any real sense of those years, and the only hope I have of keeping the chronicle clear for you is to separate them into two chapters—this one and the next. But as you read, keep in mind that they were not separate at all but piled one on top of the other. First let's look at these years as I lived them out in my mother's house. These were my public school years, and I refer to them generally as my Enid adolescence.

The Year of the Bicycle

One of my hopes was to have my own bicycle and a paper route or maybe even a job delivering medicine for the local drugstore. Just such a job was offered to me by Mr. Oakley at Oakley Drugstore on East Broadway Street in Enid. But how could I even entertain such an offer with no bicycle with which to deliver the drugs? Then it happened: the kind of coincidence that can only be born in heaven itself.

On a very ordinary day in my twelfth year, I passed the window of John B. Dykes Sporting Goods Store, and there glistening in the window was a bright blue Shelby bicycle. It was the epitome of all a boy might hope for. As I look back on that bike, it was the only pre-puberty lusting I ever did. It was more than a bike—it was whitewalls, chrome rims and sprockets, and red-white-and-blue streamers flowing like Niagara from the white rubber grips on the handlebars. It had a headlight that used two D-cell batteries for night riding. A reflector rose like the red planet from the proud rear fender. This vehicle must have been assembled by the bicycle gods of Mount Olympus.

It was glorious. It was also thirty-nine dollars, plus tax.

But I was twelve, and it was time to take my place in the working man's world. And thirty-five cents per hour was a salary "not to be sneezed at," my mama always said. So I asked Mother if I could take a job with Oakley Drug Store. "I will need a bike," I told my mother, "if I'm going to get a job delivering prescriptions to the elderly around Enid."

"Now, son," she said, "you know that we can't afford a bicycle for you."

"Mama, maybe Mr. Dykes at the store will let me pay it off over the next few months and let me buy it on time. I have five dollars in my El Producto box, you know."

"Well, son, maybe we can talk to him about it," she agreed.

I will never forget dressing up as good as I could and walking with my mother down to John B. Dykes Sporting Goods Store and talking to him about this. I was afraid to talk to him, because he was so successful.

"Mr. Dykes," I said, "I have a job offer that requires me to have a bicycle. That's the one I want." I pointed to the Shelby in the window.

"Well, son, it costs thirty-nine dollars. Do you have thirty-nine dollars?"

"Sir, I do not. But I have five dollars, which will leave me only thirty-four dollars to pay over the next few months." I saw his brow cloud up. "I assure you," I went on, "I am a credible person of business, and will not default on any payment during any single week that you carry the balance."

It was the best I could do, and I had used pretty good business language.

He thought for a moment, looked at my mother, and said, "Is the boy good for the balance?"

"He is, sir," said Mama.

"Then let's write 'er up, son!" he said.

I got the job.

Riding my 1948 Shelby all over Enid was a level of status, I fashioned. I made my bicycle payments right on time and was generally feeling better about my life.

Then one dark night, while I was out on my bike delivering prescriptions, a group of ruffians caught me in a dark alleyway and literally beat me to a pulp. Both of my eyes were black; my face and lip were split. My body was covered with bruises. I made my way home pushing my Shelby, which had been battered and the chain ripped from the sprockets. I was crying when I came up in front of our house. When my mother saw me, she broke into tears. She insisted that I tell her who had done this. I refused, simply telling her that going after the ruffians was no way to solve the problem, for if I got them in trouble, my troubles would likely only increase and more reprisals were likely to result.

The bike was more easily fixed than I was. I managed to get a new chain and put it on. The fender braces were easily straightened, and the chain guard pried back into place. It rode as well as ever. Still, I hated to go to work the next day because of my facial bruises and cuts. Nonetheless, I did. Mr. Oakley was also grieved at my appearance and, like my mother, wanted to take action against the battalion of bullies who had pulled off the abuse. But I never revealed their names to anyone.

I stayed in the back of the store until it was time for me to take out deliveries. Mr. Oakley, sensing my reluctance to enter the world, gave me a pair of nice sunglasses that largely covered my black eyes, though not much could be done with my split lip. Within a week or so I was back in school and facing my enemies once again. I was determined to not let them win in their effort to destroy every vestige of my confidence. And I may have done better at this than I thought I did, since the gang attack of 1948 was never repeated. But that was not the last beating I would ever get.

LEARNING HOW TO LIVE QUIETLY

As enthusiastic as I was about reading and learning, I soon grew to hate school. This hatred occupied the center of my life, for I spent so much time at school. I would have dropped out of school as most of my siblings had, had I not known how much this would have hurt my mother. She was most anxious that I keep going, for she understood its importance. This I did, but my obedience to her wishes was the most painful part of my life. This was because all that she had taught me to treasure seemed to me to be of no great worth in public schools. I was generally seen as an oddball in Woodrow Wilson Grade School anyway. I was never good at sports. Being raised in a house full of women with no male role models to guide me, I had no idea of either the rules of any sport nor the general mystique as to how I should go about playing them.

I was the last one to be chosen on any school sport that I ever played, and was the frequent target of bullies. I was good at all the things my mother taught me were important, but those things— reading, writing and 'rithmetic—didn't much matter at school. What did matter were football, baseball, and basketball. The horror of always being chosen last when we were choosing sides for thirty minutes of recess sports was humiliating day after day. Physical education in schools can be a kind of violence to a shy child. From the earliest days I hated kickball, an odd sport where you kicked a soccer ball and ran around the bases to try and score just as you would in baseball, except that it could be played by third graders. I could never kick the ball hard enough to get on base without being put "out" at first. This failure was greeted with hisses and boos and sometimes by being the object of a "dog pile"—a Gestapo-like torture where everybody piled on top of some weaker brother and pummeled him with their fists. I would cry, and this only deepened the bullies' enjoyment of their art.

One boy in particular was my nemesis. He was strong and he was cruel, the arch demon of all my grade school and junior high school years. I absolutely hated to look at him, for when my eyes met his, it seemed that would be enough of an excuse to cause him to wait for me after school. And there after class and off the school yard, I would really pay. Perhaps he could have been beaten, had it been my mind-set, but I was not a fighter, and when I tried to do it, I lost to the point where it was easier simply just not to try it. Still, just the sight of him caused me to tighten up inside and to vow to keep out of his way and out of his sight as best I could. Not every "coward of the county" has his day of triumph.

From my earliest days in music class, my experiences were miserable. Friday in music class was request day, and each of us got to request our favorite songs. Most of the boys wanted to sing "Old Black Joe," which for some reason—I could never understand—was their favorite. But not mine. I requested "Somewhere over the Rainbow," which put me in solid with the girls and the teacher, but the boys were waiting for me at recess.

It was a sin just to be smart. Once, in a mock quiz contest in the sixth grade, I named all five Great Lakes, in alphabetical order, for which I won the grand prize of one dollar. For this I was severely beaten by the toughies, who were waiting for me at recess. I withdrew from any attempt to win approval just by being smart or knowing things. I got to school as late as I could, so that there would be no opportunity for an encounter with any of the gangs that waited around the doors. I stayed late, so that they would often be disbursed before I left.

Once in reading class I recited the entire "Wreck of the Hesperus" by memory. The boys thought that the line "Her bosom, white as Hawthorne buds that ope in the month of May" was "frooty" and I was too. They were waiting for me at recess time. I never recited poems after that—it was just too hazardous.

I learned to sit quietly at my desk, preferring a seat in the corner of the classroom, or at the back of one, unless the alphabetic arrangement of our seats forced me toward the front. But even if it did, I grew accustomed to a coping lifestyle. To hide from hurt was a matter of living the quiet life.

HIDING FROM LIFE IN A LATIN CLASS

Still, I faced a good bit of hostility in my choice of classes. I was the only boy I can ever remember being in a high school typing lab. However important I felt it was to anyone who thought about being a writer someday, it was a course for girls only. The catcalls and sexual slurs I received just walking in and out of that typing classroom were horrific. But by high school I had quit crying over persecution. Even being bullied rarely brought me to tears. It hurt to be insulted, but I was generally doing better because I somehow never let them see how much it hurt.

I took Latin and did very well at it. English literature was straight-A stuff. In the last years of junior high school and all through high school I discovered and loved Shakespeare, often memorizing long sections of his plays.

Miss Addie Fromholz was perhaps my favorite of all teachers. She was a spinster who had taken notice of my isolationism, I suspect. She, too, had probably spent a lot of her life alone. I worked hard on Latin composition, and she appreciated it. Privately she bragged about my work in a class composed primarily of me and the brighter girls of Enid High School. My semester paper, which I wrote on the conquests of Julius Caesar, was called *Exercitus Caesaris*, the "army of Caesar," and was in Miss Addie Fromholz's opinion the finest Latin compostion she had ever seen. I'm sure it was not all that great, but it was a golden moment for me, as surely as if I had been the quarterback who scored a touchdown in the state finals.

Still, being complimented at Latin was a real perk. I loved the days when we spoke minimal Latin phrases to each other and answered our roll call in Latin.

"*Ad estne, Calvine?*" asked Miss Fromholz.

"*Sum,*" I answered, as did all the others. Then we would read a line or two from the Latin poets or orators. Ovid was my favorite: *O Sorror, O conjunx, O femina sola superstes,* or "Oh, Sister, O wife,

O woman surviving alone," said Decaulion to Pyrrha upon leaving the ark in the Roman account of the Great Flood. We wannabe Romans always had a great time in the class.

But such moments were rare for me.

SISTER CLOSE AND SISTER ROGERS

The church was of great help to me during those years. I was deeply moved by my conversion and the radicalizing of all by values and my allegiances. Miss Thompson's Highland Church closed in the late forties, and the tent revival where I was born again soon surrendered its excited converts to the Pentecostal Holiness Church. Pentecostalism was for me a haven, where the adults said kind things to me and the children I attended with were, like myself, somewhat struck with the virtues of Christianity. In short, I found in church a place to heal from the weekly brutality of my classmates.

I know now that the heroes I found among Pentecostals might seem quaint, unstudied, and naïve if I were to meet them today. But Sunday by Sunday, they provided a cozy, if odd, camaraderie that nourished me. We were friends, boisterous in praise, athletic in worship, but given to long, frequent hugs and earnest praying and good firm pats on the back.

My pastor was once again a woman. Her name was Sister Close and, of course, she was married to Brother Close. Brother Close always seemed too distant to have earned his warm name, but Sister Close was both pretty and affirming. Like Aimee Semple MacPherson, some decades before, she always wore a white and no makeup, which she called the devil's paints. She inner radiance, or so it seemed to me, that made her especially pretty. She would often stop mid-sermon and lift her arms toward the ceiling of the church, and break into tongues punctuated with radiant and loving hallelujahs. It always seemed at such moments that she was looking into the very court of God, where she said there were the twenty-four elders and stadia full of angels. She said it so convincingly that I came to believe that with some practice, I might train my eye to see them as well.

She wore only long-sleeved dresses and practical Cuban heels. She never wore jewelry, for she believed that those who did harbored pride and arrogance and had made a side deal with Jezebel, Ahab's devil woman, who like the Great Whore of Revelation would one day be cast into hellfire forever. But Sister Close was too severe in her faith to appeal to Mama. Miss Thompson had been much more permissive in her doctrinal view concerning jewelry and cosmetics. Mama didn't go to church much there, for her dresses were too short-sleeved to allow her to find any kind of spiritual reputation among Pentecostals. She was also divorced and wore a minimum of "godless jewelry"—until her death, Mama never went without the engagement ring that Papa had given her in 1920. Besides, Mama also used a little Pond's Cold Cream when she could afford it. It not only made her skin prettier, Mama felt, but the Pond's jar made a very nice family "till" once the cold cream was gone. But unlike Mama, I wore neither jewelry nor cosmetics, so I had no big doctrinal barriers to cross by dipping into Pentecostalism.

I always felt a little sorry for Brother Close. He was the ugliest man you could see for free, and he did not seem very spiritual. I never saw him go to the altar a single time to confess anything. He never spoke in tongues, and it seemed to me he dozed a bit during his wife's sermons. Maybe being married to a gospel princess, who dressed like the snow queen and could look up through the Celotex ceilings into the court of God, was a lot more than he had bargained for when they were first married. Most of the men in our church were quiet, and I don't remember that any of them were good at talking in tongues. But many of them were good at hugging a lonely little boy, and I much appreciated them. During the first twenty years of my life, the only place I ever felt a grown man touch me (except for Arthur Roelse) was in church, and I must confess, their warmth was a dimension of life I treasured. They were warm souls, and if they could not speak in the unknown tongue, so what! Sister Close and the heavy women who attended her could take care of that sort of thing.

Take Sister Rogers, who could break into tongues anytime she wished. And when the Holy Spirit was speaking through her, he never whispered. She said, "*Shandala-luiah!*" like she really meant it. She seemed to me to be—as we said in the country—about three bales short of a load, but if she was psychotic, she was certainly sincere in her madness. I remember her saying during public testimonies that she had a psychiatrist. This struck me as strange for two reasons. Number one: psychiatrists were expensive. Until I met Sister Rogers, I had never known a Pentecostal who coul[d] afford one. Reason number two: it was generally felt am[ong] Pentecostals that if you trusted the Lord—really trusted the [Lord] you would never have any illnesses, and this included [any] kind. *So, if* anyone confessed to having a psychiatri[st] always knew that they were shallow and "covering their sins" with pretense.

One night, when it seemed the Spirit was tarrying in his visitation, Sister Rogers stood up and said, "I went to my psychiatrist, and he said to me, 'Mrs. Rogers, if you don't give up all this Jesus stuff. you are going to go crazy.'"

She paused as she gathered the widely separate parts of her fragmented reason back together. I remember thinking how I had never heard anyone call her "Mrs. Rogers." She had always been "Sister Rogers" to us in the church. But I also realized that if her psychiatrist had called her "Mrs." she must be married. I fell to prayer instantly on behalf of the husband I didn't know she had. *Poor man,* I thought. And if I were God, I would award him heaven, just on the basis that no one should have to live in hell for both lives.

Mrs. Rogers went on, "But when my psychiatrist told me that I would go crazy if I didn't give up my belief in Jesus, I just looked at him and said, 'Well, Doctor, if I can go crazy praising Jesus, that's a wonderful way to go crazy.' *Gloria Shandala-lujah, en callip-toria!*"

It was moments like these when I had the hardest time with Pentecostalism. I wanted to go up to Sister Rogers and congratulate her that she was finding such a rich depth of meaning in schizophrenia. Plus I wanted to tell her that a banana is still a banana even if it's a religious banana. But I didn't.

The Vixen Transition

it was this kind of thinking that eventually led me to grow
being a Pentecostal. There was one person in the

never saw him go to the altar a single time to confess anything. He never spoke in tongues, and it seemed to me he dozed a bit during his wife's sermons. Maybe being married to a gospel princess, who dressed like the snow queen and could look up through the Celotex ceilings into the court of God, was a lot more than he had bargained for when they were first married. Most of the men in our church were quiet, and I don't remember that any of them were good at talking in tongues. But many of them were good at hugging a lonely little boy, and I much appreciated them. During the first twenty years of my life, the only place I ever felt a grown man touch me (except for Arthur Roelse) was in church, and I must confess, their warmth was a dimension of life I treasured. They were warm souls, and if they could not speak in the unknown tongue, so what! Sister Close and the heavy women who attended her could take care of that sort of thing.

Take Sister Rogers, who could break into tongues anytime she wished. And when the Holy Spirit was speaking through her, he never whispered. She said, "*Shandala-luiah!*" like she really meant it. She seemed to me to be—as we said in the country—about three bales short of a load, but if she was psychotic, she was certainly sincere in her madness. I remember her saying during public testimonies that she had a psychiatrist. This struck me as strange for two reasons. Number one: psychiatrists were expensive. Until I met Sister Rogers, I had never known a Pentecostal who could afford one. Reason number two: it was generally felt among Pentecostals that if you trusted the Lord—really trusted the Lord— you would never have any illnesses, and this included the mental kind. So, if anyone confessed to having a psychiatrist, you almost always knew that they were shallow and "covering their sins" with pretense.

One night, when it seemed the Spirit was tarrying in his visitation, Sister Rogers stood up and said, "I went to my psychiatrist, and he said to me, 'Mrs. Rogers, if you don't give up all this Jesus stuff. you are going to go crazy.'"

She paused as she gathered the widely separate parts of her fragmented reason back together. I remember thinking how I had never heard anyone call her "Mrs. Rogers." She had always been "Sister Rogers" to us in the church. But I also realized that if her psychiatrist had called her "Mrs." she must be married. I fell to prayer instantly on behalf of the husband I didn't know she had. *Poor man,* I thought. And if I were God, I would award him heaven, just on the basis that no one should have to live in hell for both lives.

Mrs. Rogers went on, "But when my psychiatrist told me that I would go crazy if I didn't give up my belief in Jesus, I just looked at him and said, 'Well, Doctor, if I can go crazy praising Jesus, that's a wonderful way to go crazy.' *Gloria Shandala-lujah, en callip-toria!*"

It was moments like these when I had the hardest time with Pentecostalism. I wanted to go up to Sister Rogers and congratulate her that she was finding such a rich depth of meaning in schizophrenia. Plus I wanted to tell her that a banana is still a banana even if it's a religious banana. But I didn't.

THE VIXEN TRANSITION

I suspect it was this kind of thinking that eventually led me to grow uneasy about being a Pentecostal. There was one person in the church who gave me hope. It was a girl named Rosemary, who told me that I could call her "Rosie" if I wanted to. I wanted to and did. I liked Rosie. She was friendly and seemed to like me too. We both sat on the back row of our little church and watched as others praised themselves into a dither. We must have appeared as agnostics to the rest of the church. Neither of us could talk in tongues, and this was quite a handicap in our church. Everyone there believed that when you really got the Spirit, tongues would gush forth. I just couldn't do it. I tried and tried, but nothing would gush forth. Thank God, Rosie couldn't do it either.

So there we sat during our early teen years. Rosie—no jewelry, no makeup, long sleeves and long dresses, a long cap, and generally a very long face. When I look back on it, I realize that pretty much everything about Rosie was long. She "neglected the paints" and wore all those long clothes so she wouldn't be sexually stimulating to anyone, and it worked pretty well for her. I was never tempted to lust after Rosie in all the years I knew her. As far as I was concerned, her main virtue was that—like me—she was also unable to talk in tongues. But I always felt uneasy wondering what would happen if Rosie suddenly got the gift and I didn't. Then I would be the only one in the church who couldn't, and that would be unbearable.

In my sophomore year in high school I met a Baptist girl who was what Rosie would have called a hussy. She wore makeup and jewelry and high heels, but she taught me the virtue in a frequent criticism that Baptists made of Pentecostals: "Any old barn looks a little better with paint on it." So my intrigue with Baptists had nothing to do with biblical doctrine. I was won over by a hussy.

I went to church with her, and lo, the whole youth department was full of hussies. Short dresses too! Their dresses were respectable, but not so spiritually long that their hems left no room for imagination.

There I found myself—smack-dab in the middle of a libertine assembly filled with lively singing and enough hussies to make me want to investigate the Baptist church. Where the Pentecostal church had been filled with mostly women, the Baptist church had a goodly number of men. In fact, there were as many men as there were women. Even the preacher was a man. I couldn't help but feel a bit odd listening to a man preach. This particular preacher was bald, like Brother Close, and not at all pretty like Sister Close. And what of all the rest of the men present? I wondered if they had all once been wanton Pentecostals who weren't just out church shopping for a flock of religious hussies.

BAPTISTS

But the preacher preached a great sermon with a lot of passion. Most of what he said was not new to me. He said if I died in my sin, I would go to hell. That if I lusted after strange women, I would go to hell. I felt a bit guilty here because I had been drawn to hear his sermon in the first place by a teenage vixen. By the time he was down to offering the invitation, I knew I needed to get saved, if only to try not thinking about hussies for a while. So I went forward "just as I was, without one plea!"

The preacher met me at the altar and asked why I was coming forward, and I told him I was coming forward to get saved "again."

"Again?" he asked. "You been saved before?"

I thought he was kidding. I got saved every week at the Pentecostal church. "Yes, I've been saved many times. I never have had much luck living above sin."

"Well, son, it's not possible for you to be saved more than once. Jesus died once, and that's the same number of times you can get saved."

"But," I protested, "every year when your church brought us a Christmas basket we all got saved. We thought that was the only way you would leave the basket."

"Nonsense. You should have told us you were already saved, and you wouldn't have had to get saved all those times."

"Well, bring us another one next Christmas, and I'll tell Mama she doesn't have to get saved even one more time just to get a basket. She'll be glad."

"Once saved, always saved" was an odd doctrine to me. But in some ways, I was glad to hear it 'cause I was getting pretty tired of getting saved every week or so. I really liked Baptists. Not only did they have lots of pretty girls, you didn't have to get saved all the time.

So in time I was baptized into the Baptist church.

I went totally under the water too. Baptists, like Pentecostals, went all the way with everything they did. When they wore makeup, they wore a lot of it. When they baptized, they didn't use teaspoons. The pastor told me I would have to give ten percent of my money, and I told him if I ever got any money I would. And as soon as I did, I did.

ETHEL'S AXIOMS

When I was a senior at Enid High School, my two younger sisters went to Hollywood to represent the state of Oklahoma at the grand premiere of the movie *Oklahoma!* They were both members of the Legionettes, a drill-team drum-and-bugle corps famous at that time in Oklahoma for their concert-style performance and their outstanding precision marching. When they came back they brought with them a 45 rpm album of the musical. I had never heard a Broadway musical, but because we finally had electricity, I purchased a few cheap components and wired an old radio to a new turntable to make my own "hi-fi," a pop name for a "high-fidelity" record player. I'm not sure how "high" my "fi" really was. I don't think very. But for the first time in my life I listened to a whole record album all the way through. I was entranced. I told my friend Alvin that they "had made a whole story up out of songs," and he was not inclined to believe me. So I invited him over to my house to hear my homemade hi-fi and listen to the musical *Oklahoma!* He was as overwhelmed as I had been.

The whole affair began a new interest in me in the arts. It was so simple a start that I myself would not believe the tale, had I not lived through it. But as I once had been entranced by the visual arts, I suddenly became captivated by music. I am ashamed it took me so long to fall under the force of its spell. But it was just never a part of our church, school, or lives.

The six agonizing years of secondary school came to an end during May of 1954. I was to graduate from high school. Mama insisted that I must have a new suit to fit the occasion. For all that the previous years had put upon me, I somehow felt that a suit of armor would have been more appropriate.

Enid High School gave me my diploma, but it was Mama who gave me an education. I have never entered those conversations about whether homeschooling is better than public education, because I was fortunate to have lived with the full measure of both. But if I had to choose between, let's say, Miss Fromholz and Ethel Miller, there is no doubt about which of them did me the most good. There would be no contest.

Latin was good—and dear Miss Fromholz, as you take your place in heaven, know how much I appreciated all you did for me—but, Mama, you gave me the code by which I've lived, believed, and served.

What was this code? And how did it become a part of me?

Before school ever began, you taught me that to cry over my lost brother meant this—

Ethel's Axiom #1: I will spend as many tears for you, son, if ever your need requires it.

In the first grade, when Mrs. Duerksen gave me the galoshes, you taught me this—

Ethel's Axiom #2: Your needs are too important for me to deny you anyone's insights in helping you to become a man. After all, it takes a village to raise a child.

In the third grade, I learned that Grandma had greater needs than I supposed—

Ethel's Axiom #3: A mother may have to commit her own mother to an asylum in order to build a sanctuary of safety for her children.

In the fourth grade, I learned I was an American, and that's a birthright worth cherishing—

Ethel's Axiom #4: Wars are winnable if you get enough little kids buying ten-cent savings stamps.

In the fifth grade, I learned that God was knowable in Jesus Christ—

Ethel's Axiom #5: When the role is called up yonder, it's possible to be there.

So, year by year, Mama built into me this interior code for survival. And her code was implanted on tablets of flesh in the center of my life. At the center of her code was Christ. He, above all, is Lord of the storms in life. He makes sense of the senseless things. Time always moves in one direction. It's a rare opportunity that passes us twice, and we only pass the road not taken once. We must decide and grab on to our best future, and if we miss it, we may live a long life, but we will never live a consequential life. The carousel passes the golden ring but once. Grab it, and the horses leave their circular death and become steeds of purpose that you may ride where you will. Miss the ring, and life is at best just a merry-go-round.

SEVEN

Coming of Age in Pond Creek

IN THE LAST CHAPTER, I MENTIONED THAT IN 1946, I BEGAN SPEND-
ing every weekend and all my summers and vacations with the Dillons
in Pond Creek. I took rather naturally to farm life. The Dillons ran a
small dairy and kept a herd of cows—Guernsies, Jerseys, and
Holsteins, which had to be milked twice a day. Jerseys and Guernsies
were quality cream producers, and Holsteins were good at volume.
By the age of ten, I had learned to milk cows. But I did not have to
milk them by hand for very long. Shortly after the milking parlor was
built, we got a Surge electrical milking system. With the new electrical milkers, we could milk the entire herd much faster.

Once the milking was done, we delivered milk throughout the
stores and homes of Pond Creek. This was unpasteurized milk, of
course, or what was called in those days "raw" milk. Our delivery
system was a 1937 Chevrolet whose trunk lid had been removed
and the trunk fitted with a kind of short pickup bed large enough
to hold several cases of bottled milk. This had to be delivered to
homes and stores, so my sister would drive the car while I ran the
milk up to the doors throughout the little town.

The milking itself was done at five thirty in the morning, and
before the bottling and delivery was done it was usually nine thirty
or ten in the morning. This was all right during the winter months
when the farmland lay fallow or was sporting a new green lawn of
winter wheat. But when spring came, there was plowing or cultivating to be done, and then, after harvest in late May or early June, the
field work was hard upon us. I learned to drive a tractor by the time
I was twelve, years before I learned to drive a car.

My sister, brother-in-law, and their three children did not attend
church in the years following the war, so when I went to stay with

them I didn't attend church either. This delivered me from trying to figure out how to please God with my life, which since my conversion in 1945 had become a constant pursuit of mine. I took the issue very seriously, and yet, when I was away from Enid, the question did not bother me as much as it should have.

One day in 1947, the Christian church in Pond Creek caught on fire. It was impossible not to think about the fire without thinking about the ins and outs of the problems of evil. It was the first church I ever heard of that actually burned, and its flames rose high into the sky, without the slightest hope of ever being put out. The local fire department just got started too late in their attempt to save it, so it burned to the ground. It may have been started by faulty gas pipes, and the resulting explosion gave such an initial impetus to the blaze that the volunteer fire department might as well have not volunteered.

It was the Disciples of Christ building, and local Baptists had been feeling for years that the Disciples of Christ were going liberal, just like the Methodists had done earlier. They had begun to say the Apostle's Creed, just like the Catholics. Some Baptists surmised that God might punish liberal churches by seeing to it they had faulty gas pipes to get even with them for their mushy doctrine. But I couldn't believe that Jesus would burn down any church just for having crazy notions. I had been acquainted with several Baptist churches with crazy notions and they never burned.

That same year, Jesse got the idea that the dairy wasn't making much money, and he came up with a way to earn more. We would not just use our combines to cut our wheat; we would subcontract our machines and ourselves to other farmers to cut their wheat. Farm

lock in the eve-
. We always said
e harvest—and
reek, we moved
ny, Kansas, . . .
braska, . . . and
ven went on to
e in late August
t it ready for the

had to be pulled
propelled" com-
he new machines.
ly make a lot of
hat appeared, the
of cutting wheat
ir. But the profits
achines as on

it som
he har
re w
camped
rom
as
rs were
to putting

d War II, so plenty of people
cut their wheat. We were
was making a lot of money
ng," or contracting to har-
rain not only had to be cut;

because they had an inte-
from the pit where it was
cylindrical storage tanks.
the decade following the
ere being raised all over
country village had two
the town's grain and a
h water. In these years,
oth of which were in a

NORTH

tage of combines, my brother-
the harvest. We contracted to
middle of Oklahoma almost to
was good, especially right after
to eight dollars an acre for us
ripened later in the more
sse taught me to drive a
gal driver's license. I
d we worked all sum-

mer long from five in the morning until eleven o'c
nings. There was money to be made in going north
it just that way—we were "going north" with th
once all the wheat had been harvested in Pond C
our trucks and combines and cut wheat in Antho
then in Grainfield, Kansas, . . . then in Alma, Ne
then Presho, South Dakota. One summer we e
Mandan, North Dakota. We always returned hom
to begin cultivating the soil on our own farm to ge
fall planting.

We worked hard.

By 1949, "pull type" combines—the kind that
behind a tractor—began to be replaced by "self-
bines, so we ditched our tractors and pull types for t
Now we could really go fast and we could rea
money. Of course, the more of these machines t
more the competition stiffened, and the price
dropped steadily from eight dollars an acre to fou
evened up by the speed of the new, faster field m
on we worked.

I never liked scooping wheat in the hot sun, bu
delicious to travel to exotic places and mix with t
who worked on combine crews. Eventually th
involved in the business that the competition be
of the crews would try to buy your business out f
offering to cut their price-per-acre rate. Some se
in open war between the crews. The fistfights at
frequent between quarreling crews. Some woul

sugar in each others' gas tanks, destroying motors on both trucks and combines. We managed to avoid any of these struggles, and our customers remained faithful to us, never yielding to those who tried to undersell us.

In spite of all the competition, the camaraderie among combine crews led me to understand how wonderful people could be. In all my years of being abused by school peers, I never once was mistreated by any of the combine crews we met. I began to cherish this macho way of life, and each year I eagerly looked forward to the adventure of going north. I found it exotic to be in a bar—underage as I was—with truckers and machine drivers. They chawed tobacco and spit, missing the spittoons more than they hit them. They were full of bad language and lusty stories, some of which had their origin in the daughters and wives of the farmers who hired them. Most of their stories of sexual conquests took place under truck beds or accommodating tarps, and were fantasies they freely lied into existence. But coming into puberty as I was, I found their tales entertaining and in some psychosexual way, they even appealed to me.

Their one-track minds all went together with beer and music. And since in all my years in Enid, I had not yet saturated my mind with Tchaikovsky, Ernest Tubb was all right with me. In fact, while waiting to dump my truck in the long, long elevator lines, I got used to crooning with Ernest:

I'm walkin' the floor over you,
I can't sleep a wink, that is true,
I'm tossin' and turnin', while my heart breaks right in two,
Walkin' the floor over you.

And Kitty Wells, who could out-nasal a TB patient, testified from every rural Kansas jukebox:

I didn't know you wasn't free, when you fell in love with me . . .
And now I'm payin' fer that backstreet affair.

Adenoids do, in a way, make a singer seem sincere. And it is only musical snobs who fail to see the importance in country love affairs that end when a good-hearted woman falls in love with a good-timin' man.

When Hank Williams asserted it was God who made honky-tonk angels and led men to lose themselves in the "wild side of life," Kitty Wells affirmed in a second recording, set to the same tune, that "it wasn't God who made honky-tonk angels, it was the men that God put here on the earth." It was the battle of the sexes set in denim and boots. It was an almighty dialogue about who was to blame for the spoiling of Eden. I could tell that the harvest workers rather appreciated me for appreciating their kind of culture.

They were amazed that I could also quote a few Latin lines of *De Bello Gallico*, although they were not convinced that I was saying real words. Still, these good wholesome brothers of the chaw were intrigued and often asked me to say things in Latin. So I did. And they'd always say, "Well, I'll be *damned*."

"Could be," I'd say. "The key to not being damned is, of course, to accept Jesus as your Savior." I felt it was important to witness to them, and they didn't mind. I've always found that country people who knew they were going to hell liked to be reminded, even when they had no intention of altering their lives.

"Now who is it that speaks Latin besides you?" they asked.

"Miss Fromholz, my teacher," I'd say.

"Anybody else in Oklahoma or Kansas?" they'd ask.

"Nobody else I'd know about," I said. "The Romans did it." Then I'd tell them about how Latin was a dead language, and I'd quote for them the little cliché:

> Latin's a dead, dead language
> As dead as it can be,
> It killed all the Romans,
> And now it's killing me.

This was poetry of a sort, and this impressed them.

I'm convinced it was the dust and grit that bore testimony that we were brothers. When you pull into a hot, July truck stop in South Dakota, and you're sitting there covered in chaff and sweaty wheat dust, you are automatically attracted to anyone else who is covered in chaff and sweaty wheat dust. I think there's even something so exotic about it, for it does somehow appeal to a farmer's daughter.

On one occasion, I was scooping wheat up over my head and tossing it into a private wheat bin inside a barn in Oklahoma. The farmer's daughter approached me with a pitcher of ice-cold lemonade, and she handed me the glass and bid me take a little break and drink the stuff. I was mortared to the truck bed with my own rank sweat and could hardly stand the smell of my own body. And I thought of Danté's *Inferno* and the lovely Beatrice who walked him through hell and seemed not to mind the stench. I remembered, too, the tales that the other harvest hands had told about how they had gotten their jollies from capricious women who liked grimy guys. I wanted to have a story like that, but I had just never gotten any woman to force herself upon me under a truck tarp.

Could this be your moment? I asked myself. I suddenly became emboldened. Still, I hadn't gotten enough come-hither looks in my life to be sure that I was getting one from her. But she seemed almost aggressively available as she stood there in a starched pinafore, looking somewhat like Aphrodite as I remembered her in Bullfinch's mythology. I was a Christian and felt like I should witness to her, just in case she had any ideas of seducing me. And the thought, while delicious, was also incredulous. And for one fleeting moment I was possessed both of a spirit of aggression and yet a deep sense of remembering what happened to David when he saw Bathsheba sponging herself on a rooftop.

It wasn't till three or four decades later that evangelicals started asking themselves "What would Jesus do?" and wearing little WWJD bracelets to remind themselves to ask the question. The wheat truck temptress edged ever closely to me as I sipped the lemonade. When she was so close that all spiritual restraint had been abandoned, I was sure I was a goner. Had there been WWJD bracelets, and had I been wearing one, I would have ripped it away, poured the lemonade sizzling in steam over the fires of hell, and joined the cruddy crew at the chicken fried steak bar of the Harvest Café with a tale of my own.

To this day I cannot explain my sudden lurch into self-control. But I could hear the screeching of my inner brakes and smell the rubber of the tires locked into a skidded stop on the road to perdition.

It never happened.

Temptation retreated.

It could have been because she suddenly felt guilty about the come-hither deceit of her lemonade ministry. It could have been because, when I lifted my arm to return the empty glass, she was directly downwind from my armpit, which by three o'clock on any summer afternoon would make the maw of hell seem like a roll in sweet clover. What was so sad about it all, was that I—being a preacher—really never thought about trying to win her to the Lord till my body odor had rendered any thoughts of either evangelism or sex pretty much impossible.

ART IN SOUTH DAKOTA

Harvest crews are not the place you go to experience the arts, and I cannot ever remember having a discussion about van Gogh anywhere north of the Kansas state line during harvesttime. But I do remember a rainy season in South Dakota when the incessant rains kept the grain too wet to cut and the fields too muddy to hold a combine. Alas, we sat and could not harvest the crops, which were in some danger of being lost if the rains kept falling, for sooner or later the wheat would "head over" and fall too low to the ground for the combine headers to retrieve. In one of these dismal seasons, when we were playing a lot of poker and dominoes to while away the rotten weather, Jesse said, "There's not much to be done here. Why don't we go over and see this new mountain carving they call Mount Rushmore?" It wasn't all that new. In fact, the year was 1951, and the sculpture had been finished for ten years. But it had not yet found time to fix itself in the patriotic center of American esteem.

We all—truckers and combine operators—piled into our cab-overhead GMC truck and readied ourselves for the ride. Only three could sit in the cab of the truck, so the rest of us loaded into the bed of the truck and drove more than two hundred miles westward to see this new world wonder. The incredible sculpture had been finished just at the outset of World War II. But in the five or six years since the war had ended, it was still short of the kind of infrastructure that would provide the monumental work the roads it needed to make it accessible.

To this day, I will never forget the impression that Gutzon Borglum's sculpture made on me. The towering white faces, bold in the morning sun, would leave me forever in awe. I would later see Michelangelo's *David* and Bernini's cherubs, Rodin's *The Kiss* and the endless treasures of Greek statuary. But nothing blazed its glory into the center of my life more than Borglum's mountain. Once I saw it, I was overcome by the power of four sets of eyes. The sculptor had bored the pupils of the eyes deep into the granite. But he left at the top of each drilled cavity a shaft of stone slightly recessed. This meant that while the pupils appear deep set with understanding, the shaft of stone at the top of the pupil catches the light and gleams as though it is a ray of light falling on the glistening surfaces of real, gigantic eyes. In later years, I would visit the site many times and often do a fourteen-mile hike from Harney Peak down to Borglum's triumph, but nothing was ever to compete with that first view from the bed of a GMC truck on a rainy day west of Presho, South Dakota.

THE SCHMIDTS OF PRESHO

It was that same year, after the rains stopped, that we actually began cutting wheat for John and Sophie Schmidt. They were generally vibrant people and yet they were disconsolate about going to church. For the longest time I couldn't figure out why they were so depressed about church. Then one day I went inside their home for a drink of water, and I noticed a stack of books on the Second Coming. Each of the books carefully detailed the second coming of Christ and focused on how Hitler was the Antichrist. Hitler had now been dead for six years, and I think in an odd way John and Sophie missed him. I have long pondered what made this prophecy-driven couple so despondent. Had they somehow sold their souls into a picture of how Hitler would end the world, and when he didn't end it that way, they were disappointed?

I think it all results from the pain you feel when you turn out to be wrong—right out in front of the whole world. I wondered if John and Sophie had committed themselves to the view that Adolf was the Beast of Revelation. But then Hitler had the audacity to die and leave them so openly wrong.

John and Sophie taught me that it is not enough to believe in something sincerely. It is also important to be informed. This was one of the most important things I ever learned. The difference between being passionately wrong about a thing and being coolly informed is the wide chasm known as naiveté. Most all of my life, it seems I have been helping people past the outcome of disconsolate policies they picked up from being zealous about former errors.

The rain that fell at harvesttime left John and Sophie's wheat fields too sodden to be entered with combines and trucks, but in addition to their extensive wheat fields, they had a ten-acre patch of oats, which they threshed to make food for their livestock. John and Sophie were old, and they could not thresh their oats. So we, having no wheat dry enough to cut, entered their oat field and cut and bundled their grain before we trundled it on wide, rubber-tired wagons to the thresher where the reaping was finished. It was free work for us, but that's the best kind. And Sophie cooked and baked for us. What pies! What cakes! What fried chicken! The flow of icy lemonade, like Niagara, never ceased.

"John," I said, during a harvest break, "I couldn't help but notice all your books on prophecy. Were you disappointed that Hitler didn't turn out to be the Antichrist?"

"It looked like a good bet to us, back in '38," he said disconsolately.

"It looks like it would more likely be Khrushchev now," I said.

"Maybe," he said. "Them fellers say on the radio that Jesus won't be coming back till they build the temple in Jerusalem. Now that the Jews done took it back over maybe they'll just start any day to build that temple."

"You know, John, back in 1656 there was a group of religious prophecy experts called the Fifth Monarchists. They had it all worked out for Jesus to come back in 1656 and end Cromwellian rule by setting up his throne in Westminster Abbey. Well, of course, he didn't do it. There were a lot of people back in merry old England disappointed when Jesus didn't show. I guess, for my part, I believe Jesus is coming again, and nobody knows for sure when it's going to happen. Ever notice that all these people who say that Jesus is coming back again always say it's gonna happen next week? None of them ever say it's going to happen next year or fifty years from now. You can't get a crowd by prophesying that Jesus is coming later.

"In our little church, our pastor always threatened us with the Second Coming. She'd say, 'Do you want to be in one of those godless movie houses when Jesus comes again?' You have no idea how her words would scare the fire out of me. John, would you believe that Snow White and I are the very same age, both born in 1936? But if she looks better than I do, it's because I risked hell-fire to go see her at the Mecca Theater in Enid, Oklahoma. I would walk up to the ticket booth at the theater and I'd look at the sky, and if it was cloudless, and it didn't look like Jesus would come back in the next couple of hours, I'd put down my ten cents, buy a ticket, and go in and watch *Snow White*. But I was nervous. I knew Jesus just might come again while I was in there. He might split the skies over Enid, Oklahoma, where we believed he would show up first when he came again. It would be just like my pastor said: Jesus would come a-whooshing in to blow the roof off the Mecca theater, and there I'd sit ashamed of my sin while the seven dwarfs sang, 'Heigh-ho, Heigh-ho, it's off to hell you go.'"

John laughed a little.

"But, John, if those radio preachers have anything to teach us, it must be they don't know any more about it than we do. But they gotta make you feel ashamed if you don't believe they're right about things. Nobody would send 'em any money otherwise. They would never be able to keep scaring people and pick up the bucks if they got too casual with their predictions. Nope, it's gotta be today if you want anybody to send you their money. Know what they say that Martin Luther said?"

"What's that?"

"'Even if I knew Jesus were going to come tomorrow, I would plant an apple tree today.' I can tell by looking at your books that you and Sophie bit pretty deep. I say Jesus can come back anytime he wants to, but for right now it's a pretty clear day outside. It looks like I'll have time to get these oats back to the thresher before he shows up."

John and Sophie took a special liking to me after that. Next time I walked back into the house, all their books of paperback prophecy were gone. And one night after supper I heard John tell Sophie maybe they'd put out a little orchard in the fall—an apple orchard. "We're old, but we might just live long enough to get a pie off those trees before we die."

We never cut wheat for them again, and I lost track of them over the next few years. I don't know if they ever planted those apple trees or not. I just know that when you can't get Jesus figured out, you can always enjoy a good piece of apple pie if the cinnamon is thick and butter has made the crust a bit of heaven, even if you haven't got the inclination to go there anytime soon.

The Last of the Ugly Years

In August of 1954, the final summer before I was to begin Oklahoma Baptist University, Jesse asked me how much money I had to use to pay my tuition with, and I told him. It was three hundred dollars, and a bit short of what I thought I would need to get into the school. "Well, Calvin," he said, "I've got a haying job, putting bales into the Davies barn. Like everybody else he'll pay us ten cents a bale to get them from the field into his barn. I want you to do the job, and instead of working for me, you work for yourself. The GMC cab overhead is full of fuel. All the money you make today is yours. You can have a couple of my hands, and I'll pay them. Their pay won't have to come out of your profits."

"Why would you do that, Jesse?" I asked.

"Let's just say I think you're a good boy, and what you want to do with your life is obviously pretty important to you. Who knows, there may be a day when I'll be proud that I gave you my truck for a day."

Never with just one truck and two guys had we had a 600-bale day. But I began early and worked as hard as I could. So did the two hands Jesse had given me for the day. At the end of the day we had put up 890 bales, and Jesse paid me eighty-nine dollars for that one day.

He could be a hard man, pushing me from early morning to late night when there was work to do, but all of a sudden I saw him in a new way. I saw him as the generous benefactor he really was. I saw him as a man not so fascinated by his own entrepreneurial need to get ahead that he couldn't take time to serve my interests above his own.

I left Pond Creek, looking back over my shoulder at that plump silver water tower and a white concrete elevator, the two customary skyscrapers of every Oklahoma hamlet. I smiled. I knew there were the Dillons, who took a miserable kid from a lonely high school and gave him the room he needed to let go of the plow handle and pick up a Bible. I was never a good farmer, but that was all right; God wanted me to be a shepherd anyway.

EIGHT

Beating the Underwear People

IN 1953, I WAS SITTING IN A CHURCH SERVICE WHEN I HAD THE OVER-whelming feeling that God intended me to be a preacher. It was pretty hard to imagine myself in front of a crowd preaching. I was often a withdrawn kid who was surviving my adolescence by making myself as unnoticeable as I could among my peers. I had learned that when-ever I made any attempt to enter a circle of conversation, it usually turned out bad for me and left me the brunt of some kind of bullying. Just getting along with the hostile world was my goal all through adolescence. The best way to do this was to keep a low profile.

THE FIRST, WORST SERMON

So it was little wonder that Brother Daley was surprised when I told him I had begun feeling I was called to preach. I could tell he was unenthused. Preachers were highly sociable types who lived at the centers of their religious communities. My sister Shirley was also sur-prised, saying that if the Lord had called me to preach, he must have had a wrong number. Only my mother seemed unsurprised and seemed to affirm me in my calling. My friend Alvin thought it was all right for me to be called, but not having a particular affection or admiration for any preacher he had ever known, he simply shook my hand and said, "Good!" The announcement generally came without any comment or evaluation. So within a week or so I had quit talking about it altogether.

However, Brother Daley soon called me on the telephone, which we only lately had come to own, and asked me if I would like to preach my first sermon at the Garfield County old folks' home. I wasn't sure I was ready at seventeen to begin my public ministry. Jesus was thirty when he began his, and I had been thinking that would be about right for me too. But when the pastor said "next week," I could see his idea of beginning was about twelve years earlier than I had in mind.

"Look," said Brother Daley, "there's no need to be afraid of this. The Garfield County old folks' home would be an excellent place for you to try your wings in the ministry."

"Well," I said, "I don't know if I can do this or not. I was thinking of starting a bit later, say when I was thirty or so. That's how Jesus did it."

"Well," said Brother Daley, "that may have been when Jesus started his public ministry, but he very likely preached a great deal before he began to preach out in the open. John 21:25 says that Jesus did many things that were not written down, and that if every one of them were written down even the world itself would not contain the books that should be written."

This stunned me. I thought the Bible was the complete record of everything Jesus ever did. I was surprised that Jesus did a lot of things we would never know about.

"So you see," said Brother Daley, interrupting my probing of his last sentence, "it's possible, maybe even probable, that Jesus preached a great many sermons when he was young, maybe even seventeen like you."

Drat it all! I thought. *Why did he have to start so young?*

"He might even have preached at the Nazareth old folks home," laughed the pastor. He laughed more than I did.

"But what would I say?" I asked him.

"No need to worry about that," he said. "Most of the old people who live there can't hear very well, so don't worry about keeping your voice level up. Most of them don't remember all that well, so the content of your sermon will not be all that important. They don't see too well, so you don't need to worry about eye contact when you preach. I would caution you to remember, however, that they often drool, but this should not be taken as a sign that they are eager to hear more. A short sermon would be best."

After our conversation, I began work on my first sermon. I used our old typewriter to type out five single-spaced pages of notes. I thought I had enough material for a twenty-minute sermon at least. But when I actually stood in front of the crowd, I was so nervous and talked so fast that I mumbled through at a lightning pace and finished with my head down in less than three minutes. I was horribly embarrassed. I sat down red as a beet, ashamed that I had ever announced my call to preach. After I sat back down, Brother Daley took over and kept the sermon going for twenty more minutes or so and closed the service.

We left.

I was never so glad to get out of anywhere in my whole life. And I determined that whatever call I thought I had, I was going to put the whole thing on hold for a while. Maybe until I was thirty. Even if Jesus had started earlier, there were some pretty clear differences between me and Jesus. He was the Son of God, for instance, and as such had a bit of an edge on me, even if he started preaching at seventeen.

THE MIRROR'S GIFT

The horror of the experience kept me from attempting to preach for two more years. In the meantime, I enrolled as a freshman at

Oklahoma Baptist University. Believing it was imperative that I learned to speak in front of others, I took a course in public speaking. Dr. Opal Craig was my professor, and I had heard that she could work miracles with stutterers and lispers and in general with all students who struggled with low self-esteem.

Our first speech was to be a two-minute talk introducing ourselves to the class. I was amazed at how easy that was for most people. I got up and bumbled through a one-page manuscript in half a minute, not two. I bit my lip to cover up my emotions.

The class was embarrassed. So was I.

I felt sorry for Dr. Craig, who must have felt like it would never be possible for her to help me become a preacher. She smiled, but said nothing. She wrote an F on my manuscript and handed it back to me. I knew she had only given me an F because it wasn't possible to assign me a grade further down in the alphabet.

Our next speech was to be delivered on a current event. I selected to speak on whether or not General MacArthur should have gone against President Truman's command and crossed the demilitarized zone into North Korea. It was a subject that had been hot on the news, and I think it was a fine topic as current events go. But I stumbled over the word *demilitarized*, saying it was a "delimiterized," no a "demizzarlized," no a "de . . ." The class began laughing. That time I choked up emotionally, stopping just short of tears.

Why hadn't I just said "the DMZ"? Even Chet Huntley said that on NBC. Why not just use letters? Why was I so stupid, stupid, stupid? I sat down and never finished the speech. I have hated the word *demilitarized* ever since and have never tried to use it again. I really felt the burning hot shame of my public failure. Dr. Craig scratched another F on my outline and handed it back. Since she couldn't write any lower grade, she just wrote this F a little bigger than the last one.

Our third speech was to be a demonstration speech. Every class member had to do a show-and-tell speech. We had to talk while we demonstrated how to do something like a hobby or a sales exhibition. I decided to demonstrate how to paint miniature chessmen, a hobby of mine at the time. I cannot describe to you the fullness of this disaster. I knocked over a bottle of red enamel and mostly painted my trembling fingers, getting almost none of the paint on the chessmen.

More embarrassment.

Larger F.

The last speech was to be a ten-minute "hopes and dreams" speech. My ten-minute speech lasted only two. Most of the class had beautiful hopes and dreams, of corporate careers and lives of gallantry. My main hope was to get out of the class without a coronary, and my main dream was to die before I was old enough to ever become a preacher.

I got the largest, reddest F ever handed out at that university.

I think it is still listed in Guinness. But it was almost Christmas! And I looked forward to going home. I envied Alvin for going into engineering. I felt I should have rethought my career field. Somehow I knew I had missed it. There must be some other way to make a living. But try as I might I couldn't shake that miserable feeling that I was called to preach.

I tried to bargain with God. "God, send me to a leper colony to love the eroded," I prayed. I had come to envy Saint Francis, who denied himself and threw his fate to the wind by kissing a leper. I would rather have kissed lepers, one after another, in long unending lines, than ever take another speech class.

Dr. Craig caught me after class and said, "Calvin, this has not been easy for either one of us or for the class. Your test grades have been good, so I am going to pass you on one condition."

"You name it," I said.

"You must promise me you will never take me for another speech class!"

"It's a deal," I said. "I will never, never, never take another speech class from you or from anyone else. I'm through with public speaking, forever!"

"Good call," said Dr. Craig.

I sincerely meant the promise, but I found myself struggling with the Lord over the Christmas vacation. God assured me that I had made a stupid promise to Dr. Craig. God told me I should have checked with him before I ever swore such an oath. God further said that I must not keep the promise.

Naturally, I hated going back to school in January.

When Dr. Craig walked into her advanced speech class in January, I was there. Her face fell. I felt very sorry for her. "You promised!" she said.

"I know," I said. "But God wouldn't let me off the hook."

"What about the rest of us? Has God got a way off the hook for all the rest of us?"

She paused.

"Calvin, I know you are desperate about this matter. I'm going to give you a little advice. I don't know if it will help, but it's all I know that might. Buy yourself a mirror, put it in your room, and practice every speech out loud at least thirty times before you bring it in here. Always practice the same way. Stand in front of the mirror and look directly into your own eyes as you practice, each and every time you practice. Never take your gaze from your own eyes as you speak. Will you do that?"

"I will, Dr. Craig," I said as the class gathered in for the first day of class. Our first speech assignment, due in two weeks, was, "How I Intend to Pursue Excellence in My Life." I hated the subject, but at least I wouldn't have to paint chessmen.

I bought a mirror.

I wrote the speech on how I intended to pursue excellence.

I began to practice, saying the words over and over.

I found it hard to look at the mirror.

I looked so stupid. I looked like I was trying too hard.

Alone in my room I tried practicing in my underwear.

That was horribly debilitating. *Why?* I wondered.

Answer: nobody looks good in their underwear!

Then I remembered what a friend had told me. He said when he became frightened in front of an audience, he just imagined everyone in the audience sitting out there in their underwear. "It's easier to preach to people when you think about how they look in their underwear," he said.

It may not have been the most orthodox of devices, but the notion had a mesmerizing hold on me. Dr. Craig? Did she not also wear underwear, and what would she look like in her bloomers? And what right does anyone have to pass out big red Fs when they themselves were hardly centerfold icons? I reflected long on the matter before I put my jeans and a T-shirt back on, and went on practicing how to pursue excellence a little better dressed.

Then a most wonderful thing happened!

I saw my eyes.

I was no longer just looking past them, I was looking into them.

Odd as it may seem, I don't know that I had ever looked into my own eyes. They were pale green and fairly piercing, yet I had never noticed that. And my face was not Humphrey Bogart perhaps, but it was reasonably strong. My cheekbones were bold, and my chin was just two marks short of what might be called rugged.

In an instant I was healed. I had seen myself, not like Narcissus fondling his ego, but like a demoniac who had just been exorcised.

God had called me to preach, and what I had just seen in the mirror, God had seen all the way along. I somehow wasn't a kid to be bullied any longer. I was new! Just like that! I had a magnificent new conversion to self-esteem.

The great thing was that Dr. Craig must have known I had never really seen myself as a man in the mirror. And once I did, I saw him so suddenly and clearly that I would never quit seeing him in any other way for the next fifty years.

On the day of my speech, I got to class early. I watched my peers assemble, and I mentally undressed them, not to lust after them, but to bring them down to my level of being. There was James the jock, who lived in my section of the dorm. Never took a shower. I could only imagine the green state of his underwear. There was Billy who himself wasn't very manly. What kind of shorts would he be wearing? Trimmed with lace, perhaps? The women who entered the class, particularly the hefty ones, gave me great hope as I saw them as clearly as if they had gone through an X-ray machine. And last of all, Dr. Craig came in. I did admire her and it was hard to dress her down to her essentials, but no one was sacrosanct. She, like all the others, had her own special price to pay.

When the vision of horror was complete, I stood to speak.

"Excellence is a pursuit never to be achieved," I said, thinking, *Poor little underwear things! Listen up so that you may hear the full scope of my rhetoric.* "For the more you reach for it, the more it recedes from your grasp."

They listened. They moved forward in their chairs. "Yet it is not the grasp that creates success, it is the reaching." They propped their chins on their elbows, and their elbows on their desks. I believed in public speaking for the first time, for I now felt the public was listening! Dr. Craig wasn't looking at my manuscript; she was looking at me. And we understood each other, and neither she nor I was any more than God had made us to be. And we both had weaknesses and we both had mirrors. We each in our own ways had practiced life somewhere else so we could live it openly before the world. And there was no use weeping over our inferiority; we were all, at our barest minimum, underwear people. And only when we have learned to respect ourselves in our inner souls can we ever speak with force in the larger world.

In a single speech I went from an F to an A. But it was more than that. It wasn't just that I believed I could succeed in a speech class, but that I was ready to take my place in the calling that I was sure I had known was true but had only recently come to believe as I stood before a mirror practicing the art of my life.

At the end of my sophomore year, I was nineteen years of age, and a vigorous country church in Hunter, Oklahoma, "came open." Our district superintendent, or director of missions as we usually called him, said I should candidate for the pulpit. So I agreed to try.

DEALING WITH LEPROSY IN HUNTER

In August of 1956, just before my twentieth birthday, I borrowed a 1948 Chevrolet sedan from my brother-in-law and drove up to preach in the Hunter Baptist Church. I had decided to preach from a passage in 2 Kings 5:1–15. The passage contains the story of Naaman, the leper general who was healed of his leprosy by Elisha the prophet. I had worked hard on the sermon, and it lasted for eleven minutes. This was not only the first sermon I had ever preached in a church; it was four times as long as my earlier sermon preached at the Garfield County old folks' home.

It seemed to go quite well. I began the sermon by dealing with the fascinating ins and outs of leprosy—its symptoms, treatment, and disfigurement. I explained how leprosy in the Bible was a kind of metaphor for sin, and how Naaman tried to hide his disease for as long as he could. He knew that as soon as he was discovered to be a leper he would be driven from his high position of power. He would then languish in the wallows of the "unclean" who cried among the tombs and died in ignominy and isolation. It really seemed more like a mandate from the Center for Disease Control than a strong sermon. But in spite of the fact that leprosy was not all that common in Garfield County, the sermon went over extremely well. They asked me to come back and preach for them again the next week.

Over the next three weeks, I preached three more eleven-minute sermons, and while the last two were nothing to compare with the first one, the congregation seemed to be enthralled. Part of my success was majoring on the things Dr. Craig had taught me, for I continued to practice in front of a mirror (and occasionally before a crucial appointment, I still do). Or it may have been that I followed their previous long-winded preacher, whose hour-long homilies had over the years worn them out with too much thunder and too little light.

So they hired me. Why wouldn't they? After that first sermon there was not a single case of leprosy anywhere in the county.

The Hunter Baptist Church was a white frame building, and like so many in the late nineteenth century and early twentieth, it was gothic carpentry in style. Its steeple once held a heavy bronze bell, but the weight of the bell had so stressed the timbers in the steeple that the bell had to come down in the 1930s. The steeple, as a result, was foreshortened to remove the most stressed of its sagging timbers, and yet it retained a rural charm that is often hard to find in more modern churches. The windows were high and arched-gothic, though not of stained glass. The long circular pews were dark walnut and matched the pulpit furnishings.

They paid me thirty-five dollars per week, enough to buy a late-model used car and keep my tuition paid through my junior and senior years at the university. Seventy people attended the church on a good Sunday. And they seemed attentive in every way. I must confess, I loved my work.

Being only twenty years of age, I was popular with the young people of the little town, and while the bulk of the town's youth belonged to the Christian church, both those from the Methodist church and the Christian church often wound up in our building for the Sunday night activities.

The funerals held there were frequent, and the weddings occasional. The building, except for the shortening of the steeple and bell removal, had not been redecorated or added to since it was completed in 1907, the year of Oklahoma statehood.

The building had never had a baptistery, and most of the recent converts had been baptized in a member's farm pond. We redesigned the beautiful chancel area and a bit of the twenty-four-seat choir loft to put in a new baptistery—a seven-hundred-gallon tank where converts could be baptized.

The most interesting feature of the new design was the baptistery painting. Baptists in those days were accustomed to having an artist paint a large picture of a stream that flowed down right to the edge of the baptistery so that it appeared the new convert was being baptized in a stream. Often these paintings had a mountain in the background, which was my preference, since our part of Oklahoma was so flat. We hired a local German artist to do the painting. And he did it quite well, except that the mountain in his painting was rather Alpine, snowcapped, and looked like the mountain on the Busch Bavarian Beer bottle. I'm pretty sure that very picture had been the inspiration for his work. Still, he had done a good job on the painting, and most of us were happy to pay him his fee and happily baptize our children and the believers before "beer mountain." Once we were used to it, we rarely thought about the Busch Brewers, or how on some Sundays we denounced drinking beer even as we gazed at the beautiful mountain that rose behind me like a Sinai of sin and corruption.

RALPH THE PROPHET

It was the people of this rustic parish who most fascinated me. There was Ralph Greenman, an old bachelor who had lived alone all his life. His solitude had given him room to grow his theories into philosophies.

Ralph was snaggle-toothed and bristle-chinned; as his teeth had never known a brush, so his hair had seldom known a comb, nor his chin a razor. But he was the Oracle of Hunter. His mind had never been complicated by striving to fit in with the modern world nor had he ever struggled with changing styles. But as the Oklahoma wind can blow a conscience clean, or the rain can wash life into a wheat field, he was tanned and straight, skeletal and simple.

I loved to catch up to him in a new furrow and ride around his fields while we shouted over the popping drone of his green tractor. The tractor was loud (the old John Deere, two-cylinder machines were affectionately known throughout the county as Johnny-Pops). We could only make each other hear by shouting our ends of the conversation over the roar of the tractor. But my favorite moments came when the conversation was too delicious to be shouted and he would stop plowing, idle the tractor to a whisper, and tell me what I needed to know to survive in the ministry.

"Calvin," he said to me on one such occasion, "you have picked a life that will be filled with criticism. Much of it will not be instructive, but listen to it all, then sort through what you need to build a bulwark of survival."

"How do I do that, Ralph?"

"Use your nose, not your ears. The ears itch to hear the good stuff, but they will deceive you, for you will want to believe every good lie you hear. But your nose, that's your best evaluator: manure always smells like manure."

He took his long, bony finger and placed it on the tip of my nose. "This is the periscope, my boy. Keep it above the water and sniff your way through the palaver of your critics. But always listen to your critics. For they—not caring too much for you—will often tell you the truth, while your friends sugarcoat, so as to stay on your good side. Remember what Polonius said to Laertes?"

I could never remember what Polonius said to Laertes.

But Ralph ended all his oracles with a poem, and his poems were the best part. "Well, old Polonius told his boy: 'Those friends thou hast, and their adoption tried, Grapple them to thy soul with hoops of steel'" (*Hamlet* I, 111, 61).

"That's *Hamlet*, boy!" he said, straining his words slowly around his lone front tooth. "Keep the Prince of Denmark right next to the Prince of Peace, and you'll live a better life."

Once, after a church business meeting, when I had been especially pushy about renovating and building on to the church, Ralph was waiting for me. He pushed me up against my car and wagged his finger at me, and said, "Hey, boy, what is the pushy stuff? We Baptists take a little while to digest stuff. Slow down, or you'll outrun us. When a leader gets so far out in front of his people they can't see him, they also can't see his vision. Don't mistake the rim of the rut you're running in for the edge of your horizon."

"And the poem?" I asked.

"It's simple, boy! 'Lord, teach us to number our days, that we may apply our hearts unto wisdom.' That's Psalm 90:12 (KJV), and it's just a reminder to pace yourself, watch the clock, and remember very few things have to be decided in a hurry."

I have tried ever since to remember to keep every dream I wished to sell to the church coming at people at a reasonable pace.

But I think the best advice Ralph ever gave me for leading the church came one time after he had shut off the tractor and we were walking back across a newly plowed field toward my car. "Calvin, my boy, the best part of your leadership is that you seem to get everybody included in every plan you make. That's essential: no secrets, ever, in the church, right?"

"Right," I replied, although I had no idea what was coming next.

"No secrets," he repeated himself. "Never have any special group in your church who knows the critical ins and outs of your dreams, while the bulk of the people are in the dark. The janitor should know everything the chairman of the board knows, right?"

"Right," I answered, but more hesitantly.

"Keep every plan out in the open, and you'll never get in trouble. Keep the church finances that way too. Let everybody know freely everything you know, and don't have any special people you try to placate by giving them information first. When everybody owns the church and its dreams, the church is healthy. When there are little secret pockets of informants, decay is in the wind. Paul said over in 1 Corinthians 1:10 that the church must be perfectly united in its reasons for existing. The leader and the led are equal partners in the union. The church has got to be owned by everybody, son!"

"And the poem is . . ."

"I guess Kipling will do here," he said.

> Now this is the law of the jungle,
> It's as old and as true as the sky.
> And the wolf that shall keep it may prosper,
> And the wolf that shall break it must die.
>
> As the creeper girdles the tree trunk,
> The truth runneth forward and back.
>
> The strength of the pack is the wolf,
> And the strength of the wolf is the pack.

Ralph was the sage. God's odd, John-Deere clairvoyant. I listened carefully through all his out-spillings of advice.

THE MIXED-BATHING CRISIS

Country people were very faithful in their attendance at church. They took their religion and politics seriously. Every country chapel flew both the American flag and the Christian flag in those days. An open Bible rested in the center of every communion table, and the register board of attendance was on one side of the platform, while a hymn board announcing the numbers of the hymns to be sung was on the other. I was generally in agreement with the flock on what was right and wrong and what Baptist doctrines were most crucial to believe and which could be the most easily dispensed with.

One doctrine I just couldn't subscribe to was the Baptist ban on mixed bathing. Baptists in Oklahoma didn't believe men and women should swim together in the same pool at the same time. This was not a doctrine that caused a lot of trouble, as there wasn't a swimming pool within twenty-five miles of the church. But the argument raised its ugly head in the summer of 1957, when I took a group of thirty young people to Falls Creek Baptist Assembly.

The boys from our church swam in the boys' pool and the girls in the girls' pool. The funny thing about this was that there were always a large number of boys who walked around the girls' pool and watched them swim, and an equally large number of girls who were walking around the boys' pool, studying them. Such holy voyeurism seemed to me to defeat the purpose of the mixed-bathing doctrine. So on Thursday of that week, I decided—and the decision clearly was mine—to take all the students, boys and girls, to Turner Falls, a public pool only a few miles away, so they could all swim together. Generally we all had a good time, but one of the ranchers in the church became extremely upset that I was leading the youth of the church into sin by allowing them into the same pool of water at the same time.

Two of our adult sponsors at the Falls Creek Assembly that ill-fated week returned to Hunter early and called a special meeting of the deacons to report my sinful behavior to the church. By the time the story circulated the community, some interesting new fictional items had been added to the story. The tale was that I had allowed them to behave extremely eroticly and that I was no longer moral enough to be allowed to continue as pastor.

One sponsor said he had personally watched me lusting after many of the young women in their skimpy bathing suits. He told them that I had deliberately led the youth into spiritual compromise by taking them to Turner Falls, where I encouraged them to dive into the sin of mixed bathing. He also believed that this kind of bathing could lead the youth into sock hops, school proms, and other forms of godless behavior. After my ministry was over, he said, there would be nothing left for our youth but to backslide into the hideous descent of rapid moral decay.

The incident nearly destroyed my sense of propriety. I quit visiting the elderly and sick, for I knew the kind of wild tales that must be flying about between people in the church—and for that matter the people of the town. I was looking for a way to get out of the church and to keep from embarrassing the fine people who worshipped there from having to struggle to defend me against this charge of mixed bathing. I did love the church and just prayed that God would let the whole experience go away.

When I had neglected my ministry in the hamlet for almost a month, the brother of my accuser came to Enid to make an unexpected call on me at home.

"We haven't seen much of you lately around the parish," he said. "Is anything the matter?"

"Didn't your brother tell you that I let the kids go swimming together and that I was there with my eyes bugged out in raw lust?"

"Yes, he told me. He told almost everyone. But you don't know him very well or you would know that he has chased nearly every skirt in the county whom he could buy or get free. If he said all that stuff about you, it's only because that's what he would have been doing if his wife hadn't had him by the ear during that week at camp."

"You think my reputation has been hurt?" I asked my encourager.

"Not in the least," he said. "Pastor, we miss you. Come on back to us. You're the best pastor we've ever had, and, frankly, I think there are some doctrines we Baptists need to rethink—starting with mixed bathing."

When I entered the church the next Sunday morning, I got a standing ovation. I was home! Nothing ever came of the gossip. But I learned a valuable thing that summer: it's a good idea to watch your backside. I didn't do anything wrong by taking the youth to a community swim. What I did wrong was not getting all the people in line on the decision first. Ever after that, I learned to lead by consensus. As Ralph had already reminded me, a good leader doesn't go anywhere by himself.

THE GIRL IN GOLD

A wonderful thing happened to me Easter of 1958. Next to my conversion, it was the most significant event in my life. A teenage member of my church showed up in a new Easter frock. I knew her well, for her parents were prominent members of the church. It is odd that you can know someone very well and yet never have really seen her at all.

I think it was the dress that caused me to see her for the first time. It was a light beige sheath dress, low at the neck and delightfully form-fitting, though in no way crass or intentionally inappropriate. About the waist was a gold cummerbund, with pinpoint polka dots set in a sheen of the shimmering damask out of which it was made.

I was amazed. Could this Aphrodite have really been a member of our church and I not seen her till this very moment? I stammeringly told her at the door that her new dress looked great, and I wondered if she would like to have dinner with me on Friday night at the El Sombrero, Enid's premiere restaurant that served everything from Mexican food to barbeque. She agreed to this, and a year later we were married, though this segment of the tale belongs on other pages of this account.

I know there are evangelical writers who say you shouldn't kiss until you're married, but they obviously never knew Barbara. Who could wait that long? Not me. It is true that when we kissed I often wondered what lay beyond the kiss, although we never went all the way until we both wore rings that told the world we were legally going all the way.

But a lover's kiss, for all the prophecy of fire that it contains, was not the best signal of our devotion. Think me not corny, but it was holding hands. I have now made a five-decade study of this issue, and I'm here to tell you that those who overrate a kiss, do it on the basis of Cyrano's description. A kiss may be "a rosy dot over the *i* of loving," but if so, it is only a dot. People who only kiss are too much interested in the fire that lies beyond it. Watch those who opt for holding hands instead. These know the life of partnership and offer the hand at every patch of ice that threatens life. Hand-holders survive. Kissers slobber and move on to other empty promises of fire.

For the moment, it is enough to say we have now been married for forty-nine years and have found ourselves amazed at the glorious story we have written together. I suppose the issue of just how glorious it is will be for you to consider, and Barbara and I would like to leave it at that.

In May of 1958, I finished OBU. With my bachelor's degree in hand, I readied myself to attend seminary, and the seminary I chose was Midwestern Baptist Theological Seminary in Kansas City, Kansas. I got a clergy pass on the Rock Island Railroad and made the five-hour trip into Kansas City every Monday, returning every Friday to preach and continue my ministry in northern Oklahoma. Barbara often drove me to the depot in Enid, where I boarded what we used to call a "streamliner" and rode by rail into Kansas City. She kissed me good-bye—to arm me against loneliness—as I swung up into a railway car. She handed me my jacket to warm me against the weather. And, finally, week after week she handed me a box of cookies to arm me against hunger. The train pulled away from the train station, and I knew that lovers can cope with separation if they have a good supply of chocolate chip cookies. I could get milk in the club car, and before I opened my Greek New Testament to study, I could munch my way into a stupor of reminiscences.

The Rock Island Rocket—the oxymoronic name of the train I rode each week—connected Minneapolis with Houston, and I took only the most charming three hundred miles of it through the flattest, most beautiful farmland in the world. I was rich. Who wouldn't have been? I had it all: a good church, a great woman, and years to fly the wide fields of God.

The winter of '58 was mild enough for next summer's dreaming. And I had seen enough of providence to know that the best dreams always come true.

I only served as pastor in Hunter for three years, but those three years gave me a foothold in the ministry. The church furnished me a snaggle-toothed prophet who told me what I would need to survive the next thirty-five years of ministry. The church had given me an explosive affirmation that enabled me to hold my reputation. But best of all, the church gave me a woman, in a beautiful dress, who would walk with me like Ruth of Bethlehem, like Hannah of Israel, like Esther of Persia, like wind, like fire, like truth, like love, like a cloudless sunrise washing my doubts with enough self-confidence to keep me at my calling. Perhaps it was on a train ride each week that I solidified life's most important doctrine of survival: the sacred act of holding hands.

This simple act has kept our union safe.
Anything can happen, when you forget to practice the art.
You can slip, or lose your way, or be run down.
We have practiced the art until we have refined it.
We never cross a busy street without the counsel of this clasp,
'cause in the uncertainties of this life, you just never know.

PART TWO

Staying Human While Being a Pastor

1956–1991

NINE

Dearly Beloved, We Are Gathered Here a Bit Confused

THE MOST DIFFICULT SEASON FOR CELIBACY IS THE ONE THAT ends with the marriage ceremony. I suppose there are no "chastity meters" that objectively measure whether the wait is harder for the man than the woman, though that is general presumption. Like Augustine of old, most Christian men, before marriage, find themselves praying, "Lord, give me chastity, but not yet." Yet the best of them struggle with the notion that sex belongs inside of marriage and not before it.

THE SEX WRANGLING

Barbara and I had agreed to safeguard the virtue. Nonetheless, the season of waiting is a difficult one. Ashley Montagu said men think about sex 75 percent of their waking lives, to which I can only mutter "At least." But the other 25 percent of the time I was generally turned toward God, and this allegiance kept my convictions intact throughout our courtship.

It was also during this season I read Sinclair Lewis's *Elmer Gantry*, and I was amazed at how the fictional Gantry bargained with his value system in such a way as to keep his spirituality and his libido both active at the same time. Gantry, like most pastors, I think, thought about sex a lot, and at the same time he also thought about Jesus a good bit. This seemed to be Augustine's lifestyle as well.

Robert Heinlein, in his *Job: A Comedy of Justice*, says religion and sexuality are the two strongest drives in the human heart. Of the two, I believe religion is the stronger, for it motivates us from the very center of our lives. It is a slow and steady light. The sexual need, on the other hand, is a matter of appetite gone mad only for brief minutes of indulgence. But religious passion motivates us through a lifetime of difficult and demanding service.

I believe it is a special problem for men, because puberty and Christian conversion arrive often in the same years of our lives. Like most Baptist men I know, I was saved only shortly before I came into puberty. Most evangelical men are rarely able to integrate smoothly these two powerful forces. Why? We have been taught that Jesus and sex are somehow opposing realities and must be kept widely separate in our thinking. After seventy years of kicking this around, I think Christian men are wrong in failing to integrate them. I have known only a few Christian men who did not duck their heads or blush at any mention of their sexuality. And the subject almost never comes up in sermons at church. Of course, sex, like every good gift of God, is sacred and given as much for pleasure as procreation. Most mature Christians agree to this, I think. Still, they don't agree to speak of it very openly.

Most of my own failure to integrate these drives I inherited from Christians who couldn't integrate theirs. So my preconditioning to love Jesus while avoiding all sexual thought was a church conflict I found hard to resolve. Like most young ministers, in my twenty-second year I still kept the drives in separate pockets of my discipleship. I can still remember a dorm discussion over whether or not Jesus ever had an erection. This is the kind of conversation Christian students have when they should be studying their chemistry. But the conversation seemed relevant enough to those of us who were coming back from the girls' dormitory every night wondering why we didn't often think much about Jesus until after the girls' dorm had closed. The dormitory lights blinked under the grand portico at precisely 9:55 each night, except on Saturdays when they blinked at 10:55. There was time for one grand good night kiss before the girls went inside and the boys were standing there in the dark wondering whatever happened to *La Vie en Rose.*

We walked back to the men's dorm proud we were "sin free" but ashamed we didn't always want to be. We were there to serve Christ, and yet there was this awful wrangling over these two primal drives. It was after one of those dormitory closings, no doubt, that we had the conversation about whether Jesus ever had . . . well . . . you know.

One of the students said Jesus must have known the condition because Hebrews 4:15 said he was tempted in all ways just as we are, yet without sin.

"Can you be tempted without lusting, or is being tempted, lust?" asked another.

Still another said, "No, brothers, temptation is lust."

But another boy preacher said, "Brothers, let us not lower our dear Lord's sexuality to our own lusty estate. Fie upon such nonsense! Jesus never once thought a lusty thought. He was the Son of God and the Savior of the world, and he would not distract himself with any evil thought because he was so bent on redeeming a fallen planet."

What a cheap shot!

But then, that's what theologians always do. Just when you're doing your best to figure things out . . . *wham!* They drop the theology bomb. This statement cut off all conversation immediately. Who could argue with him? He was right. When the vote was taken, it was six to two. Six in favor of the big theology bomb and two in favor of the wholly implausible notion that Jesus must have lusted or at least been "tempted to" and still not sinned. The two who were pro-lust were in the fine arts curriculum, and very libertine compared to us who were pro-theology.

I remembered this horrible dorm debate well into the next fall when I began dating Barbara. I was her pastor as well as her lover, and the prior dormitory rhetoric was always at the forefront of my mind. I had determined that I would always live free of any permissiveness in our relationship.

There was only one area of our lives that stalked me with compromise. It was the cedars that lined the lane that led to her parents' home. When the cedars were dropping their green spores and the harvest moon was full, my werewolfish second-self struggled with the issue of "Isn't engagement close enough to marriage" to grant myself a bit of license.

Barbara said, "No, it wasn't," and I said, "Darn it!"

Really, I think it was the automakers in Detroit who were responsible for saving me from myself. The blessed gear shift that rose from the differential hump in the center of my Chevy separated our convictions on the matter. And, in fact, the gear shift had roughly the same effect as a chastity belt. Once, in a fit of passion, when I tried to leap across the transmission, Barbara opened the car door and let me fall out. So I can honestly say, though it was not entirely to my liking at the time, I did better than Augustine did with chastity. In his defense, however, there was no gear shift in the center of Roman chariots to help him keep his commitments.

In the "olden" days before the new morality, young couples always went to their family doctor, who would tell them all about the "birds and bees." This was something that was deemed necessary, because truly Christian parents didn't generally talk about either species out loud in the home. Nonetheless, I felt that Barbara should go and talk to her family doctor, who would clarify for her how sex was to be done. I felt that this was not necessary for me, since—while I had never done it—I had some rough ideas on how to proceed with the activity.

"Are you going to see the doctor too?" she asked.

"No, of course not. Don't forget that I was a biology major in college," I said. "I just don't think it is all that necessary. I think all I needed to learn about sexual function, I have learned."

"Where did you practice? On the frog?" she asked.

She was a tad snide, but I—being as spiritually mature as I was sexually wise—said little more of it. She went to see the doctor, and I counted on the schematics in my anatomy book. It all worked out just as it should have in the long run. However, it introduced within me a feeling that sometimes the swaggering, know-it-all masculine mystique could stand a few lessons in humility.

The Marriage Jitters

I think it was in part this unsatiated fire that caused me to get a bad case of the jitters before our wedding. Maybe a better phrase would be "cold feet." I cannot say exactly why. It was just that I became unsure that I was really in love, or for that matter what love was. I even held inner court on the differences between love and lust. Marriage is in some ways a leap of faith. Half of all first marriages end in divorce. And in half of those that don't end that way, people say that if they had it all to do over again, they would not marry the same person. Something like only 7 percent of marriages have a sense of lifelong rapport, that the journey is and was ever beautiful. Since this was the only option either of us believed in, I suddenly felt like marriage was too grand a leap from someone who was unpracticed in leaping.

Nonetheless, I was the pastor of the church, and Barbara and her family—mother and father, aunts, uncles, and cousins—were all pillars of the congregation. This left me reluctant to back out of the engagement only a few days or hours before the wedding.

So we were both a little busy with the mechanics of marriage to consider whether or not we should put the whole thing on hold or not. The engravings, the bakery, the tuxes and formals had all been ordered and were in place. For these and other reasons I held my tongue and kept the war of doubt entirely within myself.

On the day of the wedding I was standing in a little clot of tuxedos in the back of the church at two o'clock, waiting for the marriage processional to begin. My best man, a good college friend, who had doubtless been in on the Jesus and sex discussion, leaned over to me and said, half in a whisper, "It must be wonderful to be in love!"

"Yes, it must be," I said vacantly.

"Aren't you in love?" he asked. The music was playing; the bridesmaids were about to move down the aisle. I tried to shake all the formality fuzz from my mind enough to answer his question.

"This is a bad time to ask," I said.

"Not bad at all," he said. "No, not bad. It's a good time to ask. If I didn't know whether I was in love, I'd march in there right now and call this whole thing off."

I looked in the door over the back of the packed church.

"Did you ever hear of Richard Lovelace?"

"No," he said. "What's he got to do with this?"

"Well, he wrote *To Lucasta, Going to the Warres . . .*"

"Who is Lucasta, and why was she going to the war? Get your head together. You're about to marry, and you have no idea whether or not you're in love?"

"You're hysterical," I said. "Calm down. Lovelace wrote Lucasta and said, 'I could not love thee, dear, so much, lov'd I not honour more.'"

He seemed to be listening.

"All marriages begin with people telling each other how in love they are. Most of those marriages die in divorce courts. I'm going in and making a promise to my woman, and I'm going to spend the rest of my life living up to it. 'Cause if you've got honor when you're making a promise, you can find love just about anywhere. Honor is the bedrock of every real promise, and I believe it is the bedrock of every marriage that lasts. I will never love Barbara any more than the sacredness of my promises. In a minute I'm going to look her in the eyes and say, 'For better, for worse, in sickness and in health, till death do us part.' And when I say that, I'm going to mean it as no one standing at any altar has ever meant it. I believe that somewhere out there in the future, I will be more certain about love, but I will never be more certain about integrity than I am right now."

The officiating minister tapped me on the shoulder, and the file of groomsmen walked in. I was surprised with all my wrangling how easy the ceremony was. And I felt a huge relief that I didn't have to wrangle anymore inside myself with how unsure I was about love.

Barbara and I walked out of the church in the recessional at the head of the line, and we were buoyant, probably because it was all over. In a moment of passion, I scooped her up in her beautiful dress, and we kissed tenderly, then with enthusiasm, and then with a kind of anticipatory violence. The photographer was suddenly there and took our picture—unposed it was . . . and real. I have it yet, for it remains one of my favorite photos of all time.

THE HONEYMOON

It was after the reception when we got in the car that I had the oddest sensation. I couldn't take her home anymore . . . at least not to her home. I always had after every date, but dating was past. Her parents didn't want me to take her back to her home, which meant I could only take her to my home, an upstairs apartment we had picked out on North Independence Street in Enid, above the radio repair shop. But before all that, we had planned a week of honeymooning, driving around Oklahoma and spending time in its state parks.

So we left the church, heading off into la-la land. As we left the church, Barbara asked, "What do we do now?"

"I've got an idea or two. I'll tell you about it a little later . . . heh, heh, heh!"

"Tomorrow's Sunday. Where will we go to church?"

"Maybe we'll sleep in like normal heathens, and maybe we'll just lay around and well . . . heh, heh, heh!" I said.

I felt funny checking into a motel with a woman, and couldn't escape the feeling that somehow it just wasn't right. But once inside the motel room, I quickly changed my mind about that.

Lest I paint an over-elitist picture of our honeymoon, we agreed to spend our honeymoon money wisely and tried to pick the top local motels we could find. Those large franchise motels had not been born yet, but we could find some pretty little "knotty-pine" cabins for six dollars a night. We bought a carton of 7UP and two heavy glasses, fluted beer mugs really, and dubbed them our "honeymoon glasses." We have always been teetotalers, but on our honeymoon we achieved that drunken sense of addiction and euphoria that just goes with beer glasses. It is odd that of all the junk we have collected that has some sentimental meaning to us, these two cheap, odd glasses—now almost fifty years old—have the highest place in our esteem. For years we toasted each other annually with the heavy things and looked forward to the next years of our lives together.

Oreos—God bless 'em—were the cookies of choice during our honeymoon, and while Oreos and 7UPs are not a great diet, the combination somehow still has a warm appeal to me. Cheap motels and chocolate cookies were just what we needed to launch the beginning of the best days of our lives. It was the very richness of this fare that makes me still feel sorry for Donald Trump and the billionaires who have wasted their lives trying to find joy by smearing eight-hundred-dollar caviar on rye crackers. Poor things! I always want to loan them an Oreo and a beer glass just to show them true wealth.

When we got back from our honeymoon, normal life began. It was wonderful! An unending date! I still continued to preach on Sundays in the parish I had served all through the summer. My day job was serving as a cereal chemist for the Union Equity Grain Exchange in Enid. Summer was busy in the laboratory, but evenings were all ours. I could scarcely stand the wait till I got home every night. Barbara stayed home all day long and read. We had no television, though they were becoming increasingly popular. But because they required an outside antenna, hardly any apartment dwellers had them.

Our suppers were simple. We ate a lot of pizza. Pizza was new to the Midwest and largely to the nation. Since Pizza Hut and Dominos were still far in the future, the only way you could enjoy pizzas was to buy them off the shelves of the local market. The trade name was Appian Way, and each pizza came in a carton— really a kit—that contained a little can of parmesan sprinkle cheese, a second little can of pizza sauce, and a cellophane package of flour with which you made the crust. Never having been exposed to anything better, it seemed like a real treat to us.

But wait, there's more!

If you bought the package for thirty-nine cents, they would also give you a free aluminum baking pan. So we ate pizza a good bit.

Pizza was not the only thing that was new to us. Sex was too. It seemed like a definite boon from God that both of these first-time things would come into our life experience the very same summer. But so it was. We would eat our pizza and then go immediately to bed. Sex and pizza. This was our double glory, born to mark our summer with wonder.

The only problem was that our little apartment was very hot. We had no air conditioning. The mean temperature of Oklahoma in July is posted daily just outside the gates of hell to remind the damned just how blessed they are. The only relief we could find was to fill the bathtub with cold water and sit in it, while our only appliance, a ten-inch fan, blew cool air over us. The bathtub was small, so we had to take turns sitting in it, and we zealously guarded our individual turns in the tub.

So went the summer.

Of Manna and Crisco

In August, sadly, I resigned the Hunter parish and left for my middle year in seminary. We had been a little profligate with our resources during the summer. Between our pizza and contraceptive bills, we had, to put it biblically, "wasted our resources in riotous living." Now it was time to face the music with not much money to move to Kansas City and begin school. So it was agreed that I would go to K.C. ahead of her and find a part-time job and an apartment. In a couple of months, I would send for Barbara, who moved back in with her family for the time being. All fun was clearly in the past. After arriving on the train in Kansas City, I searched the newspaper for a place to rent, and I found a garret apartment for which the owner wanted to be paid fifty-five dollars per month. I told him that I only had twenty-five dollars but that he could have it all. He seemed tentative, but agreed to the deal. I told him that I expected to get my first paycheck in a couple of weeks and I would pay him some more.

After being turned down at the Ford assembly plant in Claycomo, Missouri, I took a lesser-paying job at Hallmark Cards in Kansas City. I was running a die-cut machine eight hours a day in the plant. Hallmark's slogan was "When you care enough to send the very best." I worked there for the next two years, but never a day without resenting that slogan. If you cared enough *to send the very best*, you would not send a card; you would send flowers or money. And money was what I was short of.

I had barely worked at the plant for a week when the bologna sandwiches I was constantly eating began to settle in my disposition with huge resentment. I would stand at my die-cut machine burping bologna and wishing I could see Barbara. I would work as hard as one might while stewing in my lonesome misery and wondering why I had not been wiser and saved enough money to bring Barbara with me when I moved to the big city.

After our glorious beginning, I was now living out a wretched marriage. After only two weeks of work, I went to a pay phone and tried to call Barbara, who was staying with her aunt. Barbara had gone out with her mother to shop. And so I said to her aunt, "Look, Aunt Peg, they are going to cut this call off after three minutes, and I haven't got the coins to extend it. I'm going to meet the eight o'clock train tomorrow night at the station and Barbara had better be on it. I'm not asking you, Aunt Peg, I'm telling you! I haven't any money to send. And I don't really know how Barbara can raise the train fare; she can borrow it, or steal hubcaps, but I'm telling you, I want to see her on that train tomorrow night! Got that? Good-bye, and God bless you."

I hung up the phone.

I went back to my miserable garret apartment and then lived through the longest day I had ever experienced. Would Barbara be on the train or not? The next night I was standing at the top of the escalator when I heard the train rumble in on the tracks below. I watched as people unloaded and came up the escalator. There were a lot of them, and most of them seemed unnecessary. Eccentrics talking too loud, mothers dragging screaming young'uns, bleary-eyed business-men. This ascending queue of trolls and goblins never stopped. Up the escalator they rose as if they had a right to. What possible business did all of these underachievers have in Kansas City?

Then I saw it. A beautiful young hand on the black, rubberized escalator rail. Was it? Could it be? Then I saw those beautiful brown eyes, and I knew why I was at the train station and even more why I was in the world. We embraced in the ecstasy of honeymooners, whose honey had for one awful moment been emptied from their moon. She had a little money, $5.35. Which was about all I had. Ah, but pooled we had over ten dollars. On the way home to our skuzzy apartment, which she had never seen, we stopped at a store and bought beans, buttermilk, coffee, potatoes, and flour.

There is a kind of manna most people don't know about. It doesn't come directly from God, but it is born at the fringes of heaven. Biscuits and fried potatoes and beans.

It issued from the combined resources of lovers, and it set a feast each day before I went off to work the second shift. Do not pity us for the meager fare, for to this day I enjoy simple things that are brought forth from the stovetop of a beautiful woman. And spiritual she was too. It was like being married to the offspring of Saint Francis and Betty Crocker. As the Scriptures say of Elijah in the care of the widow of Zarephath:

When he came to the town gate, a widow was there gathering sticks. He called to her and asked, "Would you bring me a little water in a jar so that I may have a drink?" As she was going to get it, he called, "And bring me, please, a piece of bread."

"As surely as the LORD lives," she replied, "I don't have any bread—only a handful of flour in a jar and a little oil in a jug. I am gathering a few sticks to take home and make a meal for myself and my son, that we may eat it—and die."

Elijah said to her, "Don't be afraid. Go home and do as you have said. But first make a small cake of bread for me from what you have and bring it to me, and then make something for yourself and your son. For this is what the LORD, the God of Israel, says: 'The jar of flour will not be used up and the jug of oil will not run dry until the day the LORD gives rain on the land'" (1 Kings 17:10–14).

All that may be said of flour and oil in Zarephath may be said of flour and Crisco in Kansas City. And for us it became a kind of life metaphor. I measure the beginning of God's care for the both of us from a bag of flour and a can of Crisco. And it was even as the Scriptures said: God's good sack of flour and this can of Crisco have never gone dry in our lives. We have eaten from his bounty, and our children too, and now our children's children. Paul also knew the metaphor, for he said, "And my God will meet all your needs according to his glorious riches in Christ Jesus" (Phil. 4:19).

I know there have been moments of disagreement between us, but for the life of me in looking back on our forty-nine years, I can barely remember any of them. One such instance did occur when our marriage was three months old, after classes had resumed in the seminary and Barbara had taken a clerical job in a plastics factory. Financially we were doing swimmingly. But I was studying hard and trying to master Saint Augustine's *City of God*. I read and wrote papers, and then one night when I was reading Augustine, Barbara slipped her arms around me and asked, "Honey, do you still love me?"

"Yes, of course," I said, and went on reading.

"It seems like you love Augustine more than me," she said plaintively.

"That's nonsense," I said. "The man has been dead sixteen hundred years."

"Well, I'm alive—kinda—and it seems like you love these old, dead theologians more than you love me."

"Honey, please. Give me a break! I've got to write a paper on Augustine. We'll talk about love tomorrow."

"You're a toad . . . a great big, theological toad!"

She went to bed.

I learned that night, when I was torn between focusing on Augustine or Barbara, the best of choices was, of course, Barbara. It took awhile to repair the breach, but not too long. In a couple of days things were pretty much back to normal, and once again life was as warm as a Crisco biscuit.

THE SNOWS OF '59

In the seventh month of our marriage, we decided to join another couple in planting a new church in Ames, Iowa. Our wives both took jobs at Meredith Publishing in Des Moines, while we husbands kept our Kansas City jobs and seminary classes during the week and drove on weekends to rejoin our wives, who kept the young Iowa church going all week while we were gone. It did offer a kind of madness, but a bit of joy too. We felt like we were doing the right thing.

For our church's meeting place we rented a Seventh Day Adventist church. The Adventists, of course, used their building on Friday night and Saturday morning, allowing us the opportunity to use it on Sundays to begin a new Baptist church. We were part of the Southern Baptist advance, where the denomination was set on planting five hundred new churches all over the northern half of the United States. So we went with the other couple to Iowa, some two hundred fifty miles north of Kansas City. We worked at establishing a church, which still exists there and is thriving these forty-eight years later. But it wasn't the church that was most significant in our story.

I still wrangled with the old issue of whether I was in love or, more properly, what love was. I still had never felt all those butterflies that people regularly talked about when they spoke of being in love. I could clearly see this magic in Barbara's eyes. There was no question that I needed her, admired her, and wanted never to be very far from her, but what was this magic substance that people called love? Did love have to come all at once and be all overwhelming? Perry Como in those days sang a song whose lyrics included the line: "You start to light her cigarette and all at once you love her."

I was looking exactly for that . . . that "all at once you love her."

But Barbara didn't smoke, so if I were ever to get that feeling, I would have to get it in some other way than by lighting her cigarette.

It snowed often and much that Iowa winter. And on Sunday

nights we would often walk in the snow and talk as we always had. Then one night when the snow was falling and all the world was magic, we stopped under a street light, in the swirling world around us. We kissed, that was all. It was not a hungry kiss; it was more as Quixote said, "Pure and chaste from afar." Still, it was warm with promise. It didn't invite a sexual episode; it was holier and more real than that.

Then, *bam!*

It hit me!

I was in love!

I knew it.

Some would say it was about time.

But it was a good time.

My mind flew back to that time in May, when my best man asked me about whether or not I was in love. But that was in May, in hot Oklahoma, and this was seven months later, six hundred miles north, in snowy Iowa. Cyrano was right:

> And what is a kiss when all is done?
> A promise given under seal—a vow
> Taken before the shrine of memory—
> A signature acknowledged—a rosy dot
> Over the *i* of loving—a secret whispered
> To listening lips apart—a moment made
> Immortal, with a rush of wings unseen—[3]

So Cyrano had also done it my way! He promised under seal, then came the rush of wings unseen. The snow had turned my world upside down in white, and all that I had struggled to understand in May swept into me with new life. And I walked home that night with Barbara. I don't remember whether we had sex or not. I only know that when you see love all at once, sex is somehow only a shallow need, rooted in the barren ground of "what's in this for me."

I was in love, and a summer wedding in Oklahoma had finally found its soul in the snows of Iowa's good affirmation. And so I wrote that night:

> When first I saw the distant winter sun
> Set gently free the auburn in your hair
> With softer light, I knew I had begun
> To understand the depth of our affair.
> A country church in summer held our rite,
> Some "legal" pledge that droned a legal love,
> I could not know, until that crystal night
> I stooped to kiss a snowflake from your glove.
> Its strange December would confirm the vows
> We made in May. Nor could I really know
> The promise stood, till in the chill somehow
> It came to me. I held you in the snow.
> What summer but conceived, the cold allowed
> To be, and winter nourished love will grow.[4]

And so it has. I am much afraid that those with other definitions of love are often forced to admit on the very porches of divorce courts that their biggest moments of love were somewhere back around their honeymoons. After that the greatness of all they called love shrinks into transactions and mechanics. Someone mows, someone does the laundry, and both go to bed wishing for five real minutes of conversation that says something is still left of their marriage vows. And the "dear" becomes "drear." And the drear dwindles down to an uninteresting finish.

But ever and anon, as I kiss Barbara good-bye and start off to honor some lecturing commitment, I feel the whisper of her heartbeat. I like listening to it when my head is on her shoulder at midnight, and I know, that while the blood flows through her heart of hearts, I am hers and she is mine. And I have known it ever since that night I first felt it in an inverted snow globe of wonder. I know now that when you mean your promise and feel its glory, you have truly become a lover, for besides honor there is no other porch before that grand house called love.

TEN

The Umbilical Stretch

Our daughter, Melanie, entered the world before Lamaze classes did. Husbands entering fatherhood after me would hold their wives at the moment of delivery, help them breathe right, and otherwise talk them through the agony of childbirth. But this practice was not common in my generation.

Where Fathers Were Unwelcome

When our children were born, fathers were not welcome in the birthing rooms. This was all right with me. After the Lamaze movement was underway, I had a lot of excited fathers tell me how wonderful it was to be right there helping out when the baby was born. Most of them would then say, "Would you like to see some swell pictures of the birth of our child?" Then, before I could answer, they would shove their KMart double prints at me. Then the bloody umbilical shock would hit me. I was bludgeoned dumb by their gory close-ups. There's just something about afterbirth that makes me think more about *Friday the 13th* than the Nativity.

"How wonderful!" I would say, trying not to barf in the middle of their ecstasy. Then, as the blood drained from my face over their obstetric photo ops, they would ask, "Were you with Barbara when your children were born?"

"Well, no, not right with her. You took some very interesting pictures, but aren't you supposed to help them breathe and help them push and talk them through the pain and not just take photos?"

"I did that mostly, but wow! Just look at these pictures."

"I can't," I'd say. "There's something about Lamaze photos that has an ipecac effect on me."

"Tsk! Tsk! Too bad you weren't with Barb when your children were born! You could have taken some swell snapshots."

"I do have some nice photos of Mount Rushmore and the Grand Canyon."

"Well, they're nothing like Lamaze," they would say.

"I can see that!" I would say. "But, honestly, I've seen a lot of Lamaze snapshots. Maybe with your next child you could do a watercolor."

THE PITTER PATTER OF LITTLE FEET

Discounting the Lamaze photo ops we missed, we had planned to have our first child after we had been out of seminary for a year or so, and little Melanie came right on time, on a snowy day in February 1962. Tim was born a year and a half later, on a balmy night in July.

Procreation is one of God's miracles that parents get to assist in. Properly enjoyed, it is fun getting a baby started, and then fun swells to a kind of awe as mothers-to-be begin swelling with that grand grotesqueness that says we have joined in a partnership with the Almighty. Then comes the wonderful joy of feeling the baby kick about in the womb. The mother feels their bustling from the very center of her inwardness, and the husband feels the tiny legs kicking against his hand just on the surface of the womb as the child gets eager to kick his way out of it.

When little Melanie was born, I looked down at the world of stress that comes hooked on to the umbilical cord. But after the cord was clipped, she was free. Every human starts life with that cruel unhooking: the scissor clip that says, "Welcome to the brutal world. You are now on your own." And every parent smiles down at the joy of what they and God have pulled off. But just behind the joy, there is that little ache of honesty that makes us wonder. After all, every ripper was once a child born bright with hope. Don't the parents of every serial killer look down and dream of a son who would make the world proud? Had they known the coming shame, they would have started their weeping early. But umbilical cord clipping comes in the brightest light hospitals have to offer. And so our hopes are born untarnished by any dark fears.

The churches I pastored were extremely small when our children were young, and we had to be most resourceful in planning ways to help them see the unpleasant side of human nature without letting them dwell on the unchristian things that Christians sometimes did. We wanted to keep our children from dwelling on how ruthless some people in the church could sometimes be. Baptist business meetings sometimes have a rather hellish ring about them. Our business sessions came on the first Wednesday of each month. Every month on the day of the meeting, I would tense up, because I never knew exactly what firebomb might be brought in and what the consequences might be for me and my family.

This was particularly true of the February business meeting. It was at this meeting every year where the church met together to decide whether or not to raise my salary. They almost never did, but every February they always discussed the issue. For me it was always a long walk through acid indigestion to sit through all the arguments as to whether or not I actually merited a raise, which most generally felt I didn't.

February of 1965 was particularly memorable. It was snowing

furiously when we met for our business meeting. The blizzard had permitted only a smaller-than-usual crowd to attend. The storm managed to stop the "pro-raise" people from getting there but not the "anti-raise" people. The general consensus was, therefore, that I was already being overpaid. There were a few who spoke up and said that I had always been underpaid and should certainly have my pay raised to a livable amount. Someone also said that "livable" was not as important as "spiritual."

When the meeting was over and I had been refused a much-needed pay raise, I left church longing to get home to my beloved Alka-Seltzer and Anacin. We trudged through the snow-packed parking lot and climbed into our 1958 Volkswagen Beetle—a five-hundred-dollar rattletrap car our church had so generously provided. The children shook the snow off their boots and crawled into the back. Barbara and I crawled into the front.

There was only one family rule that we applied to every bad business meeting, and certainly to every February budget meeting: there would be complete silence on the way home from such meetings. No one was to talk. The children understood the rule. The one great thing about having a Volkswagen for your family car was that it was easy to discipline the children. The cockpit was so small you could easily reach the children no matter where they were in the car. This motivated them to keep quiet. There was fear in their wide eyes as we drove silently home. Only the windshield wipers slapping at the heavy snow made any sound.

When we finally reached the house, we parked the car in the drive and crunched up to the house through the snow. We walked into the house in the same silence in which we had driven home.

But no sooner had we got inside the house, than Barbara grabbed up our little boy, shoved him down in a chair, and said, "If you ever become a preacher, I'll beat you to death."

I could not help but wonder what kind of effect this would ultimately have on the boy. He was only three at the time. But at nineteen he dropped out of college and joined the Green Berets. I've always wondered if he considered his mother's threat and saw the military option safer than becoming a preacher.

GOING TO CHURCH WITH THE CHILDREN

When the children were about to enter school, we moved to Omaha to plant Westside Church. This church would consume the next twenty-five years of my life. One of the great things about being pastor of a church was that the entire family went to work with me and came home with me, particularly on Sundays. I felt great that the children knew exactly what I did and how I went about my job. So many men go off to work in a plant or office where their families cannot visit, so the fathers' work lives are always separate from their family lives. The children never see inside their fathers' careers or what they do in any aspect of their work.

But going home on Sundays we all talked about the sermon. Every church business meeting they were there, and at least on the way home from the folderol, when the meetings went relatively well, they offered comments and opinions on how I should lead or alter my management style. But I found them far less tolerant of church hypocrisy than Barbara and I were. Melanie's comments were usually on target, and offered freely so as to help out. One Sunday as I was preaching my way along toward the benediction, I stated, "One out of six people will at sometime during their lives spend some time in a mental institution." Melanie, sitting in a group of young people at the back of the church, began to point out those individuals she felt were most likely to spend such time in such institutions. Fortunately, most she pointed out never knew that they were being pre-designated as mental institution inmates, but the young people around her were "amening" her appointments with laughter.

By Tim's sixteenth year, he was very dedicated to "evangelizing wayward chicks," as he put it. He was awfully good-looking and tended to think of himself in the vernacular of the day as a "chick-magnet." In his own mind he really tried to date girls with the express intention of "winning them to the Lord." But we began to notice that he was breaking curfew night after night to be sure that he had adequate time to present the gospel to the wayward and gorgeous. I asked him if he was sure he was keeping his motives straight and he assured me that he was. He believed that as long as he had his Bible along on a date, that it would be the talisman he needed to ward off temptation. Several girls he witnessed to did in time become baptized. He would date just about any girl in an attempt to "win her to the Lord."

I asked him if he had ever considered leading some young men to the Lord, but he didn't believe that God was leading him to this particular target group.

Everybody has a target group, I suppose. Or at least I tried to rationalize this in my mind. Saint Francis was clearly good with lepers; Mother Teresa was good with Hindus; Tim was just good with the gorgeous.

THE FINAL CODE RULE OF SURVIVAL

Surviving our children's teenage years caused Barbara and me to practice a five-fold code of survival, though we wrote down none of these precepts while we were actually practicing them.

1. *Discipline.* I personally believe in spanking. I know that psychologists are divided on the subjects, and many say that you should never physically discipline your children when you are angry. Christian psychologists often suggest that you pray first. But the few times I asked God if I should wait or do it now, he said, "You've got to be kidding!" So for me, the best time was to gather what self-control I could and go ahead and do it while God concurred.

This was a technique I learned from my mother, who never really switched us until she was angry to the point of fury, and then she nearly dismembered us outside the kingdom. We had a neighbor woman who used to say to her kids, "I'm so mad at you I could tear off your head and spit down the hole." She never did this, however, and soon two of her kids were in prison. I think she should have hit 'em first and spit later.

I have no idea what is the best age to quit spanking your children. In the parents' opinion, it's probably eighty; children, of course, would say much younger. My son is now forty-four and someone recently asked him when he quit getting spankings. "Thursday," he said.

2. *Expectations.* Every set of parents should have a set time—ours was a weekly Saturday morning breakfast—when you can plan your method of survival for the following week. At these meetings parents should discuss their levels of tolerance, and minimum and

maximum penalties for juvenile delinquency within the family. Jews have always had a relatively low rate of juvenile delinquency. I think it all harkens back to Deuteronomy 21:18–21.

> If a man has a stubborn and rebellious son who does not obey his father and mother and will not listen to them when they discipline him, his father and mother shall take hold of him and bring him to the elders at the gates of his town. They shall say to the elders, "This son of ours is stubborn and rebellious. He will not obey us. He is a profligate and a drunkard." Then all the men of the town shall stone him to death.

There is something about this kind of thing that discourages juvenile delinquency. It takes a lot of parental planning to keep our kids off the scrap-heap of life.

3. *Freedom*. If a child wants to run away from home, help the child pack. Children should be told that they are free to run as far as they wish, only they will have to get together their own return fare if or when they decide to return. They need to be told they will have to walk to the airport or bus station as you don't provide transportation for runaways.

Our Tim ran away from home when he was sixteen, taking his two tuxedoes and his trumpets with him. I'm not sure what kind of career change he had in mind, but we encouraged him to go and helped him pack. He was back by suppertime, darn it, spoiling plans Barbara and I had made to have dinner at a real nice restaurant while he was out of town.

4. *Caution*. Try to keep them from being vehement about their

future. It was after one of those February kinds of business meetings in her teens that Melanie was fed up with the church. I was, too, a lot of the time. But she said, "Churches are the pits!" I agreed, particularly after business meetings.

"Mom, why did you marry a preacher?" she went on. She was getting pretty loud and very personal now.

"Because I loved him," said Barbara.

"Well, I'll tell you one thing: I will never, never, never marry a preacher."

This kind of talk is a psychological setup.

"Look, honey," I said, "never say 'never.' God could be listening and the devil could be taking notes."

"Well, I'll tell you this, I'll never marry a preacher."

Barbara and I shook our heads. She had taken too strong a stand. She was doomed. In the fullness of time, she married the first preacher who asked her, without even waiting for a second one to propose. Not that Barbara and I are sorry about this; he is indeed a wonderful man who probably is endowed with all the strengths Melanie needs to keep her propped up throughout the marriage years.

5. *Expecting the unexpected.* Anything you think your children might do, they won't. This final code is the hardest to practice because it feeds totally on superstition and innuendo. It eradicates Murphy's Law that if something can go wrong it will. I don't believe Murphy's Law. I've never found it to be true. In fact, regarding children, if I can think of what might go wrong, it will probably *not* go wrong.

During adolescence my children were always surprising me with off-the-wall ideas that I never would have thought they could think up. My daughter said one day the two of them went behind a local service station and smoked some cigarettes. I would never have thought they would do that kind of thing. But every morning thereafter I woke up and thought, *My kids could go down behind the Texaco and smoke today,* and they never did it again. It seemed my merely thinking of it made it impossible for it to happen.

When my son was a sophomore in college, my daughter, who was a junior, called me and quizzed, "Guess what Tim did today?" I guessed and guessed: joined an African safari, studied trapeze, entered the Iditarod in Fairbanks. I was frantic trying to think of all the things I would never want him to do.

"No," she said, "he joined the Green Berets."

"What in the world caused him to do that?" I asked.

"He saw three Sylvester Stallone movies in a row and came to believe it was God's will for his life."

But secretly I knew the real reason that he joined the Green Berets: it was because I had failed to get up that morning and say, "Tim could actually join the Green Berets today." So you must do what I learned to do. Think of every wild thing they could possibly do, and you will spare both them and yourself from doing the bizarre thing you were too dull to imagine.

A Soldier and a Maid

On the day Tim left to go to basic training, I thought my heart would break. We took him to the airport. We generally just dropped people off and went on about our business as they flew away, but that day was different. Barbara and I watched Tim until he walked down the ramp. They wouldn't allow him to take any luggage. He didn't seem to be the 220-pound giant I once felt him to be. He seemed a little boy as he walked away with his cotton T-shirt pulled down inside his dungarees.

Then we stood silently and watched his plane. We watched it pull away from the terminal, taxi onto the apron, and then move toward the runway. We watched that plane as it roared up into the blue sky until finally it was just a black speck against the burning blue, and somewhere within that black speck was that little boy we loved so much. But oh, he was small, and then the black speck winked off and was gone.

Because the training for Special Forces lasted a year, it was twelve long months before we were to see Tim again. When he returned, he was unquestionably different. Again we watched for the plane, scanning to pick up the first blur of a spec that interrupted the burning blue. Finally, when our eyes were sufficiently teary, our straining vision pulled it out of the sky, and in a bit it became large enough that we could actually say it was a plane. It was like watching the departure video in reverse.

It finally landed and we saw the little touch of smoke that flew from the singed rubber as the wheels grabbed on to the runway. Then it braked and turned toward the terminal. In a more lumbering way it rolled to a clumsy stop at the end of the ramp, and then we looked down the Jetway as far as we could until we saw him.

No longer was he a boy.

He was a man! Nay, a soldier.

He had the beret. He had the uniform. He was soon to report to duty as a part of the United Nations peacekeeping force in Sinai. He was more ready than I thought he would be for the lonely outpost and the years of books he would read while he made friends with the oceans of sand and desert that would be his home.

And Melanie was soon to marry her preacher man. And I realized that we never have all the time we need to get everything we need to help us toward tomorrow. It gets here so quickly, and so I wrote . . .

> They left us both at once, became as one
> The age for leaving . . . and yet, didn't they
> Seem young? We woke them from their naps to run
> And they leapt decades on a summer day.
> They hurried off with luggage, nothing more!
> Were his shoes tied? Did he forget his lunch?
> And did her ribbons match her pinafore?
> And dare we draw the noisy lock and chain
> To seal ourselves in all these empty rooms?
> Can our door watching bring them home again?
> This lonely night we have our debts all paid
> And given life a soldier and a maid.[5]

CONTEMPLATING KIDS AT NIAGARA FALLS

Not long before the soldier and the maid were gone, I took Barbara to Niagara Falls. We went in winter, which was always our best season. We had been before in summer when the place was mired in tourism. As I look back, I can see it was near the mid-mark of our marriage when the children were about to leave us. We were older, but the lessons the children taught us were worth the aging. But somehow they could only be understood when we were away from them . . . at a lovely place like Niagara in winter. As Hamlet remarked at Elsinore, there was "a nipping and an eager air." Nothing was frozen. I could see the neurotic waters, green and angry as they were, move across the icy froth as it hurried from Erie to Ontario. I had concealed a new diamond ring in my glove, not to replace the one I had given her much earlier, but to set a second diamond at the front of the second section—the childless section—of our lives.

Barbara seemed even more beautiful than she had on the day we were married. The crisp air and the screams of the gulls were as shrill as a trumpet in the desert. The cold air froze the radiance in her face. She was wearing her age like a crystal vestment.

What would our lives be like when we had crossed the winters out ahead? Neither of us knew that for sure. We only knew that love is not worthy of the name unless it can pass the test of twenty winters. I removed the glove from her right hand. I took the diamond from my glove and placed it on her finger. "This is for the last half of life," I said. "It is for the decades we have yet to go." I kissed her there while the frost was all about us. At that moment I knew why bread is always tasteless in summer. I knew why stars never really shine until the snow has washed the air.

This was us, two diamonds two decades apart, with decades more to go.

> The frost hung there—do you remember how
> The January air stung your young face?
> With all the warmth the wind chill would allow,
> I kissed you by the cedars. The embrace

Was all I needed to confirm the vow.
I slipped the small, cold ring inside your glove.
The years fled by and stole our youth. We heard
Our children cry—beheld our parents die.
Where have the flowers gone? Was it absurd
To let the frozen decades pass us by?
For twenty winters I have loved you so.
I long to bring you diamonds in the snow.[6]

In the heart of my heart I can see that the end of all procreation is a simple symmetry. The children were never ours. They came from God through us to take their place in the Kingdom of God. And when they were gone, all that once had made us rich, left us richer still. And I can see that when we sit alone surrounded by the thousand ghosts who made our lives full, we shall be real in their midst and agree that God meant for us this thing called parenting. And we are proof that once our children were gone the only treasure left was our togetherness.

ELEVEN

Bloody Sundays

I LOVE CHRIST AND I LOVE HIS CHURCH.

There it is!

My whole confession out at once. I do not love it casually. In fact, I think there is no such thing as casual love. So I love the church the only way I can: violently.

THE IMPOSSIBILITY OF LOVING MODERATELY

Friar Laurence in Shakespeare's *Romeo and Juliet* advises: "These violent delights have violent ends and in their triumphs die, like fire and powder, which as they kiss consume" (II, vi, 9–11). But I've tried loving God with lesser passion and found the fire too faint to warm me. Those who fervently love God are intoxicated by his warmth and live out their addiction like moths drawn to flame. I, too, at last hope to be consumed by the passions I pursue. It is not tyrants who make martyrs. It is the love that martyrs cannot abandon that chains them to their final, fiery stakes. Love lights the kindling about the martyrs' feet and all because they can never follow the good friar's advice and love God moderately.

Most who have fallen in love with Christ didn't choose to be fervent. They have just seen the Son, high and lifted up, and have no choice but to fly in his direction. Such remarkable passion is a kind of gift. I have known many Christians across my span of years. In fact, most everyone I have worked with has called themselves Christian. But among all the Christians, I have known only a few of them who seemed to have that natural—or supernatural—inclination of clinging to their God. But it is this God that holds the center of my passion. He is the object of my chase.

I say all of this with no sense of arrogance. Yearnings—even those we spend on loving God—are somehow urges we take no pride in. It is wretched work to try and fill our empty yearnings for God. It is a chasing after the winds of Pentecost, knowing we can never quite hold on to God long enough to be content.

I could solve my God need if I could only be a little more "how to" than I am. Countless books tell pastors how to build empires, collect stock portfolios, preach in a clever fashion, and stay in the saddle during a church crisis. But I don't want to succeed at any "how to" I can think of. Not primarily at least. I just want to be friends with God—close friends!

And there's the rub! Like Francis Thompson's *Hound of Heaven*, I run from him while he pursues me. And then when it's my turn to chase him, I run in his direction, only to see him farther up the trail. I would give anything to be able to quit my God-chasing and go play golf or watch a video on how to be a winner.

Some of the "big" pastors I know seem to enjoy being "big." They own a sense of success and fame that satisfies most of them. And they are revered generally for being deeply spiritual men, even loving men. But the best of pastors realize that good sermons are not just flashy rhetoric. Sermons are only noble when they are so "see-through" that the pastor's need for God is clearly visible through his words.

Now that my hindsight is 20/20 I can honestly admit that I was never a very good pastor. Perhaps I didn't want to be one all that much. It was him I wanted, this exalted Christ, this perfect end of all my imperfections. This gentle Jesus was my quest.

I now know that all who want to really know him must walk the edges of fear. It is not an easy thing to carry the burden of wanting such knowledge. It is like being a nine-year-old boy in a roller-coaster line. He fears the ride but craves the experience. He must know it. He must feel the force of the Gs, the rush of adrenaline, the churning bravado of rocketing into sky, the inverted tracks that hang you from the straps and beg you admit that you were not as brave as you thought. Loving God is even as Frederic Faber wrote:

> They love Thee little, if at all
> who do not fear Thee much,
> If love is Thine attraction, Lord,
> fear is Thy very touch.

When I was a boy, Padre Pio in Italy was afflicted with the stigmata. His hands and side bled at every holy season. I was intrigued by the photographs of his bandaged hands. His love for God had actually furnished him with the wounds of Christ's identity. He was a literal picture of Philippians 3:10, where the apostle cried out of desire to "know him, and the power of his resurrection, and the fellowship of his suffering, being made conformable unto his death" (KJV). This, I think, is what I have always wanted, far more than growing a church, or installing JumboTrons so the church's program might blare like a Las Vegas come-on to entice people to be busy rather than to crave union with the Savior.

Being a pastor was never easy for me. It's funny, but I always thought it would be. Given my penchant for loving people and my rather natural inclination to worship, I seemed to have just the right recipe for living the pastoral life. Unfortunately, I am also a perfectionist, and in the ministry, my dependence upon imperfect people made my perfectionism a fatiguing art.

Besides the student pastorate at Hunter, I only served as pastor of two other churches in my thirty-five years of pastoral ministry. My misadventures with the church began in 1956 when I was a sophomore in college. It was the very year the Russians put up the first unmanned space satellite. The odd orbiter was named *Sputnik I*, a Russian word for "comrade" or "fellow traveler." It did nothing but beep as it circled the world, and was not a very sophisticated satellite by today's standards. But it was the first one in space, and the very fact that Russia had beaten America to the punch created a kind of crisis in western science. America appeared to be behind the Soviets in science, especially in the training of science teachers.

It just so happened that I was at the university right then preparing to become a science teacher. Don't ask me why. As I have already reported in this work, I was having a tough time with public speaking, and yet I wanted to serve the Lord. It looked like the best way for me to serve in my early college days was to become a teacher on the "foreign mission field," as we used to say. Most of the countries where I felt I might go on mission were not open to missionaries. I decided the best way to get into these closed countries would be to become a teacher. Therefore I graduated from college with a double major: education and science. By 1960, I had changed directions and decided that I would probably be a minister here in the homeland, and try to convert the pagans who lived all around me in the good old USA. Then, too, as I neared graduation from seminary, I was actually the pastor of a church, and my science degree didn't really fit my calling as a minister.

FIRST PULPIT

My first church after ordination was in Plattsmouth, Nebraska. After I graduated from seminary in 1961, Barbara and I drove north from Kansas City to Plattsmouth. When we approached the little town from the east, we stopped on the bluffs of the Missouri and looked across the wide river to the little town that was to be our first real assignment together. I mockingly sang a few phrases from "Shenandoah": "Old Shenandoah, I long to see you, far across the wide Missouri."

"This is where we are going to begin our first church," I said. "Think of the joy of it all. Barbara, my love, do you remember what David Livingston's last request was?" I knew she remembered, for we had talked about it several times.

"He wanted his heart buried in Africa, didn't he?"

"He did," I said. "When I die, I want my heart buried right over there in Plattsmouth, Nebraska." I pointed dramatically across the Missouri river.

"When the time comes, I'll try to arrange that," she said.

We crossed the river and started the church.

It was not a particularly happy church, and I hadn't been there long when I discovered the deacons also wanted my heart buried there. Only our timetables were different on the matter. I was thinking of being buried *after* I had died of natural causes.

Plattsmouth was one-hundred-three years old when I moved into town, and I was twenty-four. The church began with ten or twelve couples, and we held our first services in the Plattsmouth Community Hall. In 1963, we moved out of the community hall and into our first building, which we built for twenty-five thousand dollars. It was in many ways a poor man's project, and while the church had been erected on a rather imposing hill, we had no money left to excavate parking lots on the slope that ran down steeply toward the highway. It was hard to climb the hill during a rain. The nature of the wet clay soil left it all but impossible to climb the slick surface. On a rainy Sunday morning, the ladies complained that their high heels were befouled with mud as they stumbled to reach the apex where the church imposingly rested.

But a wonderful and terrible thing happened that very spring. The Missouri River, swollen by the melt-off of a very snowy winter, went out of its banks, and the river became a brown ocean that roared into town from the east, flooding the low-lying stores. Hundreds of thousands of acres of farmland and future crops were destroyed. Once the water receded, the county began looking for topsoil to rebuild the washed-out infrastructures of our county. We just happened to have a hill that we didn't want and the Corps of Engineers just happened to have roads and levees that needed to be rebuilt out of useless hills. They asked us if they could have the hill we didn't need and offered to build our parking lots free of charge in exchange for the dirt they would excavate in the process. We struck an immediate deal.

Many of our people referred to it as "the miracle flood" by which God gave us two much-needed parking lots. "Isn't God good," they said, "to give us just what we asked for in our prayers? It was a miracle."

"*Miracle?*" I questioned, "What was so miraculous? Would God destroy half the farms in Iowa and Nebraska so he could give us parking lots? I doubt if those who have lost their farms would see it as much of a miracle." The parishioners seemed dejected when I explained away their miracle in such a non-miraculous way. But at last we had a parking lot. We paved it with big hunks of crushed limestone. And the mud was all gone. I thought the ladies would be truly happy because they no longer got their high heels muddy when they came to church. But they immediately said the crushed rock on the new parking lot was too coarse. It tended to break off their high heels when they walked across it. So we brought in some pea-sized gravel that would not break off their heels. But they said that while they no longer broke off their heels, the small gravel was just too dusty and left a white film on their shoes when they walked across it.

It was the first time I noticed how hard it was to please people.

I wondered what it took to make people happy. In the first century, people worried about facing lions in the arena, and in the twentieth they worried about getting dust on their high heels. It was during such moments that I wondered if there were not more meaningful ways to serve God.

The little church seated some one hundred fifty people, and by the time we moved into it, it was full, which led us to begin plans for an additional building that was completed for fifty thousand more dollars and seated around three hundred people. The church was never large, but then the community itself had only about twelve hundred homes. The first year I was pastor, I called on all twelve hundred homes and quickly discovered that almost all of them had an attachment to some church that was already in existence when we came to town to start ours.

I began to feel discontent with the Plattsmouth parish and felt there must be some larger place with more than twelve hundred homes and more of an opportunity for church growth.

SECOND PULPIT

Then it happened.

Unbeknownst to me, one of our Baptist churches in Omaha was experiencing a congregational split. Group A in the church was a group who was very bitter toward Group B in the church. Group B also had a root of bitterness toward Group A. There they were— Group A and Group B, trapped in the same rich love of Jesus in Baptist Church C. The four or five families who constituted Group A desperately wanted me to come to be their pastor.

I had a much larger church, but, having visited every house in the town, I knew that my current church was not much of a frontier for evangelism. My romantic notions for Plattsmouth were all expended, and I rescinded my earlier resolve of wanting my heart buried there. In fact, I didn't want it buried at all—and most certainly not there. So the new project opening in Omaha seemed a welcome dream to me.

In 1966, I was twenty-nine years old and about to end my first three decades on the planet with a substandard estimate of myself. I felt ashamed that I had never published an article in *Christianity Today*, never been to Europe, and never pastored in a city. I began to plan how I might right these personal inadequacies. Barb and I left our children with grandparents and went to Europe. I wrote my first book (which would not be published for a year and a half), and, most important, I accepted the call of these five families to become pastor of the newly organized Westside Baptist Chapel of Omaha.

The work began in rich acceptance. The five founding couples loved me! They gave me gifts: gloves, a scarf, and an attaché case. They were furious in their compliments. They were fond of comparing me with their former pastor, who was—by comparison with my "godliness"—a demoniac. My sermons, they said, were true. His were liberal and false. My life was open and free. His life was closed and cliquish. I was gloriously evangelistic; he prayed to the American Civil Liberties Union. I preached the book. He gave book reviews. Further, they said that while I had gone to a conservative seminary, he had attended an ultraliberal Baptist seminary.

Deep down I knew that all the evil things they said about their former pastor they would one day say about me. But I put far off that evil day and basked in the praise. Ours was a vigorous young mission meeting in a kindergarten cottage of the Oak Valley public schools. The first year we added forty-two members, and twenty-six of those were first-time converts who were baptized as new congregants into our enthusiastic fellowship.

In 1967, our little fellowship had grown to such an extent that we began to look around for some property where we would someday build our very own building. We were enthusiastic about the notion, and somehow I was able to find a hilltop for sale in one of the burgeoning suburbs on the west side of Omaha. Feeling extra religious at the moment, I decided to do something spiritually bold. I decided that I would lead twelve men out to the top of that magnificent tract of land and claim it for Jesus. I had decided to take twelve for two reasons: first the number was symbolic. It was the exact number of Jesus' apostles. And second, it was all the men we had.

We thirteen went to a muddy hilltop after a spring rain and knelt in the mud and claimed Matthew 18:19: "If two of you on earth agree about anything you ask for, it will be done for you by my Father in heaven." We prayed and rose and left the hilltop having marked our interest with a covenant with muddy knees. But the actual truth was that sometimes when two or three agree on buying a piece of land, the good Lord will give it to an agnostic real-estate developer anyway. Which is what happened to our tract of land.

I must confess I felt very foolish, having led such an obvious crusade that didn't work. I thought the twelve men would abandon me altogether, pronounce me at least naïve and maybe devious. But that didn't happen. When I apologized to them, they said, "That's all right, preacher, we'll just go claim another piece of ground somewhere else." What I specifically learned was that people can forgive a leader whose vision may be errant, but they will never forgive a leader who isn't visionary.

But what I noticed halfway through my second year was that those who at first seemed jubilant over my leadership had cooled a bit. It seemed to me that they resented all the new people who they once said they wanted to convert. Once these newcomers began to serve in the church, they didn't seem to be as accepted by the founding group as I would have liked them to be. I got no presents that year. They quit contrasting my attributes with that of the former pastor and began to see more and more similarities between us. My sermons, it seemed to them, were growing more liberal and sounded a lot like his. Then one of the founding group asked me if I was sure I hadn't graduated from that ultraliberal seminary. I knew I was in trouble.

THE SCHISM

The first sign that I was about to be fired came in the form of a vote on my beard. There was a motion of the four deacons for me to shave my beard. I had always worn a beard, nearly since I was in utero. It had never been all that important to me, until the day the deacons took a vote on it. Then it became a precious beard, a beard of glory, a beard of principle.

"Why," I asked, "should I have to shave my beard?"

"Well," said the chairman, "all the despots and criminals of history have had beards: Karl Marx, Czar Nicholas, Genghis Khan, Fidel Castro, George Custer . . . Judas Iscariot for that matter."

"Yeah," I said, "but what about Jesus and Santa Claus?"

My cry was to no avail. The vote passed 3 to 1.

"Gentlemen," I told them, "in spite of your vote I will not shave off my beard. If it was good enough for Jesus, it's good enough for me! Besides, if I allow you this amputation, next year you will take my chin and sooner or later my whole head."

My response to the beard vote of '68 stirred a coming storm.

The chairman of deacons then called another meeting of the other three deacons, the trinity from hell, and told the flock that I was going liberal. As evidence of this he said that I often quoted from Norman Vincent Peale in my sermons. "This is bold proof that our pastor is liberal," he said. "He should be quoting the apostle Paul, for as all of you know, *Paul is appealing* but *Peale is appalling.*" There was a motion that I should resign, and while it didn't pass, it failed by only a few votes.

The deacons said, "Even though the church narrowly supported you, it would still be best for you to resign. If you stay, many will leave the church. A man of good conscience would not put a church through the hell you will foist upon this congregation by staying when so many clearly do not want you for their pastor."

Barbara and I had never felt so low. We had no savings, no place to go. I was too old to enlist in the army, and the hospitals all had chaplains. I was still barely young enough for the navy chaplaincy, and had visited a time or two with a navy recruiter during an earlier crisis. I decided to give the navy a try, but as I drove toward downtown and the recruiter's office, I was filled with unbelievable turmoil. As I motored along toward the recruitment center, I sometimes hummed "Amazing Grace" and sometimes "Anchors Aweigh." Once I was downtown, I circled the block several times trying to decide whether or not I should go and enlist.

I never did go in.

I went home.

The church split.

Seven families left, taking their tithes with them.

Four of those who left were part of the five families who originally started the church. The defectors were those who only a year and a half earlier had felt "called" to start a *truly* conservative Southern Baptist Church. Now they once again felt called to start another *truly, truly* Southern Baptist Church barely three miles down the road from the kindergarten cottage where our little church was still meeting. They soon hired a new pastor, who didn't have a beard, and they were doubtless telling him how much more conservative he was than I was. Our membership had taken a nosedive, and so had our church income.

The Year of the Pulpit Committee

What was amazing was that no sooner had they gone than all the evil of 1968 resolved itself in a kind of joy in 1969. Barbara and I still refer to 1969 as "the year of the visiting pulpit committee." They came looking for a new pastor. They flew in an airplane to hear me preach. They took us out to dinner and bought us T-bone steaks. My children had rarely seen a steak and were frankly a little wary of anything that didn't smell like canned tuna. They loved my preaching, the committee said. They had just built a new million-dollar church building and a new fifty-thousand-dollar parsonage, which they told Barbara she was free to decorate in any way she wished. Barbara, who had known only rented housing in Omaha, immediately felt called to go to the church. "Imagine, having a salary!" she exulted. "This must be the will of God, because it seems so right to me."

When the committee flew back to their new church, I was skewered with the possibility that I could, if I wished, have a church, a salary, my own secretary, and a car—a real car. Big. With four doors and a gasoline allowance. Never since Jesus blessed the multitudes had the future of Christianity seemed so rosy. They called me three times a week, begging us to come. I was clearly God's man, they said. I didn't know what to do. I prayed while Barbara packed. While Barbara was trying to decide whether to call Allied Van Lines or Bekins, I called the pulpit committee and said, "No."

I could tell Barbara was crushed.

"Honey, I know the work is hard here, and I could never do it without you. Do you really mind?" I asked.

"Sweetheart, do you remember Ruth 1:16? I don't know Hebrew all that well but do you want to hear my translation?"

"Sure," I said.

" 'Wherever thou goest I will go. Wherever thou lodgest, I will lodge . . . S-A-P!' "

I really didn't like her translation. It played so loose with the original languages. I knew all she had been through, all that both of us had been through. I hugged her and we cried a bit. I guess we cried partly because of all that had happened but also because it was the only pulpit committee that ever came our way.

The Year of the Vast Rebuke

By our fourth anniversary at the church, we had managed to erect our first permanent building. It seated three hundred people, and we had barely half that many who attended. I approached our fourth year there with a cloud of gloom all around me. It was because of a paragraph that appeared in one of my favorite books on how to grow a church. This author of the book made a prediction that in planting a church you were prone to have a church difficulty, if not a split, at one and a half years, and a second at four and a half years. What made me so nervous was that our first split came almost to the day I had been in Omaha for a year and a half. On a hot August day on the cusp of my four and a half years, the new chairman of deacons passed me in the basement of the church at the water cooler, where I was getting my last pre-sermon gulp of cold water before going upstairs to preach. He took me by the shoulders—and he was a very big man—and said, "Have you seen the crowd upstairs?"

I nodded a yes. There wasn't any crowd. I knew what he meant!

"Yeah," I said. "It's August. The crowd always gets better after school starts."

"Not always. It depends who's preaching."

"What do you mean by that?" I asked, but I knew what he was thinking.

"I mean, preacher, that you may be good at starting a church, but you're no good at pastoring one. If you stay here much longer, I'm convinced you're going to kill this church. I think it's God's will for you to leave the church, and maybe the church will hire a new man who can keep this thing together."

"How thoughtful of you to bring this up just before I have to go upstairs and preach. I can't tell you how supported this makes me feel."

"Well, this is serious—too serious to wait. It's the eleventh hour in more than one way, pastor."

"Leave the church? Where would I go? The church is my life. How can you know God's will for my life?"

"Well, pastor, believe it or not, I and some other godly people have been praying that you would see what is so clear to the rest of us. You seem to be the only one who doesn't know God's will around here."

"I tell you what. I will seek God in this matter, and if I sense that he wants me to leave the church, I will do so. But if I have no clear word that I should leave, I will take that as a sign that God wants me to stay."

I went on upstairs and preached. It was uneventful.

All through the next week I prayed. I came out at a totally different place than our chief deacon had. "I'm staying," I said the next time we met. "Still, I'd like us to be friends if that's possible."

He never answered me, but he grunted in such a way that told me he had been to Sinai, received the direct word out of heaven, and nothing I had to say about my continuance would be the course he pursued. He was determined. His own infallible understanding of God's will would prevail.

I sensed the neighing of warhorses and the ringing of chariot wheels.

Suddenly, I could hear the last word in Barbara's translation of Ruth 1:16. I steeled myself for the rough waters that lay ahead. Congregational schisms are never about serious things we agree or disagree on. They are rarely heartfelt quarrels about theology or doctrine. They are nearly always contests about who runs things or would like to. Usually they gather around personality power blocs within the organization.

For instance, the deacon chairman, besides knowing the will of God for nearly everybody, had a darn good recipe for pecan pie. You don't have to be a real good leader with these kinds of assets. He began having most of the church leadership over to his house on Sunday nights for pecan pie and Blue Bell vanilla ice cream. Of course, Barbara and I were not invited. All that the Scriptures said of Absalom might have been said of his politics: "If only I were appointed judge in the land . . . I would see that he gets justice . . . and so he stole the hearts of the men of Israel" (2 Sam. 15:4, 6). Barbara and I and the children went home alone and popped popcorn on Sunday nights. We ate, picked our teeth, and went to bed disconsolate.

He stood on the back row during my sermons throughout the next six months. He looked out at me while I preached with a scowl that was enough to make me consider Buddhism. At the end of the service, where none could see him except for me and God, he would look at me in a way that can only be described as hate-filled. The church was still small. We had no choir, so no one else was standing at the front who could see his behavior on the back row except me. I think he knew my character enough to know that I would never gossip to anyone about what he was doing, but I gradually came to feel the alienation of almost all who attended the church. Paranoia has always been a problem of mine, but I had already been through enough church scrapes to know that some-times, when you think everyone is after you, they really are.

Once again, finances were a problem. We were paid far too little to live in Omaha's affluent west side. We struggled to keep the rent paid on our little house. Then, as if our situation was not tenuous enough, our landlord sold the house we had been renting, and we were forced to find another apartment or house or any kind of shelter that we could afford.

Meanwhile, while our moods were as low as they had ever been and we could see no clear path to the future, I found Barbara crying. No man who is a man can bear to see his only love broken and in tears. We had no friends. They had all been wooed away with gener-ous, ice-cold doses of pastoral criticism served over hot pecan pie. But Barb's tears brought me to a new dependency on Christ. In those dark hours, I gained one square foot of high ground. For the first time in my life, I was able to divorce my love for Christ from my love for his church. I had never quit loving the church, but I finally understood I could live without it. What I could not bear was to see my wife crying over my determination to win my war with hate.

Two good pastor friends redeemed me. The first told me that I would never be much good to God until I came to the place where I didn't need the church. It was an odd statement. But I suddenly saw the glory of what he was saying. I took Barbara by the hand and we knelt beside the bed and I prayed. I don't remember all that I said, but the tenor of my prayer was this:

Father,
I beg you to forgive me for what I have done to my wife and children. I have fought a dragon till I have become one. I will no longer hurt my family just to try and placate evil men, who claim light but act in darkness. In short, God, I do not know what I will do for a living, but I declare before you, Father, I do not need the church. I need your Son to be my brother, and I need this woman to be my wife. And if I must sacrifice anything to save my love for Christ and my family, I will sacrifice my service to the church first. That's how it is, God! Amen.

I made plans to resign the next Sunday, and actually wrote out my resignation. When Sunday morning came, I went to the church early, as was my custom, and then almost as an afterthought to my intention, I called a pastor friend who lived then in Atlanta and said to him, "I'm going to resign this morning."

"This morning!" he said. "Why this morning?"

"Well, I've worked this all out with the Lord, and we made a deal. That anytime the local church got in the way of my affair either with Barbara or Christ, I'd serve them and let the church go."

"But you always said it was a great church!"

"I know. I lie a lot. It isn't a great church, and I want out."

"Well, do as you will. I'll try to help you get another church. But let me give you some advice."

"Yeah, what?"

"Since you're going to resign anyway, why don't you tell them how you feel about them?"

"I can't do that!"

"Why not?"

"Because I don't use profanity in the pulpit," I said with some satire and a lot of bitterness.

"Have you ever done that? Do they really know how you feel about them?"

"I guess not," I said.

"What have you got to lose? You're going to resign anyway; why not just tell 'em?"

"I'll think about it," I said.

I thought about it.

I thought about it.

I thought about it.

Then suddenly I thought maybe it would be kind of fun to tell them how I felt about them. In fact, I thought, *How does a pack of dirty rats ever really come to know how people feel about rats if some-one doesn't point out their rodentlike character?*

It is at this point the Spirit may have left me, or maybe he didn't. But I really wanted to preach that morning, and I hadn't wanted to in a long time.

The service was soon underway. They sang a couple of hymns I felt they didn't really mean, like "O How I Love Jesus," when they clearly didn't, and followed it up with "It Is Well with My Soul," when it clearly wasn't.

And then it was my turn. It really wasn't a sermon based on a biblical text. I couldn't find a text on rats. I just laid my Bible down and began:

I'm ashamed of you people, and I think God shares my opinion. No one in the world should treat a preacher's family like you have treated Barbara and me. And you know what? I'm fed up with it! I came home and found my wife crying because of both the loneliness and the criticism you have forced upon us. Your view of the Golden Rule is so far away I don't know if you could even write it out. But I know one thing: I never taught you this kind of congregational savagery and it certainly isn't in the Bible. I'm leaving here, and I'm going to find a new congregation who has managed to take the Bible seriously and model the Christian life with a constant exhibit of love and kindness. I haven't seen much of that around here. Oh, by the way, I got down on my knees beside my wife and told God what I think he wanted me to say and what I think he wanted you to hear too. I need Jesus. I need Barbara. But I don't need you anymore. And if you ever manage to cry out your sins before God, there's a slight chance he might go ahead and save you, which is more than any of you deserve.

The rebuke was pretty good, I think, as far as rebukes go.

The problem was that I started crying. To all would-be rebukers, if you're going to do it, don't start crying. Crying weakens a rebuke a whole lot. One of the problems with my particular crying is that I get so loud about it. I like to see a good, manly movie star cry. I like to see a single manly tear crossing a leathery face, highlighted by good cinematography. This is my idea of effective, dramatic weeping. Unfortunately, when I cry my face wrinkles into a prune and healthy people upon seeing it throw up. Worst of all, I was going through an emotional meltdown right out in front of God and everybody.

But an unusual thing happened. They started crying too. It got pretty messy in there for a while. Some of the men were even uglier than I was when they were in tears. Then they began to come forward and hug me. I hugged back.

It seemed like centuries since anybody had hugged me! Then some of them fell on their knees at the front of the church and gradually the world was upside down. The only one who didn't come forward was the deacon chairman. They say that not too many showed up at his house for pecan pie later that night. Maybe pecan pie just can't compare to getting your soul back.

That week a group of men went to him and said, "It's become pretty clear to us that we can't have both you and the preacher in the same church, and if we can only have one of you, we'd rather have him." He was angry and vowed to live long enough to see me thrown out of the church.

Then on Thursday of that week, he was getting into his car when he was struck by lightning. He was so badly injured it appeared for a while he would not live. He was taken to the hospital, and after a tenuous beginning and several days of therapy, he began to improve. I was still his pastor, so I went to see him. Even in his ashen demeanor, he was hard and intractable. I'm not sure why I went to see him, really. Maybe I felt a bit of fear. Truthfully, I've never much liked lightning. And while I assigned no theological assessment to the event, it's amazing what a bit of electricity can do to help us evaluate our lives.

I think the whole church did.

This same kind of thing had happened in Acts 5. And after a couple of people were zapped, the scriptures relate that "great fear seized the whole church and all who heard about these events" (v. 11).

TWO DECADES OF SURVIVAL

He left the church.

I stayed twenty-two more years.

And I spent the next two decades proving the deacon wrong. I didn't stay with any motive of vengeance. I had no need to prove him wrong. But he was wrong. I could be used by God to grow a church! The church grew from its founding ten members to more than three thousand by the time I left. I've always wondered if that would have happened if he had been allowed to have his way. I think not.

But the decision Barbara and I made on that one desperate night, we would prize evermore. We put our love for Christ and for each other above our need to be accepted by anyone. This became our inviolate creed of marriage.

Our shoeless tour on a roadway of shattered glass was over. Today we both can say it is easier to find Christ in our brokenness than in our meager achievements. He is all in all. Barbara and I remain safe within the circumference of his embrace. Holding on to his wounded hands, I can truthfully agree with Maya Angelou, "I wouldn't take nothin' for my journey now."

TWELVE

A Blind Man Who Came to Sight

In 1967, I made a new friend. He was a young Mennonite pastor, well educated, and like myself was trying to plant a new church in the same suburban area as I was. Neither of us was having much luck. The Omaha population is only about 2 percent Southern Baptist, which is my denomination, and the city had even fewer Mennonites than that. It was inevitable that we should meet.

Bob Friezen was his name. Our callings were one. Both of us were twenty-nine years old. Bob and I began to meet for breakfast every Monday morning at a local coffee shop. When the eggs and sausage were cleared away, we lingered long over coffee cups, discussing how our churches were going—not necessarily growing. Somehow the discouragement I felt in not seeing much happen was about the same discouragement he felt in not seeing much happen.

Both of our ministries took the same form. We both went throughout the city, driven by our ardor to evangelize. We were undaunted in our zeal and tireless in our effort. We ran furiously from door to door, like an Avon agent with a thyroid problem, to try and win everyone we could to Christ.

We loved the Lord, but both of us felt that he seemed slow to love us back. Our dull months of fruitless ministry constantly nibbled the edge off our piety. Still, we met weekly, sharing our prayer time and talking constantly of our devotion. In addition to our God talk, we exchanged sermon ideas, program concepts, books, and journals.

THE REVELATION

Then one morning at breakfast, Bob said his doctor had told him he was going to be blind—totally blind—within six weeks. We were both barely thirty years old.

I remonstrated with God over Bob's condition, for I thought the man had already paid a big enough price for his calling. In the next few weeks, as his world darkened, I complained bitterly to God about his treatment of Bob. I have never been able to see truly fine people brutalized by life without pointing out their wounds to God, just in case he had missed noticing them. Gradually I moved from being terribly angry to being moderately irate with God. I asked him to heal this good man, this wonderful friend, this disciple who had given so much and whose best dreams were crashing. His sermons were ricocheting off the empty Samsonite chairs that filled his tiny chapel. Each week we met, and as we did his light slowly died. I suffered with Bob as he quit driving and began letting his wife bring him to breakfast. I watched him struggle to find the eggs on his breakfast plate, learn to cut his food in the dark, and smile when he'd ask me how much of his breakfast was now on his chin and how much still on his plate.

By the sixth week of his doctor's prophecy, he carried a red-tipped cane and struggled to keep a stiff upper lip. I was glad that he couldn't look across the table and see me, for at times my lip did tremble and I fought that odd burning at the corners of my eyes. I knew it was important to be cheerful in his presence, but it was so very hard.

I went home from the restaurant in tears.

"God," I said, "it is hard enough to plant a church when you can see, and when you are blind it must be all but impossible." Yet Bob had made it clear at our morning breakfasts that he intended to go right on trying to build his church. He didn't have many members, but all of them loved him as much as I did. None of them wanted him to leave his post. They put a stool up on the makeshift chancel of his little church building, and his wonderful wife would lead him to the pulpit area where he would sit and preach. He lived in a morass of low self-esteem and wondered if people would listen to a blind man preach. And without being able to see if their own eyes were looking back at him, he had no way to measure if he was really coming across.

When we met the next week, I asked him how the Sunday had gone. He said, "It went as well as it could. The worst thing about all this," he went on, "is that it's not going to get any better and I will never be free of the dark. I'm scared of the dark, you know. I never was, but now I am. I have no money to secure my wife and children. If I can't keep the church, or if the church doesn't decide to keep me . . ." This time he did cry. So did I.

"Well, Bob," I said, trying to talk with a huge frog sitting right on top of my Adam's apple, choking my words into croaking syllables, "we have today. Today you have your children and your wife and your church members. Today you have Jesus and ham and eggs. Today will last only until tomorrow, but if you still have Jesus and ham and eggs tomorrow, we'll start working on the day after tomorrow."

It was a stupid thing to say, but I couldn't think of anything else.

"You're right, of course," he said. "I also have Hebrews 13:8: 'Jesus Christ is the same yesterday, today and forever.'"

I liked what he had to say so much better than what I had just said, although in some ways, we had both said the same thing. "*Jesus Christos, el mismo, ayer, hoy, y manana . . . para siempre,*" I

---

said in Spanish, the kind of dumb thing you say when you've run out of sensible English.

Then I asked what I could do *for him* or be *to him*. He asked me if I would come to his house and read to him whatever he would select or whatever book was grabbing my attention at the time. Maybe the best parts of *Christianity Today*, and, above all, the Bible. "It will just be till the state office of the blind can begin getting tapes to me."

And so began a deepening of our tryst. I read to him. On Tuesdays, always. On Thursdays, sometimes. One Tuesday when I went to see him, he was all cut up. His face was lacerated, like he had fallen face-down in a hedge trimmer.

"You're a bit bloody, if you don't mind my saying so. Did you get in a fight with a Calvinist?"

"No, I'm predestined to avoid that."

"Okay, what happened?"

"Well, I was out visiting in the neighborhood and . . ." He broke down. He didn't sob hopelessly, but like a man who had gotten himself injured trying to figure out the ways of God.

"You want to tell me about it?" I asked.

"I don't want to, but I need to," he said. "It happened on Thursday afternoon. I was trying to make a pastoral call on foot, trying to feel my way through the neighborhood with my cane. I thought I was doing pretty well, remembering the corners and crossing where I had every street clearly fixed in my mind. It was the driveways that mixed me up. Inadvertently, I went to the wrong house. When I rang the doorbell, a woman answered the door and said, 'Yes? What can I do for you?'

"I didn't recognize her voice and knew I must be at the wrong house.

"'I see you're carrying a Bible,' she said, 'Go peddle crazy somewhere else. We don't want or need any of your religious stuff here.'

"She slammed the door, and in my disorientation, I missed the steps I had climbed to arrive at her front stoop. I fell off the stoop, which was only three or four feet high, but I fell through a rose trellis, cutting myself all up as you can see. The woman, noticing finally that I was blind, ran out of her house to help me up. I don't know why it took her so long to notice I was blind, I was carrying my red cane . . . Duh! So she came hurriedly down and offered to help me up. But I stood on my own, threw up my hand, and said, 'No, please, I've got to do this for myself.' After this bit of gallantry, I turned too quickly and fell over two more terraces in her yard. She helped me find my Bible and cane, and called my wife to come and get me. My wife came. I've been speaking to her since Thursday, but right now I'm punishing God by not talking to him. I can't tell you how angry I was at him . . . I still am!"

"Well," I said, "did you learn anything from this?"

"I learned," he said, "that I can't do house calls like I used to do. I learned that if it is possible to do ministry at all, it can't be done that way. I don't think I can take many more rosebushes. I don't know what I'm going to do with my life."

"Well, Bob," I said, "today you have your children and your wife and your church members. Today you have Jesus . . . How are the ham and eggs holding out?"

"Fine, plenty of both."

"Got any Band-Aids left?"

"Just the ones with Scooby-Doo on them!"

"Those are the pretty ones, Bob," I said. "Save them for Sunday."
I read to him.

The next time I read to him, he was over his fight with the rosebush.
The week after that, he actually said some nice things about God.

THE MAN WHO LEARNED TO LOVE THE DARK

I continued to read to Bob, but I began to notice that the whole
issue of ministry was flip-flopping. I wasn't the one helping him
along; it was him who was helping me. I noticed that during our
reading times, he wanted to talk about God all the time. The books
he was reading changed. He didn't want to discuss Carl Sagan or
Stephen Hawking anymore. He was into A. W. Tozer and some
of the mystics. He wanted to know about my prayer life. It didn't
take me long to tell him about that. I hated to tell him how I often
asked God to give people stomachaches when they were unrespon-
sive to my leadership.

"That's not very Christian," he said.

"That's what God said," I replied.

"How's church going?" he asked.

"We grew from forty-eight in attendance to thirty-two last
week," I said.

"You can't keep growing like that for much longer," he said.

"Don't I know it? How's your church growing, O thou Martyr
of the Roses?" I asked.

He laughed, and freely too. "I'm sorry you had to put up with
me when I was charging into the roses. I'm a bit ashamed. I asked

God to forgive me for being so snotty in my prayers. He said he might, but that I needed to grow up." He stopped and laughed, just like he used to when he had 20/20 vision. He went on, "You know that thing you said about 'today.' You were right. And all these weeks later I've still got Jesus and ham and eggs and a new box of Band-Aids—my own box, no Scooby-Doos. Best of all, I can say it: I'm blind. I always will be. But if you try to tell me I'm handicapped, I will hit you with my cane."

We both laughed.

"You're talking pretty tough for a blind man," I said "How's your church attendance? How many came?"

"I don't know. It's always so dark in my church, I just can't tell how many are there. But from the hymn singing I can tell they're either all singing louder or there are more of them there."

There were more of them there. Marlys, Bob's wife, told me they had been steadily growing ever since Bob had tangled with the roses. She told me they had over 150 of them the week before, and Bob hadn't made a single house call. "I think it's his prayer life. Now that he and the Almighty are back on speaking terms, he spends a lot of time talking to God. He hasn't read a single church growth manual that says you can grow a church on prayer, so I don't know if this prayer-and-inner-life thing is going to work out or not. Bob is always in the dark, and I have to remind him to close his eyes when he prays, because even though the light doesn't vary with them open or closed, he just looks more spiritual when he closes them. I tell him all the time he looks like he's talking to himself when he doesn't. But you know Bob!"

"I don't know if I do or not. I thought I did. But the one I used to know seems unlike the one I've come to know."

It was interesting for me to watch Bob change. It was like he had made the long, long journey from being a pastor to becoming a codependent saint. But his church grew by leaps and bounds, while my church growth was stagnant, offering me no chance to brag about how big it was becoming.

Finally his church was running around four hundred in attendance, while mine was dawdling along, showing very little growth at all. I really wanted to grow a church without going blind, but sometimes I wondered.

"Why do you think your church is growing and mine's not?" I asked him.

"Maybe you need to fall through a rosebush. It worked for me."

In desperation I asked him, "Where was that rosebush?"

He only laughed and finally, like Samson in Phylistia, told me all his heart. "I'm glad I lost my vision," he said. "Know why?"

"I cannot possibly understand why you would say such an irresponsible thing."

"Because for the twenty-nine years I could see, I loved the church, the hymns, the ministry, Sundays. In short, I loved the 'things of God.' But now, in this wonderful darkness, I love God. Do you get what I'm saying?"

"Sort of," I said.

"When you get it entirely, you can forget about the rosebush."

A New Worldview

I thought about his statement for weeks. Did I as a pastor love the things of God or did I love God? I was like so many young pastors who graduate from seminary and find themselves with a fistful of resumés no one is willing to read. I was like most every church planter I had known. All I wanted was the chance to plug into the Kingdom somewhere, preach, and be given a chance to actually serve a flock. But I somehow felt that the best way to get a church that responded to me was to start one from scratch.

I knew it was important to plant churches. All "mainline" churches are on the downturn numerically, with fewer churches each year than the year before. Therefore all American church groups are interested in planting new churches, realizing that unless the denominational dying is checked, in time it results in death.

Almost all American denominations grew until the middle of the twentieth century. Then their memberships began going the other way. Now virtually every denomination is in decline at one rate or another. Almost all of them are trying to get young preachers to plant churches, and thousands of such attempts are underway. But most of those attempts are doomed. Every week in the USA, thousands of people leave their congregations never to join any church again . . . ever!

Why couldn't I or any young preacher start his or her own church with some hope of success? Because church planting is hard work, and only about 3 percent of those churches that are planted survive to maturity. That's the statistic. The reality is that those pastors who try and can't make it happen are often too disconsolate to try to fit into Christian ministry anywhere else. They are simply wiped out by their own sense of failure.

But Bob had beaten the system by prayer. By prayer? How could that possibly work? It was so unlike what all the megachurch books

said. One of the most discouraging blocks that young church plant-
ers run into is the touted success of the American megachurch. It
is often achieved by those who have no formal theological training.
Many of these ardent but untrained ministers have no good opinion of seminary-educated men and women. So young graduates
who go to the suburbs—the most fertile place to plant new
churches—find themselves trying to appeal to small numbers of
new converts, while the huge programs of the mega-churches that
surround them are often anti-small church and anti-seminary.

Bob's steady acceptance of his dependence totally on God left
me morose and feeling somewhat defeated from week to week.
Bob's triumph and growth plunged me into despair. My Monday
morning periods of depression grew customary. Sometimes after a
low Sunday of attendance, I would sit alone in my quiet study with
my head covered and spill my jeremiads into the air. It got harder
and harder to pull out of the blue funk. It was at this time, one of
the lowest seasons of my life, that I found myself broken and often
unable to shake my feelings of despair. Not only was my church not
growing, but I anguished as every good father might over the fact
that I was a breadwinner for my wife and children, who were just
beginning their teenage years. I had no answers for how I could go
on providing for them and making the church grow.

I had two or three books in print, but they weren't making any
money. I have laughingly told my friends that my mother was buying
most of my books and giving them to church libraries. I thought my
love for the arts would carry me through with a bit of positive dis-
traction. *Jesus Christ Superstar* had just come out on Broadway, and
while I like the rock-opera format of the work, the musical portrayed

a very weak Jesus. I needed the robust God of Bob Friezen, not a weak superstar Messiah of whom the Magdalene lamented she didn't know "how to love him." She crooned she had known so many men before, and in so many ways "he was just one more."

I wondered why nobody had written of a more robust Jesus, who knew who he was and how he could strengthen his disciples with all they needed for the tough times. In the midst of all of this, it seemed I heard God say, "That's a good idea—a more robust Christ! It's such a good idea. Why don't you do it?"

If it was God, I put up a bit of resistance. "Well, God, I'm not just burning the world up with a hot church plant. Are you suggesting that I take on the world of art and literature by writing of my own robust Jesus?"

"Yes," was all he said, I think. I don't hear verbally from God, and the impressions I get sometimes confuse me. I've always believed in listening for his voice, but I've generally found that listening to God is indistinct work. You never know if it's really God or if it is your own stumblebum alter ego. So I put the impression on a back burner.

THE NIGHT OF THE SINGER

And then it happened. I was awakened at two o'clock in the morning. I heard no voice, but some words leapt to the front of my mind. The words were, "When he awoke, the song was there." I had no idea why the line came to me, but I have learned to serve my poetic psychoses. So I went to my study and wrote down the words. In fact, I wrote down several pages of words.

When he awoke, the song was there,
Its melody beckoned him and begged him sing it.
It hung upon the wind
and settled in the meadows where he walked.

I wrote for an hour and then went back to bed.

This odd pattern repeated itself a few nights later. Other lines
came to me.

From the river he moved on,
in quietness alone.
He still talked to Earthmaker
as he always had but now
he called him "Father-Spirit."
He loved the newer name.

I wrote again. Pages flowed. I remembered reading the word
Earthmaker in an American Indian myth, but I loved the word, for
it held a romance one missed by simply saying *Creator*.

I went back to bed, but there were other midnights. Sometimes
there was more to the story. I could see this robust Jesus I only
looked for in contemporary artists. He was rising from the pages of
my manual typewriter. This was a Jesus who came as a universal
melody on my favorite midnight.

In the beginning was the song of Love.
Alone in empty nothingness and space,
It sang itself in vaulted halls above,

Reached gently out to touch the father's face.
And all the tracklessness where worlds would be,
Cried, "Father," through the aching void.
Sound tore the distant chasm and eternity called back,
I love you, Son, sing Troubadour.
His melody fell upward into space,
And climbed its way in spangled rhapsody,
Earthmaker's infant stars adored his boy,
And sung his name in every galaxy.

When this particular moment of midnight madness was over and I was getting back into bed, my wife awoke and asked, "What have you been doing getting up so many nights and going down to your study?"

"I don't know exactly," I said. "I'm writing a poem."

"It must be a very long poem," she remarked.

"It is. It is already a hundred pages long and I have no idea how it's going to end. Maybe tomorrow night I'll find out some more. Stories are wonderful things," I went on. "Nobody writes them, not really. Stories just tell themselves. We who take the credit for them listen to them as they pass us by, and we have the moxie to write them down."

"Well, I wish this one would tell itself during the daylight."

"Me too. But this story is a nighttime narrative. So that's when I've gotta write it. If I wait till morning, it won't tell itself, and I'll never know how it ends." Then I stopped and realized how irrational I was sounding. "Babe, do you think I could be going crazy?"

"No, honey. People like you never go crazy; they just drive other people there."

It was, in a way, a compliment, so I continued writing, largely at night. I edited by day what I had written at night. And in an amazingly short time, the work was finished.

I sent it to Word Books, a publisher I greatly admired, but they wrote back and said that while they personally liked the book, it was too poetic to sell in an evangelical market, which was where all my readership was at the moment. Their reply led me to admire them a little less than I had before I mailed them the manuscript.

I sent the book next to InterVarsity Press. I didn't know anybody there whom I could greatly admire. But the book was assigned to be evaluated by Jim Sire, himself a Ph.D. scholar, whose focus was on John Milton. He wrote me back and said that he liked the book and was thinking about accepting it for publication. I began thinking I might learn to admire InterVarsity. When I got the letter back saying that they were going to publish the book, I was ecstatic. Dr. Sire told me it was a good book and that it ought to be published. He, like the people at Word, also felt that the book would not sell well, for it was too profound and too poetic and that Christians didn't generally buy books of poetry. "We are going to publish five thousand of these," he said, "even though we believe that in ten years we will still have four thousand of them on skids in our basement. But we are going to publish it."

I told Bob about my good fortune, or the blessing of God, however my publisher's acceptance was to be viewed. "It's what comes of thinking so much about Jesus," said Bob.

Ref#: ZV9780785297987
SKU: ZV9780785297987
LIFE IS MOSTLY EDGES

Vsn:

LP: 5652719737
ISBN: 978-0-785-29798-7

3

PALLET

TBOX:

TO: **871 – 192 – 3**

3282207201

To Loc Type:
I – EFBS

To Loc Status:
S 0

Quantity to be putaway: **1 UNITS**

Comment: BK NO PRICE CTN $18.99 USD

UNITS/CS	36	UN WT	1.080	LWH	9.000	1.100
CASES/PL	40	CS WT	39.520	LWH	13.250	10.750

Suddenly I realized that during my nocturnal visitations of the Spirit that I had not focused on my failures, or even the failure of my church growth tactics. I had left off my fruitless strivings and was totally involved with Christ. I was up all night and all day with Christ. And I had come to Bob's focus without ever seeking to own Bob's spiritual sojourn. I had quit busying myself with the things of God and busied myself with God himself. I didn't mean to quit thinking about the things of God; it just happened that my focus on God had replaced the good stuff of my life with the best stuff.

That's what *The Singer* was. It was a book of praise in which I never thought about or mentioned church growth. I had a higher focus going. I had written a long, long psalm, as a newer song of praise might come to be. When the book came out, it was widely reviewed. But the review that meant the most to me was a Canadian reviewer who had my number. "Miller, himself, is the Troubadour," he wrote, "singing a love song to his Lord." The whole issue of succeeding had nothing to do with struggle; it was instead a matter of inner music.

The Gifts the Poetry Begot

When I dropped my guard and focused on Christ, what I had tried to make happen, happened automatically. The church began to grow. And the growth made me ponder again the promise of relinquishment. Letting go of any drive releases the soul, and those who can't quit struggling in an attempt to realize their dreams will be the last to realize them. I had done nothing very remarkable. I had learned the lesson from a fellow struggler, a blind pilgrim, who taught me that the secret of success is not "busianity," it is "Christianity." None of the great saints of the church made his or her mark by trying harder, only by loving more completely. Jesus said it so well in Matthew 6:33: "Seek ye first the kingdom of God," he said, "and all these things will be added unto you" (KJV).

This was not the end of the adventure. I don't know why the events of our lives fall out the way they do, nor would I ever say God hurts anyone so that others may profit from the hurt. But in June of 1975, the year *The Singer* was released, Paul Little, whom the whole world admired for his passionate life of evangelism, was killed tragically in an automobile accident. He was scheduled to speak to the Christian Booksellers Association's annual meeting in Anaheim, California, in July. Through a series of twists and turns I could neither chart nor understand, I, as author of *The Singer*, was asked to take his place on the program. The program was the third in a series of luncheons where authors appeared to promote their new books. Catherine Marshall was speaking at the first luncheon to promote her new book, *Something More*. Johnny Cash was speaking at the second luncheon to promote his best seller, *Man in Black*. Paul Little would have been the third speaker at the third luncheon, except his life had been tragically cut short by the accident. Because of that vacancy, the program committee asked me to take Paul Little's place.

I was terrified. I had a very small church in Nebraska and had clearly not reached the level of distinction the other speakers had attained. Worst of all, I literally took Paul Little's place. When I got to the hotel in California, my room was still registered under his name. When I got to the head table the next day for the speech, his printed name had been crossed out on the place card and mine written in. When it was almost time for me to walk up and give the presentation, my InterVarsity host leaned over to me and said, "There are a lot of people here; you'd better be good!"

Why did he say that? Life was hard enough as it was.

I will never forget the dimming of the house lights and the raising of the light on the podium. My knees were knocking, but I forced myself to start off as casually as I could. I had planned an eighteen-minute monologue from *The Singer*. I had it all memorized and worked at giving the presentation more from the standpoint of an actor than a writer. I think it worked. The monologue had a rather emotional ending, and when I reached the end of the presentation, I bowed my head for just a moment of silence and walked back to my seat.

I sat down.

For a moment there was a silence—very loud silence—that occupied the crowd. Nobody moved, and I had the awfullest feeling that I had bombed. Then someone in a far corner of the luncheon arena began to applaud all alone. I felt like saying "Thank you, Mother!" when someone else joined the applause. Then everyone did. Then they were all on their feet, and my frightened personality dissolved in an inward moment of praise. They obviously loved the book, and I loved them for loving it. A book-signing party followed the luncheon, and I autographed hundreds of copies of the book.

My elation was like Simon Peter's on the Mount of Transfiguration. "Let us build three tabernacles and stay in this good moment forever." But I had to go back home. I took an airplane back to

Nebraska, but I really didn't need it. I could have flown home without it. When the Spirit is in his fullest control, airplanes are a nuisance, too dawdling and slow.

The Singer was launched, proving that what is born at midnight in the eeriest hours of God's presence can beget our entire reason to be. I have always wondered what would have happened had I not served that poetic psychosis and toddled down to the typewriter in the middle of the night. Would *The Singer* have sung? Would I ever have shaken free of the church growth syndrome? I once admired Ian Fleming, whose hero, James Bond, said in every novel, "The name's Bond, James Bond!" I have never achieved in so wide a way as Fleming did. But my hero can say something like, "The Name's Christ, Jesus Christ." And honestly, I've liked my hero a lot better than I liked Fleming's.

I don't know whether I created the book or the book created me. But it is a great joy to feel a pierced hand on your shoulder in the wee small hours of the morning. From 1975 onward, wonderful things happened. People asked me to lecture at colleges and conferences. In the next twenty years, I lectured at more than two hundred private colleges.

People who moved to Omaha often knew about *The Singer* and looked up our church. The wonderful fallout of the success was more success, most of which I had nothing to do with. People simply read *The Singer*, came to the church, and joined it. As an index to *The Singer*'s success as a grower of the church, it took me fourteen years to collect the first four hundred members of the church, but in the next nine years the church added twenty-five hundred more!

And while I do not brag about this, the poverty years were over. I will never forget my first royalty check from *The Singer*. It was an incredible amount of money. When I opened the envelope the check came in, I was shocked to see the amount of money written on the check. When I showed the check to Barbara, she was overwhelmed. "They must have sent you Francis Schaeffer's check by mistake," she said. "It can't be yours. You've never made any money writing."

"I'm sure you're right," I said.

I called the financial officer at IVP and discovered the check was mine and the amount on the check was right. "Honey," I exulted, "the money is mine. Do you know what this means?"

"What?" she asked.

"It means I can finally be obedient to God. All of my life God has been leading me to buy a Corvette and I've been disobedient. Now, at long last, I'm prepared to obey. You think gold, maybe?"

"I think we'd best pray about it."

We did and God said, "I didn't say a Corvette, I said a GM product, maybe an Impala. And get a late-model, used one. Who do you think you are, Ian Fleming?"

I saved some of the money, gave some to the church building program, and bought a late-model used car. It was pretty nice. And being frugal has a kind of godliness about it, darn it! But I had learned during the lean years that poverty is one thing money can't buy. I'm glad I learned it, 'cause once you learn the good lessons of feeling rich when you are poor, you're better able to keep God in your conscience when you're not.

Bob got his sight back only after he went to heaven. It's been awhile now. But I know when he got there he went straight to the throne to get a good, close look at Jesus. And boy, could he see good! Of course, the light's always better there.

I'm still down here getting my glasses changed every few months, but I see well enough to know that once you love God—I mean really love him—you start hearing poetry at midnight. And if you're obedient to the voices, you may not ever get a Corvette, but you'll ride without a fare and you'll fly without a plane.

It is even as *The Singer* said,

> It is strange how
> oftentimes the air
> speaks.
>
> *We are sane as long*
> *as we hear voices*
> *when there are none.*
> *We are insane when*
> *we hear nothing and*
> *worse, we are deaf.*[7]

THIRTEEN

The Year with No Christmas

IT WAS TWO LEADERS IN OUR CONGREGATION WHO PERHAPS CAUSED me first to consider leaving my twenty-five years of service at Westside Church. One of the weaknesses of my leadership has always been my lack of interest in sports, particularly local, church-sponsored sports like city-league softball. You may be surprised that I list this as a weakness in leadership. I do so only in the sense that I am a right-brained, arts-loving leader, and such leaders are not always understood by the bulk of suburban, sports-loving lay persons. Their personal lives are often tied up in endless rounds of school soccer, university and professional football, and, for that matter, church softball.

The Softball Sabotage

By the mid-1980s, our church had numerous softball teams in the city leagues, and one of our full-time ministers was managing the church athletic program. After the city church league's Friday night games, it was his custom to have the team members and their families over to the home of one of his star players for sandwiches and refreshments. It all began as a way to attempt to evaluate the church league and try to critique how they were playing—their team performance during their games. It was intended to be a time of study and evaluation. But after a few seasons it had evolved into a session of pastor evaluation. Since I was the pastor and the one being evaluated, I was never invited to these sessions. This left me at quite a disadvantage. Not halfway through the season, the anti-pastor rumbling of these meetings began to spread beyond the softball teams and filter through the congregation. There was some talk among the teams that the athletic minister was planning to start his own church with unhappy softballers who only dimly saw their own faults but clearly saw mine.

I have never been able to see a church member leave the church without feeling a lot of guilt about my leadership and, unfortunately, my Christianity. Through the years I suffered much over those gossip blitzes that focused on me. There was often not much I could do, because those who were intent on leaving the church never talked to me directly about what was making them unhappy. They never gave me the space to correct what they saw as flaws in my leadership. Worse than being shut out of these evaluations was the widening schism I could see developing in our congregation. Church divisions always develop along similar lines. In most every case, people on either side of the split begin playing the little game of Us and Them. Us and Them is a game of division. The people on one side of the split are the *Us*, and those holding the opposite viewpoint are the *Thems*. The spoken lines of those who take sides are:

If only *they* would be more like *us* . . .

Those people don't love the church like *we* do . . .

I wish *they* would just leave the church and then *we* would all be happy . . .

Once the game of Us and Them is in full play, a church split is almost inevitable.

So when the athletic minister and thirty or forty of his friends were meeting after their softball sessions for a few extra innings of Us and Them, it became clear to me that if ever I was going to have any ability to stop them from leaving the church en masse, I was going to have to be proactive. I watched the crowd of the unhappy softballers grow from week to week. When I drove by the home where these evaluation sessions (often called "Bible studies") were being held, I could see the sea of cars of these dissidents gathered together. I would say to myself, "This has got to stop." But how was it to be stopped? One of the problems of Us and Them is that those on either side of the conflict refuse to talk to those on the other side.

To stop the split someone has to cross over. While I prayed that God would send us a peacemaker who would carry an olive branch to the disenchanted, no one did. So I decided I would do this. I would wander, like Jesus, through the camp of the Samaritans and see if I could do something to bring peace. I would set the doves of peace free to flutter before me, like the pope did on Maundy Thursday. I would go to the Friday night Bible study, ring the doorbell, and say, "Hark! It is I! Though sinful and deplored, I have come to lay down my sword and shield and study war no more."

In my mind, it seemed like the peacemaking would be easier than it actually turned out to be. One Friday night, after passing the place where all the dissidents had gathered, I found my heart hurting over the division a great deal more than usual.

I went home to Barbara, my courageous wife, and said, "Now we can be like God intended us to be. You and me. Deborah and Barak, Aquilla and Priscilla, Augustine and Monica: we shall attend this godly—or maybe ungodly—gathering of our brothers and sisters, and beg the leader to lay down his arms. Then we shall all be one again, and all church division will end."

But Barbara said, "But, honey, they hate you! May they rot in hades!"

Since this was hardly the posture I needed to cross the Rubicon,

I said to her, "Honey, they are just sheep who have lost their way. Once we show them the will of God and how to be loving and kind, they will come back to the fold. You'll see!"

"But *those* people aren't like *us*. *They* don't love the Lord like *we* do! If only *they* would leave the church, then *we* would all be happy."

"Come, let us be courageous. Let us go to the Bible study and see if they will admit us. Then if they do, we can pray with them, and I'm sure they will let us do so. I have hardly met any foe so wicked they wouldn't allow me to pray. Maybe we can all pray together, for it is impossible to hate your fellow man and pray at the same time."

"Oh but he praying mantis prays! What those people need is repentance."

"Perhaps, my dear, we need that as well."

"Well, *we* don't need it as much as *they* do."

After much persuasion Barbara agreed to go with me to the prayer meeting. We drove there. It was after dark and we walked up to the house filled with lights and all the people. The disciples were gathered in the inner room and were praying, I'm sure, for all the excitement they were going to find as they started their new church. "It will not be like the one where Calvin is pastor," was a frequent line, I am sure. "No," said another, "this one will be one for *we* people who truly love God, unlike *those* people at the church who don't. *They're* not like *we* are. *They* don't love the Lord like *we* do. If only *they* were like *us*, we could be truly happy."

Putting extra starch in my index finger, I reached out and pushed the little pearl button that played a set of tubular chimes inside. The host of the home where the meeting was being held answered the door. It seemed to me his face drained a little bit when he saw Barb and me standing on his stoop. I knew what he was thinking: You're *not like* us. You *don't love the Lord like* we *do*. I know also he did not want us to come in, so he stood right in the middle of the doorway. I could smell the pizza they had been eating before we arrived.

"Uh . . . uh . . . hello!" he said, taking no warm initiative to invite us in.

It was indeed an awkward moment for him, and when I saw that he could not form the words, "Won't you come in?" I smiled and asked, "Can Barb and I join you in your Bible study?"

Again he stammered, "Well . . . well . . . well . . . ."

"Please let us come in, we won't eat much."

He smiled at the statement. "Well, okay. Come in."

We followed him back to a huge family room where a double ring of chairs filled the entire space. There must have been twenty or thirty couples there. I knew them all. I had baptized some of them, and in other days I loved them freely and we had once laughed together at church suppers and sang "We Are One in the Spirit" together. But their faces were steely gray now. Our host said, "Folks, Calvin and Barbara have come to our Bible study. Isn't that wonderful?"

Nobody said it was. What their faces said was, *They're not like us. If only they would leave the church, we could all be truly happy.*

But Barbara and I smiled, grabbed cups of coffee, and made our ways to opposite sides of the room. We began talking to those immediately around us. We did most of the talking, and they answered in monosyllables. We laughed like theater majors, like actors on Academy Award night. We did the best we could to be friendly. Gradually they loosened up and began talking with us. Finally a spirit of joviality seemed at hand, and I realized it was best for us to make our way out of the gathering. But before we went, I asked the host if Barbara and I could pray with them before we left. He agreed and we all stood and held hands—a Baptist custom quite common in prayer groups.

"Lord," I prayed, "how wonderful is your Spirit who makes us one. How much alike we are. I am so glad you were with the Joneses last year when they lost their baby, how real, and how sufficient you were. It was so much like you, Jesus, to draw near to the Halseys when their parents were taken suddenly from them. And, Lord, when Marva's troubled pregnancy at last resulted in a wonderfully healthy child." On and on I prayed for every couple in the room. I even peeked to be sure no one was left out. I've never believed much in peeking during prayer. I did it only to keep track of others who were not keeping their eyes closed as they should. During one of my extended peekings, I caught the athletic minister peeking about to see what kind of effect I was having. I can't say I really blame him. It was a spiritually motivated political prayer, and I was much more interested in them hearing my prayers than I was God hearing me.

When I got through praying, there were many people in tears, and they all were hugging and weeping as one. Hugging is a Baptist sign that things are generally all right. And after Barbara and I were back in our car and driving home, Barbara said, "That was masterful hypocrisy. You weren't talking to God; you were talking to them."

"Maybe," I said. "But God was probably listening in."

"Well," she said, "it probably didn't do any good. Those people

---

aren't really like us. Do you think they really love the Lord like we do?"

"Uh, uh, uh. I think they do love the Lord like we do, and we could all stand to love him a little better."

The group never left the church. Three or four couples did, but most of them stopped attending the Bible study and the crisis was averted. It's funny, but that night no one ever spoke about a division the whole time we were together. Us and Them, the old game, was gone. The new game was the more simple game of Us. What a healthy game it was too.

The divisive minister accepted the call to serve in another church far to the south of Nebraska. There were a few soreheads who couldn't wish him well. At his leaving, some, of course, wanted to sing "Ding, dong, the witch is dead." But most of the munchkins realized that if we're ever going to create Oz in the middle of Kansas, we must start loving the witches in our midst.

HURRYING PAST CHRISTMAS

Usually there was only one major crisis per decade, but this was a two-crisis decade, and I didn't have the time I really needed to repair my soul and thus get ready for the second storm. Two kicks in the gut need a little healing time to be managed. And I think I would have gotten over the next uprising if it hadn't followed so closely on the heels of the first.

It began in December of 1990. One of our thirty or so adult Bible study leaders in the church began to feel that our youth director was building a clique out of the popular kids that excluded the less popular kids. He told me that our youth director should be fired. Our youth director was a wonderful young man and had a reputation for being fair with all his adolescent congregation. He was popular throughout the city and had a large number of youth involved in his programs.

I have always been a little partial to church youth directors. They have a hard time. They are always living under the wrath of some unhappy parents who think their children are somehow not getting their fair share of attention in the church. They live on the cusp of annihilation and are frequently fired for no good reason, except that of all the staff members, they are the most easily cut off. They are too often sacrificed to minority opinion with little support from their pastor leader. In our own particular denomination, youth ministers are fired three times as often as pastors. They remind me of tail gunners who defended the rear ends of World War II bombers. The tail gunners hung off the bottom side of bombers in little plastic bubbles, where all enemy planes could see them and fire at them. They were essential to protecting a bomber from the rear, but they were extremely vulnerable in any attack. The average lifespan of a tail gunner in battle was eleven minutes, which by odd coincidence is also the average life of a youth director in church business meetings. That was why I felt it important to take our youth director's side. I genuinely loved the boy, and I was anxious not to see him shot down in a church squabble.

However, the adult class leader was anxious to get him off the church staff and was constantly passing out mallets and nails for his crucifixion. It was easy to see that another potential church problem was being born. The adult leader noisily announced that if the youth director was not fired then he would leave the church and take his Bible class with him.

All of this was in December, the season of Jesus' nativity. But it is also the month of furious fa-la-la, when there are hardly any silent nights on the church calendar. As usual during the month, I was running madly between the pastoral obligations of the season. There were Christmas chorales night after night. Candlelight communions were frequent. The counseling load is always heavy in December, and—joy to the world—someone was trying to get the youth director fired.

Four days short of Epiphany in 1991, as I collapsed in an overstuffed chair, praying for the Second Coming, Barbara asked me, "Did we have Christmas this year? I can't remember."

It was a simple question without a simple answer.

I couldn't remember even putting up a tree! I couldn't remember anything that had happened after Thanksgiving. The adult class leader had left the church. The youth director was still on the staff. Noel! Noel! We must have had Christmas, because it was January now.

It snowed lots that January.

I sat by the fire, staring into the flame, reading my Greek New Testament night after night. I thought and thought about Barbara's question.

There was only one casualty of Christmas 1990. Me.

I had vowed from time to time in moments of Baptist dyspepsia to leave the church. What pastor has not had his share of Monday morning resignations? But something was new in my fatigue.

I passed Barbara in the hallway of our home as I was going out to shovel snow. "You know that question you asked me back at the first of the month?" I asked her. "When I get back in from shoveling the drive, ask it again, my dear."

When I was back inside, she asked the question again.

"Did we have Christmas this year? I can't remember."

"That's what I thought you said, and I want to say, 'THAT DOES IT!'"

I paused between outbursts and went on.

"I'm leaving the ministry. I can't take it! I have three thousand members and I love them all, but I can't take it. I don't read anymore. I haven't written a book in five years. I haven't written anything. I'm running around trying to save everyone else and I'm losing me . . . at least the best part of me."

A Bittersweet Adieu

I had always said that true men and women of God have so much faith they can't ever suffer from burnout. But now . . . at fifty-four years of age, I was tired. I knew that somehow I couldn't go on giving at the level I had been giving and make it through the rest of my life. The church had become one of the largest in our city, but I wasn't captain enough to pilot her through the rough seas of congregational instability.

As far as anyone could see, the ship of faith was steady in the water. People were joining her week by week. We baptized more converts than almost any church I knew in our area of the world. We had baptized two people every week for twenty-five years. The church had grown from ten members to three thousand. And I suppose things were as they had to be or I would never have considered leaving the church. I'm not the kind of pastor who could walk out on a congregation in trouble.

In May of 1991, we held a church-wide emphasis called "Family Circle." This consisted of forming a double column of members that circled the entire church building in a ring-around-the-rosie sort of arrangement. Then once completely positioned by aides with walkie-talkies, a helicopter flew overhead and took a rather dramatic photograph of the church completely encircled by its members. I have kept the photograph all these years, for it seemed to me to symbolize the church at its unified best.

Still, I believed the church was causing me to lose the best part of me. I liked books. Reading them was life. Writing them once in a while had been most rewarding. Now I rarely read and never wrote, and it became clear to me that if I was going to save the best part of my soul, it was important for me to follow God in a new direction.

In the middle of all this floundering, I got phone calls from four different schools—two universities and two seminaries—inquiring if I would consider joining their faculties. The most intriguing of these letters came from Russell Dilday, who was then president of Southwestern Seminary. With a degree of casual hypocrisy, I told him I would pray about it. But the truth is I had already prayed about it, and had said yes in my spirit a long time before he ever asked.

I received a formal letter from the seminary regents in October, and I was able to resign immediately, making my resignation effective the first week in November.

I think people in the congregation were generally stunned. I had been their pastor for twenty-five years, and long pastorates seem like they are never supposed to end for any reason. The lay leaders pointed out to me that the church was growing by leaps and bounds. The six weeks prior to my resignation we had baptized more than fifty people. Offerings were strong. Why on earth would I want to leave?

What followed my resignation was a blitz of affirmation. All that I wanted to feel in terms of affirmation at my twenty-fifth anniversary, I felt just after I had announced my resignation. Every night, couples wanted to take Barbara and me to dinner, and we accepted as many invitations as we could. But there were too many of them. It was Mardi Gras and Carnival all rolling over us in our last few days in Omaha.

I do believe this: our lives belong to God, and I suppose it doesn't much matter what we spend them doing as long as we desire his perfect will to be carried out in our love for him. There was something exhilarating about a career change, if it can be called that. I found myself looking forward to professorhood. And the notion that it was what God wanted enhanced the days ahead.

The bitterness of spirit I had experienced in January faded. I realized I had been unusually depressed, and I determined that I would not leave the church feeling bitter. I have often been extreme in my moods—bipolar, in the most casual sense of the word. Being a man of extreme mood swings, I had always believed that I would end up either a weeping vegetable or a bitter cynic. Since I have never admired cynics, I was shooting for weeping vegetable as the best of categories. Most of all, bitterness is never appropriate. Hard times are never a matter of personal choice. Bitterness is.

Bye-Bye and Here's Why

In time I came back to a positive spirit, but with a new understanding. I needed to leave the church permanently. Not just my church, but any church that might want to call me as a full-time pastor. Thirty-five years as a local parish pastor was, after all, long enough to consider myself faithful to that phase of my calling. But the hard times had taught me this. I was trading the best gifts God had given me for the good gifts I had been using. I wanted to study more. I wanted to write more. And a university or a seminary was a better choice for this new, unfolding phase of my life.

But another set of evaluations also dogged me. I could see that the evangelical church in America was changing. The traditional culture was being swallowed whole by the contemporary age. Christians were increasingly turning from content evangelism to a mere congenial and gelatinous ecclesiology. The vocabulary was changing too! Year by year, we were hearing less and less about the transcendence of God, or the reality of hell and heaven. Sin, as Menninger had lamented in his classic *Whatever Became of Sin,* was missing as a reason for confession and personal renovation. I think, honestly, the kind of church I was good at was being replaced by a kind I didn't understand.

Besides the loss of transcendence in doctrine, the suburban church had become furiously programmatic. The new kind of churchmanship kept people busy with a calendar of activities and sociopolitical causes that did not intrigue me as much. I felt sure that the new age that was bearing down upon the church would require pastors who could live with less emphasis on the deeper life and more emphasis on a "YMCA agenda." *Relevance* was the new way of saying *here and now.* And I needed the church as I felt it had historically been where the *there and then* was always a good reason for loving God in the *here and now.*

I believed that whoever followed me would be better able to serve a society that expected less, whatever I thought they needed. Scholar pastors—which in some ways I considered to be the goal of my life—would not be as necessary in the future as they had been in my era. Maybe this was why a minister would sort through softball rolls to gather a church-planting crowd. He was not much of a scholar. I don't know that I had ever known him to read a book. But he seemed to be exactly what many of the young people needed. I recently visited a megachurch where the church bookstore contained many workout tapes on how to get buns of steel while you arrived at a full and meaningful life. This was the very kind of prophecy I made for the American evangelical church at large the year I left off being a pastor.

Throughout history everything Right has gradually marched Left. We have only to remember that Harvard in 1679 was a preacher's college. The same YMCA that in 1850 said, "Come play basketball with us and we'll talk about Jesus," was in 1950 saying simply, "Come play basketball with us." Herein lies my greatest fears for the Emergent Church: in its attempt to start where the culture is, it rarely stops and asks, "Is this where the culture should be?"

All of this introspection for me added up to a simple sense of calling. Maybe I should go to the seminary and try to be an apologist—a defender—for the old Christianity that was born in the book of Acts. Maybe I could help form young ministers to care about the "faith once delivered to the saints." Maybe I could help them see that the world still needs a faith where the sanctuary is more important than the Christian life center.

I knew why God wanted me to leave the church: it was for the sake of the church that he was calling me out of the church! Where I was going—the seminary—was the reproductive system of real spiritual vitality. The seminary stayed in touch with the past, the distant past, and championed the heroes who in every century kept reminding the church that she was in the world to change it, not to endorse it.

When the final Sunday came, the members of the church gathered in a large ballroom to hold an afternoon reception for us as we left to begin a life of teaching in the seminary. It was a wonderful day. Many greeted us for the last time we would ever see them on this earth. There were handshakes, embraces, and occasional kisses on the cheek. There were pastries and cheese balls and punch and sweetmeats. An abundance of love and vittles was everywhere evident. Throughout the afternoon people had been throwing thank-you notes in a box, and when the glorious greetings were all past, we turned to leave the long, long reception. We grabbed the box of thank-you notes on our way out.

I barely stepped out into the crisp air when a glorious sense of lightness and liberation flooded over me. I was free. Like Elvis, I had left the building. I was starting over. I had no idea how I would be as a teacher; I only knew I was eager to find out. Barb and I got in the car and drove away.

We drove out of town past the church. There it stood with its 105-foot tower, falling in the brisk light of the lawn flooders that were giving it its customary dramatic form. So much of our lives had been lived there. What would we do without the shrine? Could we live?

On we drove.

The van containing our furniture was ahead of us. An odd sensation overtook me. In the vacation times of previous years I had always defined happiness as two weeks away from the church with a thousand dollars worth of traveler's checks in my wallet. Now I defined happiness as having my furniture out ahead of me in a moving van and our bank bag under the front seat of our car, headed for a new life.

We had driven only a few minutes when Barbara asked me, "Where do you want to spend the night? Where shall we look for a motel? Somewhere here in Nebraska?"

"No," I said, "not here in Nebraska! I don't want to sleep in Nebraska one more night. I have slept the past thirty years in Nebraska. Tonight, I want to sleep in the next state over."

We both knew it was Kansas.

I had never cared much for Kansas. It seemed to have no deep purpose except to keep Nebraska and Oklahoma separated. To cross it was to wrangle with two hundred miles of asphalt—a long, uninteresting drive flanked with sunflowers, telephone lines, and barbed wire. But for once in my life, Kansas seemed to be everything Dorothy and Toto thought it was. "I'll take Kansas. The first motel in Kansas, be it pigsty or Hyatt is our home for the night."

As it turned out, when we had crossed the Kansas line, the first motel was a little more rustic than the Hyatt. Barb said as she looked at the neon lights of the first Kansas motel, "How does the Dew Drop Inn sound?"

"Wonderful," I answered.

We checked in.

We were tired and immediately climbed into bed. Almost as an afterthought, Barbara reached over into the box of thank-you notes I had placed on the nightstand beside the bed.

"Would you like me to read you a thank-you note? There must be at least a thousand notes in this box."

"No," I said, "we'll read them on the way to Texas tomorrow."

She looked as though she would put the thank-you note back in the box, and then thought better of it and tore it open.

A fifty dollar bill dropped out!

We were both stunned!

"Read me another one," I said.

She did, and a second fifty dollar bill fell out!

This was my idea of a box of thank-you notes!

We stayed up opening notes till the wee hours of the morning. There was in excess of ten thousand dollars in the box of notes. This utterly took us by surprise. I had no idea they were taking up a "love offering" for us.

"I guess they loved us more than we thought they did. Will somebody please tell me why God's people, who surfeit under a mighty surge of grace, have so much trouble telling other people they are loved?" Barb wondered.

"I don't know," I said.

"All that time they loved us," she said, "they just never let on, so nobody ever knowed it." She was quoting a line out of *Oklahoma!* where Curly sang "Pore Jud Is Daid!"

"I wonder why they never let on?"

"I guess I never gave them a reason to till I resigned."

"I wonder how many preachers resign their churches 'cause

---

nobody ever let on," she said.

I wondered too. I wondered all through the night.

I wondered all the next day.

These seventeen years later, I still wake up at midnight wondering.

PART THREE

The Professor Who Liked Teaching but Loved Learning

1991–2007

FOURTEEN

The Calcutta Kid and Tombstone Shopping

Two events marked my early fifties. They flew fast at me and landed only four years apart. They seemed so separate at the time, yet they were one in their impact. The first of these was the birth of my grandson in Orissa, India. My grandson was born exactly one decade after my own mother died.

The Child from the East

In 1986, my daughter and son-in-law received the news that they would never be able to have children. This news came as the first chill of winter for all of us. Our children, like us before them, wanted a child. But more than the knowledge they would never have a child, the news threatened to leave a gap in the Miller family history. For as long as I could remember children were born to our family. In every score of years no generation had been left out. Now, the chain would be broken. So there is a sting in the dismal confession, "We can't have children." It's the kind of loss you weep about for a moment but feel for the rest of your life.

But we were all about to learn that a thwarted motherhood can be a powerful force for good in this world. It was a gray afternoon when Melanie came to us with news. "I've been talking to an international adoption agency. A baby has been born in the Orissa province of India," she said, measuring her words. "The mother actually died of malnutrition, which is the customary way you say starvation in that section of India."

"And so . . . ?" I wasn't quite sure where she was going with the conversation.

"The baby's mother died in childbirth, and the boy she gave birth to weighed less than three pounds—not all that uncommon in malnourished mothers who carry their unborn children to a full-term birth. The baby is currently in an Indian orphanage, and will be eligible for adoption when he gains some weight."

"And so . . . ?"

"And so, we are thinking about trying to adopt him. What would you and Mom say about having a grandson of color?"

"I like colored grandsons," I said.

"I like colored grandsons too," said Barbara.

"Besides," I said, "it sounds like the child needs a life he would never be able to have if he stayed in India. I think we should adopt him even if we don't like him. It just seems like the Christian thing to do."

"But he'll be a different color than you are!" protested Melanie.

"I've never liked my color anyway," I said.

"I've never liked your color either," laughed Barbara. "Who would want a bald-headed grandson with liver spots? What can we do to help?"

"I don't know yet," said Melanie. "But it will take all of us to make it happen."

"Well, I want to buy him a little white sailor suit. I think a kid with a dark complexion really looks great in white."

"Yeah, and then when he's big he can probably get a job as skipper on the *Love Boat*!" I laughed.

But Melanie didn't laugh. When hope is at its zenith, it forbids its bearer to laugh. It is too fragile, too delicate, too all important! She was serious about this whole thing. She stood to leave, and as she turned, she tossed over her shoulder a parting word, "The child's name is Sangram."

We embraced, and she left. There was more than one way to have grandbabies, and maybe this was a way to do it that pleased God. God could take a child with little chance of ever prospering in a land of one billion citizens and give him a chance, using a white middle-class family twelve thousand miles away.

Sangram was doubtless from Hindu stock, and knowing what I did about Hindu caste, he would have been a pariah; that is, a member of the *Pardiyar*, at the bottom of the caste system. He would have little if any hope for a decent life or career. Pariahs run rickshaws all their lives or clean the homes of the Brahmans or wash the streets or work the mines. But he would be coming to us, and we would tell him about Jesus and how no person should ever be relegated to a menial hell thought up by some elitist who happened to have the good fortune to be born into a higher caste.

"He'll be darling in a little white jumpsuit," repeated Barbara.

"Maybe we should get him here before we get him all dressed up," I said. I don't think I had ever seen Barbara so worked up over the idea of having a brown-skinned grandchild, who at the moment was just three months old—and practically skin and bones—in a Hindu orphanage.

The path between this initial dream and its fulfillment was long and arduous. The differences between the Indians and the Chinese are as different as one might imagine. But they hold this in common: they treasure sons and deplore daughters, and it is a rare thing to be offered a boy. My children were elated by the prospect of having a son, not because they preferred boys, necessarily, but they knew this adoption would be special. There is one other unspoken defect in Indian adoption policies: it is taboo to suspect that they are selling their "unwanted" babies because their populations are plagued by longstanding seasons of famine and starvation.

It was clear that Sangram, even in his prenatal starvation, was the child of a woman who possibly never had enough to eat. But he was in an orphanage, and while the process would stretch on for a year before he actually arrived, he was in a place where he was now being nurtured and fed and strengthened. And then, when adoption negotiations had only been underway for a few weeks, a wonderful thing happened: a picture arrived from the orphanage.

He was a beautiful baby! He was a little skinny, but then that was my evaluation, and, in times of plenty, most of the Miller clan had lived for generations on the brink of chubbyhood. This was a fault probably handed to me by my mother during the Depression, but Mama believed God had created body fat to be stuffed here and there around our abdomens, "because you never know when you might get sick and need some extra fat just to survive." It was a wonderful rationalization I had used across the years to defend my gluttony. I wasn't overeating. Not really. I was only storing up a lot of carbs for my future survival.

What never survived were my clothes. My trousers shrank and my shirt-collars strangled me. They both tightened up until my eyes bulged out, and I felt a magnificent sense of escape just in taking off my trousers to go to bed at night. "Thank you, Jesus, for making me so healthy!" I would say as I put on my generous pajamas. So when I saw the first little pictures of Sangram, I didn't think of him as skinny, just too unprotected for the future. But I knew when he got here we would teach him the Miller doctrine of fat-for-survival.

Think me not sentimental, but I gazed at that little photo of the brown-skinned child until I could have drawn it perfectly in the dark. I could hardly think of his little frame, or of his poor dead mother, without believing that God had given him to us, even though the weeks after the photographs, like the weeks before the photographs, dawdled along like crippled snails.

The paperwork to adopt a child goes on and on. Forms, forms, forms! Another schedule would arrive from the agency, then another evaluation from the nation of India. A secondary application for the orphanage. And then a third protective custody form, then airline travel itineraries. And for our children: money, money . . . ever more money. Our children were none too wealthy, but they borrowed and spent. Borrow . . . write a check! Borrow . . . write a check! Borrow a *whole* lot . . . write a *big* check! And nothing much happened except another month crept past.

Then, after ten months, came a letter of promise and the stated day of Sangram's arrival. He was to be brought over on United Airlines, flight #407, from Calcutta. The child's delivery escort was to be the orphanage director. When Melanie was steady enough, between periods of hyperdelirium, she worked at putting together a nursery in their home. A layette. Diapers by the carton. All stacked neatly in the corner of the room that would be all ready for him when the magic day arrived.

And arrive it did. Melanie and Louis went to the airport along with grandparents from both sides of the house. Friends and well-wishers, all were there, some fifty in number. This was well before the current ban on unticketed people going to the boarding gate. So we all gathered at the Jetway ramp of Gate 15.

The night of his arrival was really a dark and stormy night. The plane was two hours late. But none of the welcoming party would have thought of leaving. Every airplane that touched down onto the rain-slick runway, we all thought would be United 407. But every time we were disappointed. Inevitably it had to happen; 407 came down the runway and then pulled up to the Jetway where all of us were waiting, just inside the terminal.

Then the passengers began to unload. The flight was very full, and ever so slowly they filed off the plane. As they unloaded, I felt those same emotions I had felt years earlier, when I had waited for my young wife in a Kansas City train station. There they came: pretentious passengers, who talked too loudly as though their pointless blabber would somehow make them more important than they actually were. Eccentrics in cowboy boots, sporting handlebar moustaches. It was uncanny that none of them seemed to have any idea how utterly unessential they were to human happiness. Finally a beturbaned man got off the plane. He was the only passenger we had seen so far who looked remotely Indian, and while he didn't have the baby we were looking for, we thought he must have left the tot sleeping on the plane. We were all so excited we broke into applause and cheers.

The man looked at us so quizzically as if to say to our applause, "I luv zees kuntry. Eet eez so wonderful!" It was not him, though he was nearly the last person to get off the plane.

Then came the very last person to leave the plane. He was a short Hindu man, dressed in what appeared to be cream-colored pajamas and a white fez.

He was carrying a baby!

Sangram!

What happened next was as much of a miracle as I have ever seen. For among all fifty of the faces that greeted him, his gaze fixed directly on Melanie, and then he held out his little brown arms to her. Tears rushed from all our faces, and Melanie, crying also, reached out to take the baby who was reaching for her.

He was so beautiful, yet strangely aware of how beautiful he was. He was a baby, that was all. But he was so much more than a baby. He was a prayer, an answer, an angel, a boy, a commitment, a reason to get up in the morning. A link, he was, between India and America, between his parents and grandparents, between the immediate future and the far-flung future. A kiss of God and humankind!

Melanie could see, as we all could, that he was wearing a little yellow cloth diaper that had never known the touch of Borax. But the little country orphanage twelve thousand miles away that had given him the diaper was no longer his domain. He had landed in the West with all its hypercommercialism and cellophane insanity. Melanie laid a small blanket on the terrazzo floor of the airport, put the baby on the small blanket, unpinned his traveling diaper, and bound him up in a snow-white, snap-tab Pamper. And then she put a brand-new pair of Star Wars pajamas on him. Eureka! George Lucas had clothed him in C-3PO and R2-D2. He was a Westerner! A one-year-old, a Star Wars-stamped Westerner at that!

A party of fifty or so walked out of the airport exalting the baby. It was a kind of noël. And the child represented what any baby represents: a commitment that we were his guardians and protectors. And as he grew, he would require from us the utmost in our love and care, in our prayers and dreams. Every area of our lives he would touch and touch again. And I thought of that long-ago, stern discouragement of the doctor, "I'm sorry, madam, but you can never have a child."

What a falsehood!

She had the child. And the umbilical cord that anchored him to India was not really clipped until he landed in far away Nebraska. Do not tell us he has not our genes, for God runs the great gene pool of humanity, and all our genes were given to us from that great God. This God has so many children that if all of them were properly distributed no family would ever need to go childless. I looked at our intercontinental grandchild and went home that night to write:

> The doctors like stern prophets prophesied,
> That barrenness would curse our anxious hope
> And heritage. But see the prophets lied—
> A dark-skinned child came like an infant pope,
> To bless the multitudes with open joy.
> I never stop to wonder at God's grace
> Until I see this primal, brown-skinned boy,
> In him God's love acquired a face.
> Not of my blood you say? Idolatry
> Of genes and DNA. This child I so esteem

Has magic power, and has demandingly
Reduced the great Pacific to a stream.
He tricked the Ocean into shallow shoals,
Then waded it across to claim our souls.[8]

Perhaps it happened at the snapping of a new diaper on the airport floor, that the name of Sangram left us. He now had a Christian name: Jared Daniel. And never did we hear his former name again. He became a U.S. citizen, and I love remembering him slumped, sound asleep under a flag that guaranteed him life, liberty, and the pursuit of happiness. That pursuit belonged to all of us, and we pursue it still.

Jared's arrival marked the beginning of a new era. There was a focus in the family that had not been there before. We talked about him. We talked to him. We babied him, which is the chief activity for grandparents, I think. He got his little white sailor suit, and he became a poster child for Calvin Klein Jr. in the church nursery. And in many ways all such activities continue to the present, and this is now his twentieth year. Some years later the children adopted a second child, who came to them at ten years of age from Thailand. The boys from preadolescence grew together and broadened our definition of Christmas, indeed our definition of life.

MONUMENT TO ROMANCE

Early in the '90s I reached my fifty-fifth year, and for some reason I was possessed of an odd drive to buy not just our grave sites but our tombstones. Obtaining four lots from the cemetery trust was easy since Barb's stepfather in his later years had become the trustee of the Hunter Cemetery. Burial lots there were twenty-five dollars apiece, a bargain for such essential and terminal real estate. We bought four lots, in case our children in their later years might choose to sleep out their pre-resurrection years alongside us. But at the moment of the purchase I think they thought it a bit weird that we were so obsessed by the notion of having them for ourselves. Then, when we bought our tombstones, they must have thought we had flipped out.

But I think I was motivated to take the step for two reasons. First of all, this seems to me to be the kind of thing you can't leave to your attorney—even as an instruction in a will. Who's to say he won't ignore your instruction and buy himself a sports car with the money he should have spent on your tombstone?

But the overwhelming reason this was important to me is that I wanted to put on that stone my regard for Barbara. I wanted it to be big enough to hold a fourteen-line sonnet on each side, and I wanted it to be in granite. I had long regarded Gutzon Borglum's remark about his creation of Mount Rushmore. Regarding his titanic granite busts of American presidents, he said, "We will raise our monuments and lift them high, so only the wind and the rain will wear them away."

I sat down with the main monument maker at Enid Monument Works and I said to him, "What is the hardest rock in the world out of which to build a monument?"

"Granite!" he said. "Without a doubt, granite!"

"Can you put a fourteen-line sonnet on each side of such a rock?"

"Is the pope a Catholic? Of course I can. But "Rest in Peace" will cost you less, and "R.I.P." even less than that. It costs so much a letter to put words in rock, you know. That's what keeps people from putting sonnets on their tombstones."

I slipped him a copy of the sonnet I had typed out on a piece of paper. "Can you do this?"

He read it for a long time. At length he said, "I'm not sure I understand it, but I can get it on a rock. Did you write this?"

"Yes," I said, "I wrote this. It's how I feel about my wife."

"Couldn't you just send her a valentine?"

"Maybe, but I want to raise a monument to her and lift it so high that only the wind and the rain will wear it away. As long as this rock endures, I want the world to know how great a person once lived in this little town. We were married there years ago," I said, "in a church that's only a few blocks from the cemetery where we'll one day be buried. I was a pastor there. I've officiated at I know not how many funerals in that little red-earth field of graves."

"That thing you just said, about the wind and the rain, did you write that or something?"

"Actually Gutzon Borglum said it."

"I never heard of him. Did he get a tombstone for his woman too?"

"No, actually, he carved Mount Rushmore."

"Oh, that Gutzon Borglum."

"How much will this cost me?"

"Well, if I do it in inch-and-a-half letters, the rock will cost you a thousand and the sonnet four thousand."

"Sounds like a bargain to me."

I paid him some money, and he said he would have the proofs ready to look at in a couple of weeks. When I got the proofs, I studied them harder than anything I have ever proofread in my life. When you're working in granite, you can't use an eraser when you make a mistake. When I was sure he had it right, I told him to go ahead with the work.

I wrote in my journal of the tombstone purchase:

> Today we bought a space beyond the tree—
> The church is but a mile away
> Where we made promises in candle light.
> We know that one of us must finish first,
> And the other one bring roses to the curtain call.
> But love's dark crepe finale unrehearsed
> Demands we live until that curtain falls.
> Let's hold each other to the edge of night.
> Our encores will be born in better light.[9]

I was teaching at Southwestern Seminary when they finally set the stone in the little cemetery.

They say that when the stone was set, people by the droves came out from the little town of Hunter to read the stone. Arthur and Ruth Roelse drove clear out from Enid to read the stone. Some drove from as far away as Pond Creek to read the poem. Some— although not all—surely understood the drive that forces poetry into granite. It had to be written, for not to speak of such a love would be a sin against the Holy Ghost. The sonnet was this:

If this be love, expect me not to wait
One day to tell of it. For life is chance
And so unsure that I must celebrate
It while I have the strength to dance.
He is integrity: if there be truth,
As I can know the time, the time is right.
The passing years have fed upon my youth
The day to testify grows short of light.
I know the risk. Love could still prove a lie.
Some future, fickle circumstance might kill
My best resolve: I do's do sometimes die.
Broken vows are spawned by weakened will.
Old promises must pledge themselves each day
Or, unrenewed, pass quietly away.[10]

A Golden Letter with a Golden Pledge

Somewhere in that season of tombstone shopping I wrote some special words to my wife, "Dear Barbara, we have with this stone faced that last plateau. And sometimes when I look at you, I see a radiance that is brighter than it was the day we met. I love you. I have always loved you. I love you too much not to say it one final time. Here then is the formal, final letter I have always wanted to write to you. Keep it in a safe place, in case you live on past me, and then read it as the last testament of an old romantic, who couldn't quit loving or even quit being fascinated with the subject."

Fifty years have so far occupied our finest watching of the seasons. And after all these years, I can't imagine I was ever so confused about the problem I had defining love. Why was I so reluctant to become engaged to you, these fifty years past? That love I struggled so to define at twenty-three, defined itself in time.

We are gloriously together and it is not dull company.

There's a crispness in the air, my darling. The night is coming on, and reminds us that we've used up the first seasons of our togetherness, and this warm, late summer that we so enjoy can't be held forever. One day, not so far away, one of us will be forced to stand alone. Only one of us must test that demonic emptiness, which will the final fruit of our lost togetherness. It's odd I always thought I would be afraid of the future when there wasn't much of it left. But beyond the granite stone, we will find a better togetherness than that which time forced us to surrender.

Maybe I'm over-romantic! I suppose that a man who puts a lot of schmaltz on his tombstone could be accused of that. But I've not been so romantic I didn't know we were getting old. The hardest part of aging is the illusion they're always trying to foist upon us down at the Social Security office: the notion that we're old and they're not. The hypocrites! How do they think people get old, anyway? We are all hurrying along taking care of summer's business, and soon it is winter. Besides, neither of us has ever thought of ourselves as old. To me you're as young as ever. I long ago gave you a ring and you agreed to spend a few fast decades exploring the world with me. And weren't we conquistadores? Planting our flags on each new experience and marking out the borders of our little kingdoms as we passed through them. And for one brief shining moment we dreamed, we loved, we were. It was just last Saturday I saw you coming down the aisle in white, breathtaking in your beauty. But that was not the best part—not just the start of our marriage. The best part is now.

I know why Robert Browning wrote in "Rabbi Ben Ezra":

> Grow old along with me! The best is yet to be,
> the last for which the first was made.

I feel sorry for all those who announce at twenty or thirty, "Yippee! I'm in love!" I have the awfullest urge to slap them out of their hysteria and say, "Hey, puppy, you don't know anything about love. Love exists only in the lives of those who have learned to kiss in the laboratory of pain. Love is the kiss that has laid aside by the fire of the honeymoon night, and found itself in the chaste hello of the cancer ward. Love is the trembling feel of faithful lips on a wrinkled hand. Love is a willingness to walk slow when our lover finds each plodding step a triumph over sluggish tendons. Come back to me you over-ecstatic, untried twenty-year-olds, when you are broken by age, then tell me of your love once you have gained the right to define it."

But for now it is even as it was with Leigh Hunt.

> Jenny kissed me when we met,
> Jumping from the chair she sat in;

Time, you thief, who love to get
Sweets into your list, put that in!
Say I'm weary, say I'm sad,
Say that health and wealth have missed me,
Say I'm growing old but add,
Jenny kiss me.

And Barbara, I thank you now for every golden kiss set in
the silver years we've known.

We knew the warm, sweet sun of love in youth.
We felt the touch that gilded every night with warmth.
We drove each false thing out with truth
We lived poor but thought of it as wealth.
My darling, you have made me rich as Troy,
You crowned my being with such gold piled high
I've pitied those who never knew my joy.
Old age is but a kind of lie
We dare not tell.
For age is unavoidable in life
But thinking old is but a choice we thinking of ourselves
    will never choose.
Please, am I walking somewhat slower now?
It's love's maturity that slows us down.
No one can run who's weighted down with dreams.

So, walk with me, my love, but not too fast.
We'll pace ourselves to carry all this gold,

We've gathered in the loving.
For the good-night kiss
We offer on our final night on earth,
Is but life's sweetest testament
Though it comes last of all.[11]

FIFTEEN

Giving What You Have, to Get What You Can't Keep

Between being Pastor Miller and becoming Professor Miller lay a broad chasm. Crossing this wide divide required a running leap I barely managed to make. And once I had cleared the chasm, my new teaching career left me uncertain that the choice I had made was a wise one. Pastors are the heads of congregations. They are in on every piece of gossip and administrative decision that passes through their churches. They are always central in their flocks. They are not always esteemed. In fact, they may at times be despised by a part of their flock. But loved or hated, they are always central.

Professors, on the other hand, are fringe people. The big decisions about their workplace are made by people they rarely or never meet. The trustees sit around mahogany tables and decide the courses of their professor's careers and their lives. They are assigned to teach out of offices they don't pick. They are mandated to use certain classrooms they never get to choose. They are given everything: their work loads, their class times, their chalk allowances.

Comedownance . . . Comeuppance

The pastor of a three thousand member church in America usually makes two hundred thousand dollars a year. The average seminary professor is making at best fifty or sixty thousand a year. Seminary professors do not take a vow of poverty to teach; it just works out that way. In most denominations, the renown within a denomination always goes to the big pastors who have the prominent pulpits and therefore get all the convention and assembly perks. Their churches pay to send them to the political centers of their denominations, where they elect each other to prominent positions. In the denomination I serve, no professor has ever been elected to lead the denomination.

But the life of a pastor-turned-professor is not all bad. The best of such men and women realize they are the heartbeat of their universities. No student ever went to a college—or, in my case, a seminary—because they had outstanding trustees. It is the teacher who knows the grassroots joy of being friends with those who are taking out huge loans to study with them. After all, this is the basic meaning of college. The "lege" part of *college* comes from the Latin *legare*, "to read or reason." The "col" part of *college* comes from the Latin for "together." Students and professors in college "think together" or "reason together," or most simply—and this is truest to the Latin—they "read together." Trustees and donors don't visit the campus to read together. They relate to the school to give it money and structure, or to control the money and determine the structures.

The biggest struggle in becoming a teacher was simply one of pacing the delivery of the matter I wanted to communicate. I could go to class with what seemed like an hour of lecturing and finish the whole presentation in half the time. Or I could go to class in fear and trembling thinking I didn't have a nickel's worth of material to present and find that it consumed the whole hour.

Once when I had finished a whole lecture in twenty minutes and could think of not one more thing to say, I dismissed the class early. Head downward, I moped my way back from the classroom to my office. On the way I happened to run into a fellow professor, who asked why I was so glum. "Oh, I dunno," I said, "I just can't get the hang of it. I thought I had plenty of material for a fifty-minute lecture and then I finished the whole thing in twenty minutes flat . . . very flat!"

"You too!" he said. "I just can't get the hang of it either," he volunteered.

"But you've been teaching for twenty years!" I said.

"Yeah! That's pretty sad, isn't it?"

It wasn't sad. It was glorious! If he, an esteemed veteran on the faculty, could gush through an hour of lecture in twenty minutes, maybe it was a common, horrible fault that stalked every professor. I cherished that exchange. Misery does so love company.

But I was only beginning to learn the real differences between preaching and teaching.

"Teaching is always done at the dangerous intersection of personal and public life," said Parker Palmer.[12] Further, he said that each time teachers begin a lecture they choose the point within themselves at which the lecture will begin. For this reason, my move from the pulpit to the lectern was highly significant. Significant but darksome. There was no clear path between the two, though I had always supposed there would be. But a sermon is vastly different from a lecture.

A sermon flies on the wings of Scripture and opinion. A sermon is always a document tightly prepared—twenty-two minutes of glistening, rhetorical sculpture. A sermon best done is an art form, produced in a quiet studio, then exhibited in bright light to do its polished work. Sermons are seen as having come from God and therefore smugly fly above contradiction. But a lecture is a piece of lore, fashioned from a mixture of the professor's personality and academic knowledge but assembled out in the open and formed on the spot by the feedback of lovers and skeptics all in the same room at the same time.

I had not been a teacher for a week before I discovered that what I *knew* was not nearly so important to them as who I *was*. They wanted to know *why* I taught, more than *what* I taught. They wanted me to *know* them rather than merely *inform* them. They wanted to know all about my affair with Christ more than the content of my lectures. So I discovered early on that good teachers teach what they are, more than what they know. In teaching I had to become my lectures, and my lectures had to be constructed from those building blocks chiseled out of my own soul. I had to become my words rather than just speak my words. I knew why May Sarton wrote:

> Now I become myself. It's taken
> Time, many years and places;
> I've been dissolved and shaken
> Worn other people's faces . . . .[13]

Parker Palmer wrote in another context: "As a young teacher, I yearned for the day when I would know my craft so well, be so competent, so experienced, and so powerful, that I could walk into my classroom without feeling afraid. But now in my late fifties, I know that day will never come . . . . Each time I walk into a classroom, I can choose the place within myself, from which my teaching will come, just as I can choose the place within my students toward which my teaching will be aimed."[14]

Teaching for me is an act of intimacy. Like all other acts of intimacy, it occurs within the hearts of two—the teacher and the learner. No matter how large a class is, the entire class is reduced to two, the teacher and the learner. No minds are chaste; all good minds lust outwardly in search of intimacy, and they copulate each time they meet. Teaching is an intimate art, filled with ecstasy and life. It occurs at the exact same place where humanity and divinity join to form a new incarnation of truth.

THE COAT WITH TWO POCKETS

A Hasidic proverb says, "We need a coat with two pockets. In one pocket there is dust, and in the other pocket there is gold." We need a coat with two pockets to remind us who we are. Knowing, teaching, and learning under the grace of great things will come from teachers who own such a coat and wear it to class every day.[15]

This coat with pockets of gold and dust demands that the teacher descend from Olympus and admit to being made of dust. It is at this point that teaching becomes most fragile. Because teachers who disclose themselves give up enough propriety at times to be hauled in before the deans and regents. But this candor awakens an honest reaction within the students, who need to know the edgy stuff, the boundaries, the chasms that lie before unacceptable confessions. Good teachers are never pornographic, but they are graphic. They are mentors who have seen and felt the cold breath of things that nearly condemned them before they passed their experiences on to their mentees.

It has long been said that the three most popular sermon subjects are (1) The Second Coming, (2) Sex, and (3) Will There Be Sex After the Second Coming? Having had any number of single

ministerial students in my classes over the years, I have seen them
wrangling over how to live holy like the apostle Paul, while thinking about sex 75 percent of their waking lives.

One seventy-five-year-old professor, wearing his coat of dust
and gold, was asked by a young single student who was having a
struggle with lust, "Prof, at what age does a man quit looking at a
young woman with lust?"

It was clearly off the subject, but then most vital questions often
are. It was a class on Egyptology, and for one small pinpoint of
time, the twenty-second dynasty of Egypt was forgotten while the
stunned class waited to see if the professor would answer such an
interruption.

"Well," said the septuagenarian professor, "I don't know exactly,
but it's sometime after seventy."

This question was obviously answered out of the pocket filled
with dust. The pocket filled with gold was the Egyptology pocket.

I happened to come to the seminary to teach during some rough
years of denominational struggles. Some fundamentalist conserva-
tives were making it hard for every professor to find out how to wear
the coats with two pockets. Everything taught had to be scrutinized
very closely, and it had to match the thinking of the powers in charge.
Any number of professors were fired for being liberal, and within our
school it was often the case that a student from a conservative church
would smuggle a tape recorder into class to try and catch a professor
saying something that might be interpreted as heresy. Then the student might take the heretical tape to a conservative trustee and it was
either "ouch" or "off with his head." The guillotines of fundamental-
ism always make teaching a nightmare.

ON BEING RIGHT-BRAINED IN A LEFT-BRAINED WORLD

In such an atmosphere, I was lecturing on heaven and hell in relationship to evangelism and missions when a student asked me to explain the basic nature of heaven and hell. I told him that while I had never been to either one, both were real, but the language that describes them in the Bible was highly metaphorical. I tried to tell him that when we deal with the transcendence of eternity, the best we have to go on are word pictures. "Heaven," I said, "is a place where the concrete paving of earth is so exalted it appears to be twenty-four-carat gold. But," I went on, "who wants to go to heaven just to gaze at such resplendence? Heaven is eternal togetherness with Christ. The Scriptures are most clear on this. Earth's gates of wood and stone by comparison become gates of pearl in heaven. The guttural grunts of sin in this world become angelic choirs in God's realm. Hell, by contrast," I said, "is the torture of being forever separated from God. Burning forever in the knowledge of lost allegiances and broken commitments. As flame threatens and destroys human flesh, Satan's fires destroy the spirit and isolate us forever from God. But from the word pictures given us in Scripture, we still cannot imagine the true nature of these eternal realities. 'For as the heavens are higher than the earth,' said Isaiah, 'so are his ways higher than our ways and his thoughts higher than our thoughts.'"

When I finished my argument, this very conservative young man stood up, clicked his cowboy boots together, and said, "My friend, when you say hell is only a metaphor [which of course I never said] you are on highly dangerous ground."

"Well, my friend," I answered, "if the only hell you can believe in is one *you* can understand, you are on highly dangerous ground. The true nature of heaven and hell are so far beyond our imagination that we are fools to say we have correctly defined it for all those we force to swallow our small interpretations of these grand estates."

Occasionally I have had the desire to belt a student, and this one came close. He was much bigger and far younger than I am, so I think belting him would have gone the worse for me. But I never forgot his obstinacy. I thought he might report me to a trustee, but he never did. After class that day, a student walked up to me and said, "Prof, I'm so glad you said that to him. I'm in other classes with this guy and it has been his way of life to intimidate every professor that has taught him. Thanks for not letting him get by with this in your class."

Besides the sullen and angry students I have known, I have often run into students who were incredibly naïve. Before I got to the seminary, I published a novel called *The Philippian Fragment*. The novel purports to be the account of an archaeologist who discovers an ancient manuscript of a martyred preacher of the first century. In the middle of the nineteenth century, Charles Finney—himself a Yale graduate—taught that a novel was only a well-told lie. But as it would happen, a young student on a distant campus wrote me a letter. This student believed the novel I had written was not a novel but an actual account of a real archaelogical discovery and the events that clustered about it. One day as I sat in my seminary office the phone rang.

"Are you Calvin Miller, the author of *The Philippian Fragment?*"

"Yes, as a matter of fact I am," I said, being perhaps a little too proud.

"Well, do you still have the fragment you wrote about?"

"No," I said, a bit baffled.

"Well, what did you do with it?"

"It never existed. The book is a novel about an event I imagined."

"Well then, did you lie about all this? . . . . This book changed my life . . . is it untrue?"

"Well, I'm glad I wrote with enough force as to change your life. What was it like before I changed it?"

"Never mind how it changed my life. I feel gypped. The book cost fifteen dollars, and it changed my life, and now you're telling me the book is untrue. What are you, a big fat liar?"

"No, I'm a big fat novelist!" I said.

"Well, if it's not true you must be a liar!"

This conversation was turning ugly fast.

"True? Yes. Factual? No! As Don Quixote said, 'Facts are the enemy of truth.'"

I wished I hadn't mentioned *Don Quixote*, which was a sixteenth-century novel that he had never heard of. Trying to explain the quote only prolonged the whole argument.

"Look," I said, "if you haven't dog-eared the copy too much, maybe the bookstore will take it back and you can trade it in for *Black Beauty*, which is also a novel, because there never was a horse named Black Beauty. But when I was eight it changed my life, and forever altered the way I see horses."

"Horses!" he bellowed.

I hung up.

Novels are now being published and read by evangelicals. But they have come very late to the scene, and many evangelicals still won't read them because they are not true, as they see it.

But there were even more serious issues at the seminary than cultural naiveté. Women had stormed to the front of America's divinity schools and were demanding that seminaries become more inclusive with them as they wrangled through the world of church to arrive at a place of service in the Christian world.

THE GENDER IMPASSE

I once had a church leadership class with eighty students in it, four of whom were women. I know they were determined to get their degrees, but among that many men—some of whom were strongly opposed to women in ministry—they always looked a little scared to me. Women are often quiet in large sections of male students. And after several class sessions in which they had remained silent, I asked all four of the women to take chairs on the raised platform at the front of the classroom. They did this very reluctantly, but they did it. Then I gave them the whole class period to tell all the men in the class why they believed they were properly following God in a ministry career.

It was a quiet session. One by one the women told of their experiences of faith and how they had come to trust in Christ, and later felt that God had called them to serve him full-time in the church. When they said they had been "called," a few of the men grew agitated and stirred in their seats. But as the women continued, even the most agitated of men seemed to settle back and grow easy. Then some of the women began to be emotional about how they often felt thwarted in the church and felt like their ministries were unwelcome in many churches. They all believed God had called them, but also felt that many men would never allow them to serve in any prominent positions of ministry in the church.

At the end of the class, I suggested that Southern Baptists—and most of us in the class were that—could profit from widening their hermeneutic on women. I suggested several biblical heroes who actually were women and led both men and women in some encounter with God. I encouraged the students to look at the coming of the Spirit on the Day of Pentecost, when both men and women prophesied. We looked at Galatians 3:28, where it clearly says that in Christ there are no men and women, only one undivided church. We examined Romans 16:1–4, where Saint Paul commends more women than men in the church, and all the women were cited for doing heroic sorts of service in the church and none were praised for being good, quiet homemakers who kept still in the church and fried whatever their husbands hunted.

It was one of my favorite of all classes I ever led. I did nothing but let the women talk and let the men listen, and listen they did. Several of the men came up to me after class. A few were mad that I would let a woman "usurp" authority over the men in the class, but most said they had never realized that women could feel the same sense of urgency and calling that they themselves did.

Of course, there are always gender warriors who go too far. One of the professors where I taught, in an attempt to wedge a little femininity into the Trinity, prayed in chapel, "Holy Spirit, come and be Queen of our lives!" In ours and other conservative seminaries, the idea that the Holy Spirit might be the feminine member of the Trinity was too much. He was fired and went to teach adjunctively on the faculty of a more liberal divinity school that could tolerate his views.

ZORRO

But gender inclusiveness was not the only front on which students struggled for balance. My most outstanding and fearsome contact came from a secretive source I knew only as "Zorro." In October of '94, I received this letter:

Dr. Miller:

I was going to preach a sermon from the passage I ask you about in the sentences below. But I have been told by some liberal professors at the seminary where you work and where I study, that this part of the Bible is untrue. I would like to know whether or not you believe John 7:59–8:11 is the true word of God. Many scholars believe that it was not a part of the original manuscripts of the Bible, and thus not being the true word, it should be stricken from Holy Writ and never be used in churches. There are so many liberals lurking about on the seminary faculty that it is up to us students to ferret out liberalism and work at getting these liberal professors back in Yale Divinity School where they belong. So I must know how you feel about this disputed portion of the fourth gospel.

Your Friend, Zorro

"Zorro" left me a post-office box number and zip code so I could return my answer while he remained incognito.

I agonized over how to answer Zorro. My answer would have to be written, and I have generally not answered anonymous mail, which could be answerable to some inquisition while affording the author the privilege of remaining shielded. My views of the passage in dispute were what he would probably consider to be heretical. He was apparently a "King-James-only" Christian, since only the King James Version of the Bible, first printed in 1611, generally doesn't mention that the passage is spurious (not a part of the original manuscript, but added later). All later versions of the Bible, of course, do.

I recognized at once that my answer would be the perfect kind of evidence an enemy might need "to prove" that I was a liberal and didn't believe all of the Bible and therefore should be fired. Looking shaky on biblical inerrancy was the equivalent of feminizing the Holy Spirit. After much agony, I began my reply to a post-office box, picking my way through the doctrinal minefields of my unnamed aggressor.

Dear Zorro:

I can assure you that all sound scholarship, conservative or liberal, agrees on the subject that the passage you have inquired about was not a part of the original gospel of John. This does not mean that the story of the woman taken in adultery is untrue. It simply means that whether it is or not, it does not garner to itself the same kind of certain authority that the rest of the New Testament possesses. John 3:16 is of course uncontested and bears the same kind of integrity that you might like to give to the passage you inquired about.

Nonetheless, the story is pivotal in looking at the nature of sin and guilt, and Christians throughout all the centuries have used it to celebrate the truth it illustrates. If you want to preach on the text, do so, but do not fail to mention that while the text is worthy, it came much later in time than the rest of the Gospel of John.

This is all I have to say on the subject, except this:

ZORRO REVEAL THYSELF!

Scripturally and infallibly yours,

Dr. Calvin Miller

Several weeks went by, when on a late November day, as I walked across the seminary campus, a thin young man came alongside me and, putting his arm over my shoulder, said, "Hi, Dr. Miller, I'm Zorro."

I looked into his eyes. He seemed about to break into tears.

"Look, Zorro," I said, "these are nervous days. Good men are being fired from the faculty over all sorts of issues of supposed liberalism and doctrinal error. Do you know what your letter did to me? Do you understand that I answered the letter not knowing if yours was an attempt to bless me or have me fired? Why would you do that to another fellow struggler? I don't get it. Shame on you!"

Now he did break into tears.

And I, being a sucker for weeping students, broke into tears too. What's to be done but to hug each other and promise we'd both try to be a little more understanding? His letter wasn't as cloak-and-dagger as I had assumed it to be. He was a young boy trying to figure out how to be true to the patriarchs in his defense of truth. If he hid out behind "Zorro," it was at least a clever way of saying,

"*Viva la Biblia!*" I was a neurotic old professor who was spending a lot of time shadowboxing with the devil, afraid that I might end up like my professor friend who had feminized the Spirit of God.

LEARNING FROM STUDENTS

Students have helped me remember that all of us are guilty of serving our hang-ups and renaming them as convictions. One day in class, we were wrangling through John Spong's book *Rescuing the Bible from the Fundamentalists.* A major portion of the book is given to his attempt to prove that Saint Paul struggled all his life with homosexuality. Spong is a better writer than a theologian, but his argument was forceful enough to have several students doubting the "hetero" nature of the apostle's sexuality. Most of us in the class were firmly committed to Paul's "hetero" sexual identity, but a few wanted to discuss it further. When the argument had reached its peak, one of the students in the class said, "Well, does it matter what his orientation was? The key thing is not what we are, but whether or not we yield to the temptations that can destroy us. The issue is not whether we are gay or straight. The point is," she went on, "that Paul—like all the rest of us—also had a sexual nature, and that like all good Christians, he had taken a stand against all sexuality outside of marital commitment."

It is statements like this where students sometimes teach teachers. Properly seen, any Christian's sexual indulgences outside of marriage are wrong. Case closed! I will never forget the clear lesson I learned from those I taught. The biblical case for sin does not dwell in any proposition that some particular sin is worse than the rest. We are, after all, all sinners. And the sins we resist are but gold in our Christian character.

In any seminary almost everybody believes that Jesus is coming again. Most believe he is coming soon. But some believe he is coming "right now." Many years before I got there, one student had actually leapt to his death from the central building of the seminary because God told him he would land unhurt. He landed dead, and thus lost his status as the campus prophet.

More recently the prophets have been a bit less dramatic. For instance, one day, just before chapel, a young friend of mine came running into my office with his trousers wet in front.

"Is that water?" I asked.

"It was before it went through my kidneys," he said, looking downcast.

"Well, what could possibly have caused you to wet yourself?"

"Well, I was standing at a urinal, whistling 'A Mighty Fortress Is Our God,' for men always look straight ahead and whistle at urinals, you know. Well, an excited man ran in and took the urinal beside mine. Then he reached over and put his arm around my shoulder, shaking me soundly and shouting, 'Jesus is coming again!' He just kept up this multitasking: of both wee-weeing and shouting 'Jesus is coming again!' He scared the wiss out of me, and I couldn't pee straight. I tell you, you just can't trust a premillenialist at a urinal. And now I'll have to miss chapel so I can go home and change clothes. He'd better hope Jesus comes before I get back to campus, 'cause if he's still here I'm going to beat the living daylights out of him!"

But most of the students I have known have been well-balanced and devoted to the call they each feel that God has given them. I think I liked them best in the seminary chapel. I loved to be among them when they were praising God. I loved the moments of revival when each of them seemed determined to affirm their commitment to God and to take their discipleship all the way to that special place they would be serving once their seminary experience was over.

In the fall of '96, we had a campus revival that was sweeping in its emotional power. Many students "got right" with God, and those who were right with God got even "righter"! The chapel was packed with nearly two thousand students, and they began to flow down the aisles in surrender. They shared their testimonies of sin they wanted purged from their lives.

You whose tradition keeps you from appreciating this kind of service, let me remind you that altars have been the places of cleansing and renewal that God has chosen to renovate his world. Altars are places where things die, that commitment may live. That day the service stretched from ten in the morning until four in the afternoon.

Many students confessed to broken home lives, to illicit affairs, to self-will. Others acknowledge their lackadaisical attitude toward the unevangelized, both in Texas and around the world. Somewhere among the hundreds of confessions—around one in the afternoon—one male student confessed to masturbation. Many an evangelical young man has been a bit naïve in this matter, generally believing that the truly born-again eschew the practice. Genesis 38:9, 10 calls this the sin of Onan, who spilled his seed on the ground and was struck dead by God. The threat of being struck dead is not big enough to keep Baptists from doing it, only from enjoying it. So the guilt that follows it began to bleed through several other confessions that afternoon. Several more confessed to masturbation, and it was a tad embarrassing that so many felt the need to say so. It was, of course, not a new revelation to most of the professors who realize that 90 percent of all young men do this, and the other 10 percent lie about it. But we gritted our teeth as some of them went on with their confessions. These confessions did not, of course, reveal anything new to me about the confessors, but it did leave me a bit reluctant to shake hands around the campus.

After the service, I told one or two of the young masturbators that there are some confessions that should be made privately to God. Further, I said that one should never confess publicly to more people than they have wronged. Even if they considered the practice odious to God, it is no interpersonal offense and it should be confessed in private, if at all. God, I have always found, is less offended by masturbation than evangelicals in general.

But the day was wonderful. I will always remember the students seeking to plant themselves firmly in the will of God and the vitality of altars where so many things change about us in so short a time. I must confess, I have relied on student prayers to get me through the most convoluted of times. When students pray in the power of their fresh relationships with God, it always seems to me I find worthy answers to my own needs.

The Little Saints

During the '93–'94 school year, I met regularly with a group of five young pastors, who besides their seminary studies and busy part-time churches, agreed to commit their Tuesday nights to a time of altar and prayers. We agreed to study the prayer habits of ten of Christianity's most influential saints, and thus embarked on a long pilgrimage of extra reading and quiet altar times in our homes. Out of that year of study I produced a book called *Walking with the Saints.* The saints we formally walked with in our readings were Augustine, Saint John of the Cross, Therese of Liseaux, etc. But the saints I learned to walk with were really students: Charley, Deron, David, James, and Chad. All of them are young ministers now, shepherding their own parishes, except for Chad, who has served for the past fifteen years in the Middle East. In a world where eight out of ten young ministers are no longer in the ministry ten years after their graduation, all five of these young men are still serving faithfully.

I used to pass Chad and his soon-to-be wife, Leah, on the campus in the spring and see them praying together and reading their Bibles, preparing themselves for the difficult parish they intended to plant in a Muslim milieu, somewhere just beyond their graduation. Even then I knew that I was the most fortunate of all men. That I should even be allowed to be with them in the same classroom was for me a symbol of my own superficiality. For I, who had paid no great price to serve the Lord, had been given the chance to teach those who really had committed all to keeping their commitment to Christ, in whatever realm he called them.

I felt the same way when I was conducting some prayer seminars among the fine Christian doctors in the country of Yemen. Martha Myers, one of those doctors, wrote me a letter after I had returned to the states. I knew her for a total of four days while I met with her colleagues in the hospital and prayed with her a few times from a guarded rooftop in Jibla. But I can still see her in her Ford Explorer, packed in tightly with Yemeni women, shrouded in black burqas. She loved them, cared for them, delivered their babies for four dollars, if they had that much cash, and less if they didn't. She wrote me a most conflicted letter, which I shall never forget, in which she sketched the character of those she served:

> Just because we worked together around the clock some days, ate together, fasted together, saved lives, lost patients . . . they have lied about us to the police, the courts . . . stolen personal and hospital goods, eaten in my home and come back later to rob it . . . Living here has made many things in the Bible real. Jesus came into a hostile environment . . . It must have hurt Jesus when he came into his own and his own received him not . . . He must have been aware of this, but still faithful to pray and love and care till the day he was betrayed and the last time he saw Judas.[16]

Ironically, Martha was assassinated by the very Muslims to whom she had shown nothing but kindness for so many years of her life. I have treasured her letter so many times since then.

Her death profoundly affected me. And yet I didn't think of her so much as I thought of Chad and Leah, serving in the same anti-American, anti-Christian world. And ever since I realized that Martha was safely in heaven, I have turned my prayers toward my students, who serve in a world that often hates them.

While I was visiting Martha, I was walking down the streets of Jibla, not far from the Christian hospital where so many valiant doctors and nurses were serving Muslim people. These Muslims needed and accepted their medical practice but despised their faith. A large group of Yemenis gathered about us as we walked along, and began throwing rocks at us who were there temporarily serving as missionaries. Someone asked me at a missionary conference what I did as I was being pelted with stones. I simply replied, "I just prayed that the rocks would hit the other missionaries." It wasn't perhaps the most charitable of prayers, but I've never much liked getting hit by rocks. The stones reinforced my commitment to love those who don't love me, for my enemies are not God's enemies.

My students understood this. Because of them I do too.

I could only pray for Chad and Leah, and this man who was once young and sat in my classes as though I had something to teach him turned out to be the teacher and I the all-too-reluctant student. Chad is paying the price, ever in love with Christ and ever in danger. It is for him I include as a part of my prayers for him the words of Robert W. Service:

Send not your foolish and feeble
For I harry them sore.
Send me men girt for combat,
Men who are grit to the core.

And I wait for the man who will win me,
I will not be won in a day.
I will not be won by weaklings, subtle, suave and mild.
But by men with the hearts of Vikings
And the simple faith of a child.

Desperate, strong and resistless,
Unthrottled by fear or defeat.
Them will I gild with my treasure,
Them will I glut with my meat.[17]

It is even as the martyr Jim Elliott wrote in his journal:

He is no fool who gives what he cannot keep
    to gain what he cannot lose.

These are my students.
Their commitment is their gift to God.
Their commitment is also their gift to me.

SIXTEEN

Good-bye, Mr. Chips

T. S. Eliot remarked that when he was old he would wear his trousers rolled and wondered if he'd ever dare to eat a peach. Jenny Josephson said she would brazenly wear purple. And most of these days—at the current writing of this book—I, too, wonder what I shall do to declare my individualism now that I am at what many people declare to be "old." Dr. Seuss lamented that at the end of every old-age physical, when we have been *properly pilled*, all of the hospital forms had to be *properly filled*, so that our heirs could be *properly billed*.

BEING OLD IS AN OPTION

The hazards of old age are many. Still, "old age" is an odd phrase, really a redundancy. Getting old is not an option; seeming old is. Nonetheless, it is a term that many people want to force upon you—a state of mandatory acceptance.

Seminary students, for the most part, avoid the excessive lifestyles of their peers, whose eccentricities offend them and me. Young people with shaved heads in low-slung pants and butterfly tattoos that show just above their rear cheeks see me—I'm sure—as a troglodyte. If I were not such a devoted Christian professor, I would tell them to dress better before they start looking down on the Social Security crowd. Near Christmas, my white beard causes little children to look upon me adoringly with that *Miracle-on-Thirty-Fourth-Street* gaze that tells me we'd be friends if we had the time. And then the late teen, gothic starers with their pierced lips, noses, and navels look at me as though I'm the one who's culturally out of step and their own metal-studded faces are the way God intended the race to be. But my students across the years have served me in ways that affirm me rather than rebuke me.

This past summer I decided to retire. It was not a step I wanted to take, but I was seventy-one, and while I was not yet drooling during a lecture, I feared that I would go on too long and I might not recognize that I was drooling during my teaching. Teaching past the edge of one's effectiveness is a common sin of old-but-reluctant-to-admit-it professors.

I had been living in two modes since I was fifty-five—the date when AARP kicks in—and I have been enjoying senior rates at the movies for more than fifteen years. I always get 10 percent off at motels, even the nice ones, where I stay. Club 55 at Whataburger has given me a thousand glasses of free iced tea over the past decade and a half, and McDonald's has served me a thousand cups of senior coffee so cheaply that I feel like I am abusing the system when I ask for two creams. And though I am now awaiting a colonoscopy (for which there is no senior discount), it is just routine; I don't expect anything to be wrong. But then I'm an optimist, whose half-empty glass has always been half-full. My pacemaker doesn't make my garage door go up; in fact, I don't have a pacemaker. My triglycerides are high (who knew I had them?). My cholesterol is moderated by Vytorin. And I'll leave you guessing about whether or not I pop Viagra.

As a lover of students and a lifelong professor, I read Ecclesiastes and *Good-bye, Mr. Chips* a lot. The writer of Ecclesiastes was a preacher (not a very happy one) who got old and writes with a tone that is a bit crotchety. And Mr. Chips was a professor who allowed his fellow teachers to catch him at the art of growing old.

Growing old gracefully! What an art it is! *Gracefully* is the word, the adverb we usually apply, but *gracefully* is an inadequate adverb, especially when you think about things like Preparation H and Dentu-Cream. While I struggle to honestly own the word *gracefully,* I continually read both Ecclesiastes and *Mr. Chips.*

Ecclesiastes reminds me:

Remember your Creator in the days of your youth,
    before the days of trouble come
        (*Now comes the allegory of aging*)
and the years approach when you will say,
"I find no pleasure in them"—
        (*The AARP years have arrived and you can't afford*
        a condo in Ft. Lauderdale)
before the sun and the light
and the moon and the stars go dark,
        (*The bifocals won't focal*)
and the clouds return after the rain:
when the keepers of the house tremble,
        (*Your biceps have slipped to the underside of the arm*)
and the strong men stoop,
when the grinders cease because
they are few,
        (*You sleep with your teeth in a cup beside your bed*)
and those looking through the windows grow dim;
        (*You squint at fine print*)
when the doors to the street are closed
and the sound of grinding fades;
        (*Your teeth are too few to gnash*)

when men are afraid of heights
  (*You hire a roofer*)
and of dangers in the streets;
  (*You never go through the bad parts of town anymore*)

and desire no longer is stirred.
  (*You're beyond the help of Cialis*)
Then man goes to his eternal home
and mourners go about the streets.
  (*Your friends say, He sure looks natural, don't he.*
  What time's the funeral dinner?)
(Eccl. 12:1–5, asides mine)

Notes on Growing Old

Mr. Chips offers me the best of counsel as I remain committed to students even in my post-seminary years. Mr. Chips also found it hard to leave his students for no other reason than he was growing old.

What a great joke, this growing old—but a sad joke, too, in a way. And as Chips sat by his fire with autumn gales rattling the windows, waves of humor and sadness swept over him very often till tears fell so that when Mrs. Wickett came in with his cup of tea she did not know whether he had been laughing or crying. And neither did Chips himself.[18]

The great thing about Mr. Chips is that he retained his student popularity to the very last. I want to be like that—or as much so as possible. On one front, it looks like I'm succeeding. I seem to be popular with my students, maybe because the word is out that I always buy lunch. Being a teetotaler, I never pay for anybody's drinks. But I like thinking that it isn't the fact that I'm a cheap date that makes me popular. I think students genuinely want to be around me. Oh, they don't want Barbara and me to double-date with them, but, for the moment, they want to be with me, because . . . well, I'm a survivor.

Those few people who survived the *Titanic* were popular for years. Until the day they died, they told and retold the long tale of their horrible icy night in the North Atlantic. So students come to me, in effect asking about my affair with the *Titanic* of the gospel ministry. "How did you make it through, Prof? In an occupation where so many perish, you lived. How? Can I?"s

"Yes," I always assure them, then pointing to my wrinkled head I say, "but this is how you will look when you get through with a lifetime in the ministry. To see the outcome of the *Titanic*, you must have someone paint your portrait, with your fair face full of wrinkles, leaving off your hair and teeth. You must learn the art of the refugee. How to live on less money than anyone else in your graduating class ever made. All of those awards you got for being the person most likely to succeed, you should burn immediately before you get too attached to them and the lie they represent. But you don't need to eat worms to try and become humble; your deacons and elders will help you with that. You also don't need to worry about crucifying yourself for the sake of the cross; your deacons and elders are surprisingly good at crucifixions too. But in spite of all of this, you will laugh more spontaneously and cry more easily than others you room with in the rest home."

Old men are the most maudlin. I find myself crying during the national anthem. Sometimes I don't know if these tears rise from deep patriotism, or the fact that in a world of rappers, Internet pornography, and television preaching, maybe someone ought to cry once in a while for the values we have lost. I play old Broadway on the piano, as a retreat from Snoop Dogg. I catch myself singing hymns when I'm alone. It's my way of missing organs and pianos in church. I am in a sense a man between worlds, the world that's being born and the one that's dying.

Mr. Chips could not adjust to the rapidly changing world of technology either. One of the wonderful developments in silent cinema—Mr. Chips's segment of history—was the simple addition of an organ to the movie itself. Not much of technomarvel as great advances go, but it was still a large advancement for Mr. Chips. It was just one more evidence that the world was changing faster than he could ingest.

THE CHANGING WORLD

"Have you been to the new cinema, sir?

"I went with my people the other day.

Quite a grand affair for a small place like Brookfield.

They've got a Wurlitzer."

"And what—umph—on earth is a Wurlitzer?"

"It's an organ, sir—a cinema organ."

"Dear me . . . I've seen the name on the hoardings, but

I always—umph—imagined—it must be some kind

of—umph—sausage."[19]

Mr. Chips is typical, I think, of those who have lived for a long time.

The world changes so rapidly that we barely have time to adjust to one nuance before we have to start working on the next one. I am seven years older than nylon hose, eight years older than steering column gearshifts, twelve years older than ballpoint pens, fifteen years older than automatic transmissions, a couple of decades older than power steering, and thirty-three years older than the first moon landing. I listen to the Andrews sisters a lot and wonder how popular rappers ever steamrollered over such talent. It's crass to say so, but I enjoyed Ronald Reagan's funeral. It was the patriotism and all the hymns played by the Marine band and fireworks and people singing "God Bless America." You miss that kind of thing in the political morass of "kill the president!" and the ACLU hunting down the Baby Jesus and knocking down his little manger right out of the city park.

I am fourteen years older than electric bills and thirteen years older than grain combines. I have a friend who simply waves her hand in front of her Toyota car door and the fool thing unlocks itself. I recently received my e-mail at Cambridge, UK, on an American phone made in Korea, purchased in Dixie, and billed to me from Chicago. The nation is growing so rapidly. When I was nine years old, there were only 119 million people living in America. Now there are 300 million people, and they all shop at my local Wal-Mart, plug the register lines, and go to the courthouse to get their car tags at the very same moment I go to get mine. Who tells them when I'm going?

But it's mostly church that has changed. Jesus shows up occasionally on our JumboTrons at church, but he doesn't look as Christian as he did in my youth. The little Pentecostal church I attended when I was young had a picture of Jesus wistfully looking out over Olivet at evening. At that time I had no idea Jesus was a Jew, and except for the beard and the purple and white toga, he looked pretty much like the last Pentecostal evangelist we had in for a revival. He was too sedate to really fit our worship style, which was fairly boisterous and sometimes athletic. But now, he has stepped down from his purple-toga esteem. Now he simply presides over our jazz bands and praise teams.

In the current round of worship wars, I find that my students worship the same Christ that I do, and yet he is not the same Christ. Their Jesus seems usually to have opted for a trapset and turned his back on the pipe organ.

Every generation has its way of changing things around to fit the times. But for my part I was perfectly content to sing the songs the church was singing three hundred years ago. The words don't always fit the times. Take the line from "Come Thou Fount of Every Blessing" that goes, "Here I raise mine Ebenezer, hither by thy help I'm come." I love this line. I sang it years before I had any idea what an ebenezer was. This was also how I felt about "Beulah Land," "O Zion Haste," and "Lord Sabaoth His Name." I particularly liked the nautical hymns: "Haven of Rest," "O Safe to the Rock That Is Higher Than I," "Ship Ahoy," and "I Praise God for the Lighthouse."

Or . . .

I was sinking, deep in sin far from the peaceful shore,
Very deeply stained within, sinking to rise no more,

When the Master of the sea heard my despairing cry,
From the waters lifted me now safe am I.[20]

Or . . .

I have an anchor that keeps the soul.
Steadfast and sure while the billows roll,
Fastened to the Rock which cannot move,
Bounded firm and deep by the Savior's love.[21]

Or . . .

Jesus lover of my soul, let me to thy bosom fly,
While the nearer waters roll, while the tempest still is night
Guide me, O my Savior guide, till the storms of life be past,
Safe into the harbor guide, O receive my soul at last.[22]

I was fourteen before I ever saw an ocean, and I am still deathly afraid of them. I guess you can't be terrorized by hymns about drowning all through your life and not be somewhat afraid of oceans the first time you actually go to sea. Whatever fears I might have escaped in singing so often about the ocean were firmly fixed by the movie *Jaws*. Lucky for me sharks didn't show up in Pentecostal hymns. At least I never had to worry about being ripped apart while I waited for the Captain of my soul to come and rescue me.

Now I can almost hear my younger students say, "The worship war is over. We won! Fling away your hymnals, Prof, and all your old-fashioned religion. Gaze upon our JumboTrons and be saved!"

They are, of course, wrong. Worship wars are never won. Neither are they ever over. For just behind those who think they've won is the next generation, who have already begun to dress Jesus in an even newer rigging and will jig to even bigger amps and brighter strobe lights and foggier smoke machines!

But the worship wars are not the only place we disagree. Fewer young men and women are going into the pulpit ministry. Seminaries seem to have about the same number of students as ever, but only a fraction of them now intend to become preachers.

Further, the rise of the Emergent Church, a largely independent evangelical movement, has usurped the shrinking vitality of the church I knew in adolescence. The Emergent Church "emerged" in the wake of dying evangelical enthusiasm, and new congregations were born in community halls, abandoned filling stations, and defunct warehouses. But they emerged with a worship style that each of them believed was unique, and yet an odd sameness possessed each of their egotistic claims of each one being "the church of what's happening now." Only a fraction (some say as few as 3 percent) of these church plants survive or thrive, and the churches that survive all look very much the same. They all have a fondness for black inside walls and graphics, JumboTrons, and soupy sermons that rarely address the huge social problems that face the culture. They are, for the most part, serving an unattached dysfunctional sort of clientele, who have neither sampled the richness of Christian tradition, nor the long history of the church.

But the few emergent pastors who do succeed, often succeed numerically so well that they cause the pastoral seminary graduates to have a lesser view of themselves. These less entrepreneurial students find their own self-esteem inadequate to help them survive the terrors of graduating and becoming shepherds of small flocks. Many young seminary graduates wonder why they can't succeed like the emergent whizzes across town who are thriving in a redecorated warehouse. Why can't they draw the Rose Bowl traffic that jams the interstate exits of their cities? In the current large-church milieu, to be small is a curse that causes a huge drop-out rate among young pastors.

One of my favorite young ministry students was refused ordination for defending women in ministry at his hearing. He wrote me a letter, part of which read, "Dear Professor, My denomination has refused to ordain me, and I am feeling most disconsolate. Please tell your young students that if they are lucky enough to survive their ordinations, they may join the ranks of those who don't make it ultimately. Tell them that 80 percent of them who become pastors will not be in the ministry ten years after their ordinations . . ." The letter is much longer than this. But since I received it five years ago, I have read it to all my classes. I want each of them to know what they are up against as they begin their ministries.

The Battle Lands of Learning

From my first years as a professor I have tried to work within the institution to make the ministry as noninstitutional as it can be. No teacher can teach without constantly dealing with what's going on in the institutional milieu that provides the teacher's salary. In this sense there is probably no such thing as academic freedom. Many of us who work in denominational schools know that a huge priority is to find acceptance among those who own or direct the schools. Denominations at civil war put a particular stress on their professors, who must teach while volleys of doctrinal fire explode all around them. There is always a war going on. Mr. Chips served during an actual war, World War I, in which the bombs were literally falling.

> And once, on a night full of moonlight,
> the air-raid warning given
> while Chips was taking his lower fourth in Latin . . .
> So he went on with his Latin, speaking a little louder
> amid the reverberating crashes of the guns and the shrill
> whine of anti-aircraft shells . . .
> Afterward they learned that five bombs had fallen
> in and around Brookfield, the nearest of them
> just outside the School grounds.
> Nine persons had been killed.[23]

May I as a professor say right up front: I love our denomination. However, it has been hard to see colleagues disappear like Columbian peons, silently eradicated by death squads in the night. Shortly before I left the faculty of my first seminary appointment, it was my privilege to spend a couple of hours with Dr. W. A. Criswell, the long-ago patriarch of our once-all-together denomination. I asked him if he thought the denomination would split, and he replied wryly, "No, I don't think so. Jello don't split," he said. And it's probably true. No one can doubt the fraying that is now going on around the edges of our long-ago, lost togetherness.

I had not been at the seminary for more than three years when one of my favorite colleagues was fired by the board of trustees. It was a sad day for me, for I very much liked the man. He was my friend and attentive to my every need as a professor. His firing was my cruel entry into the denominational war. He was accused of being a liberal, but I know for a fact he was not. He subscribed to biblical authority and believed in the Virgin Birth, the resurrection of Christ, and the Savior's imminent second coming. He could by such definition have never been a liberal.

He was replaced within a very short time by another president, one apparently more to the trustees' liking. The new president had not been in office long when an artist was hired to paint his portrait to hang in the school rotunda, where hung all those who had previously served as president. I am not particularly opposed to having one's portrait painted to be hung in whatever worthy niche is to be found in the hallowed halls of graduate schools. But this picture always arrested my attention. Each time I passed it in the rotunda I studied it. It came to stand for all that was evil in how good men die and others come to replace them. Denominations generally put up pictures of people who run them, and often their lives are not as worthy as the lives of those uncelebrated students who pass their pictures in the hallways as they leave to take their places in the dangerous world of ministry and service.

Shortly after the new portrait went up, I happened to be at Columbia International University in South Carolina. I was passing through the hallways when I came into a large room of that school. In this room I noticed that its walls were covered with pictures of men and women. One of the university students happened to pass the room at the very moment I stood surveying those pictures.

"Are these pictures of your past presidents?" I asked.

"Presidents!" he almost shouted, as though I had insulted him. "Hardly presidents. These are *the important people* who have graduated from this school. Every picture in this room is not just a graduate but a martyr."

"A martyr!" I found myself nearly shouting back.

"Yeah, man, a martyr."

"You mean every person pictured here actually died for Jesus in some part of the world under some kind of persecution?"

"That's exactly what I mean. Go read the tags."

I did. Beside each picture was a tiny tag that told where the person had died and what was the price they had paid for their service.

"This is remarkable," I said. I thought of the new picture recently hung in our rotunda. "At our school we put up pictures of our presidents."

"Presidents! At our school we put up pictures of our martyrs."

Southern Baptists have had a few rather notable martyrs, but we hardly ever mention them. Day by day, we celebrate our denominational administrators, and when All Saints' Day comes in November—when other traditions celebrate those who have died for Jesus—we are a strangely silent lot. But God celebrates those children who studied, learned, and then left and died. With those I had the good fortune to teach, I count myself both unworthy and very blessed.

My whole entrance to the Christian work occurred right after Jim Elliott passed "Through Gates of Splendor," with that odd piece of paper in his blood-soaked pocket that said, "He is no fool who gives what he cannot keep to gain what he cannot lose." So I esteem the lives of those I touched—whose lives were taken from them to set them singing in a higher world. In this realm of light the only administration is the throne. There the only official delegates are the twenty-four elders. Portraits, I think, do not exist in that realm. They fade so quickly in exalted light.

MIDWIFING THE KINGDOM

Professors, it seems to me, are those who midwife the Kingdom. They don't create the children. They don't even procreate the Kingdom. They just happen to be present in the room where preachers and missionaries are born. One of my favorite lines from *Good-bye Mr. Chips* comes when old Chips overhears a colleague putting down his childless status.

"Pity, pity, that he never had any children?"
As soon as Chips hears it he replies:
"But I have you know . . . I have . . . thousands of 'em . . . thousands of 'em . . . and all boys."[24]

I suppose, in a way, I have clutched as my own a thousand students who came through my classes and took their places in the service of Christ. In fact, every interesting chapter of my life for the past nineteen years would bear a student's name. And the gifts of esteem they have given me have borne me up through a thousand needy moments.

At the top of my list of students who have given me the gift of well-being is my longtime friend Dean Register—now Dr. Dean Register! I met him during an assigned area of a Ph.D. seminar when he was assigned by the seminary to critique my preaching. This was thirty years ago. But from his student days I was never so much his teacher as he was mine. His love of poetry and the arts brought our ministries into close rapport. But it was watching him love God that often rebuked my casual spirituality and taught me the fire that I left lying beneath the ashes of my devotion. Every act of worthy grace that has proceeded from my life was somehow born in his value system. I am older than he, but he is the student who will preach my funeral (or I, his) when the time comes. I want a student to bear me up to God in the last evaluation of my life, and he is the student I want.

Joe Woodell taught me to see Walt Whitman in a new way. Whitman's tribute to Lincoln was his postassassination cry of "Captain, my Captain." No one who has read the poem can escape being moved by Whitman's tribute. The John Keating character in the film *The Dead Poets Society* was portrayed as a unique professor who loved both poetry and students and lived to bring the two of them together. The climax of the movie was a wonderful moment when all of Keating's students stood on their desks and affirmed their professor by crying "O Captain, my Captain!"

Joe Woodell, who is now Dr. Joe Woodell, Ph.D., was once just an ordinary student whose friendship was good for a cup of coffee every morning. But his great gift came to me when on a nameless Thursday, the question came up in class, "Prof, do you think there are actually teachers like John Keating?"

"Of course," I said to my students, "but such an exaltation happens only in the movies. No student ever loved a professor so much, that he would stand upon a desk and cry 'Captain, my Captain!'"

The words were barely out of my mouth, when Joe jumped up on his desk, clamped his fist over his heart, and cried, "Captain, my Captain!"

It remains for me a warm experience that is locked in the safety deposit box of my heart, and will remain there forever. Clayton Speed, one of my students at Beeson, never passed me in the halls without quoting the same Whitman line.

During one epidemic flu time, I went over to the campus infirmary to get a flu shot. Mike Miller, a private pilot who had abandoned his wealthy status and solid income to study for the ministry, was talking to me as we walked along together. He had sold a lovely home and taken a warehouser's job in Fort Worth, where the seminary was located. Like most sacrificing students I have known, he never complained of his financial woes, and generally was so cheerful no one would have known he was financially against the wall, trying to make a living while he studied theology.

We walked into the clinic and I filled out the paperwork necessary to get my ten-dollar flu shot. "Why are you getting a flu shot?" Mike asked.

"Mike, I have to. My schedule demands it. Every weekend I'm forever traveling around America, flying here and there. I'm just plain busy. I can't afford to get sick—even for a week or two."

"I know what you mean," he said. "I've got two jobs and two kids. I'm so financially strapped that if I got sick even one week, I'd have to go to debtors' prison, and I have no idea how I'd ever take care of my family."

Suddenly my shame-colored face brightened to a neon red. What made me think I was the only one who had a busy schedule? I actually could afford to endure the flu better than Mike. Tears came to my eyes and I turned to Mike and said, "Has anyone ever bought you a flu shot?"

No one had.

I did.

Now Mike has a large church right here in Birmingham where I work. He also has a doctor's degree. He could buy me and sell me, but he remains that same wonderful man of God whose sense of Franciscan denial has made him one of the most sacrificial pastors I have ever known. We will always be friends, but I think our friendship began with a flu shot in 1994.

Ray Still is a student of my life, and while I never had him in seminary class, he declares I am his mentor. Pity he has such a low standard. Lucky for me he counts me as a mentor.

Then there's Deron Spoo, who since his senior year at the university has been my friend. He was my grader, my mentee, my research assistant, and my student in I don't know how many classes for four years. I preached in his pulpit during a recent study leave he took at Oxford. Deron named a son after both me and his real father, Jerome. While I feel sorry for little Calvin Jerome, his youngest son, I am proud that Deron so esteemed me. I will keep at the center of my heart the day both I and his real father stood in his huge church in Tulsa. There were two old men, Calvin and Jerome, holding a little baby and dedicating him to the keeping of God. Rabindindrath Tagore was right: it does take a village to raise a child, and for one shining moment I was chief of the village.

Bryant Bush was in my village. So was Brian Gill, a gifted writer still looking for a publisher who can see his gift.

Then there's Lance Sawyer, who is the best storyteller I have ever had as a student and the most creative man in the pulpit I have ever known. When he finishes a pulpit tale, God has but to show up for a moment and all who are spiritually needy hurry out past the story-teller to do God's will. I first heard him preach in a homiletics class, and was blown away by his knowledge of storytelling and his ability to sweep his hearers into a mood of intensity and joy.

Then there's Ralph West, another doctoral student of mine, who shared so much of England with me. He also has the same literary heroes I have: Jane Austen, T. S. Eliot, Shakespeare, and the like. He has a huge church but a small demeanor, and has never ceased to trea-sure our friendship—a friendship that began in class. Ralph is widely published and much sought after as a keynoter for various meetings. But his finest asset is his sensitivity of soul. He now has his own home near his church, but before he bought it, he bought one for his mother. When I asked him why he bought her one first, he said, "All through my life, besides Christ, she has been the one constant in my desire to love and serve God. We lived in what white folks call the ghettos all of our lives. Mama kept me from knowing how poor we were, but with her around we never felt poor. I promiseed God that if I ever had enough money to buy my own house, I'd buy one first for my mama. And then later if I could afford to buy a second house, I'd buy one for myself. Now Mama and I both have houses of our own."

Jim Tee graduated with honors from our school and is serving in a small Dixie town. He is a no-nonsense man with a high inten-tion of freeing the rural South of racial prejudice. Jim pastors a very small church—white, very white—where two little black children showed up recently. One of the elders grew incensed that he would allow the children in the church.

"Well, now you've done it, pastor! You've allowed two little black children in our church. What are you going to do if they try to come back next week?"

"I'm going to pick them up for Sunday school in my own car, so they won't have to walk so far."

His elder was incensed, but not Jim; he is taller than even the most frightening of deacons and so he is hard to threaten. There's always the Klan who could try to get even, but he's taller than most of them too. He could be fired—it happens to a lot of pastors—but right is right with Jim, and getting fired for the right reasons is as important as getting a raise in salary for all the wrong ones.

Jim often calls me on the phone and we talk. I was his teacher; he was my student. But now we are colleagues. And that's how profs and students end up—colleagues. But not really. That can never be. Just as fathers and sons can never end up "just" friends. In the best relationships they remain fathers and sons for the rest of their lives. So it is with teachers and students. The categories are lifelong and they are wonderful categories indeed.

At a retirement luncheon, Garrett Irby said, "Prof, you've been our teacher for three years, and next year you won't be on the campus anymore." He paused and then went on, "What in the world are we going to do without you!" Still, as I walked out of my last graduation processional, I glanced back and I could see them—all the students. They gave me a great reason to get up every morning. They were my lectures and lunchtimes. They were my counselors and yet they wanted to learn my art. They were my raison d'etre. They gave me more than I could give back. They loved me, and the romance born across a lectern is wonderful. For the better part of two decades, they caused me to see Jesus in all they were and all they hoped to be. When my last commencement ceremony was over, I walked out into the open sunlight outside the Jefferson County Arena, I slipped out of my academic regalia, and for a moment I thought about the students I was losing. I felt an obstinate tear run down my face. I echoed Garrett's question: "What in the world am I going to do without you!"

SEVENTEEN

The God of What's Left

IT IS ALWAYS HARD TO SAY WHETHER OR NOT MEMOIRS SHOULD BE written, but if they need to be, they must fit into that small window of time when you are old enough to still remember what should be said and young enough to be free of dementia and other hindrances that eliminate hindsight. So it is with me in my seventy-first year.

Kiss Good-bye Each Time You Leave the House 'Cause You Just Never Know

People should make preparation to die, and I am not talking just about being sure we've called Jesus Lord so we can find the gates swinging open when we get there. There are the other things. I am convinced that Barbara and I must live with gusto until it is time for one of us to say good-bye. In case we have to say it with too little warning, we ought to say it every day. A kiss at midnight is never an interruption to those who are trying to make their final memories a benediction. And *I love you*, just before we start for the grocery store, is crucial. Why? Many a man has had a heart attack picking up a head of cabbage and putting it in a shopping cart. Who knew you could die between the radishes and the grapefruits? I am trying to cover my contingencies. I knew of a man who clutched his chest and died, and all he said as he departed was "Holy cow!" Terrible last words. He should have said, "I love you, my darling. I'll be waiting for you on the other side." One of the most terrible epitaphs ever inscribed on a headstone was, "I told you I was sick!" It was obviously written by a man with more of a need to be right than loving.

Once when I was forty-six, in a hotel in San Antonio, I had an attack of acid reflux. I had never had such an attack before. I rolled over and gasped my last to Barbara, "I love you, but would you please call 911. I'm about to buy the farm."

"I love you too," she said, "but you're not having a heart attack. Call 911 yourself, and quit eating so much just before bedtime." It was a good diagnosis, but the important thing was that she kissed me before she went back to sleep, indicating that in case she was wrong, and I *was* buying the farm, she would have at least kissed me before I shipped out to the morgue to get my toe tag.

One of these nights when I gasp at midnight it probably will not be acid reflux. Then I will go on. The same is, of course, to be said for her. Both of us now live with that evil day dogging us. What pair of lifelong lovers hasn't? We've not been sick much in our lives. In spite of the three thousand pounds we have lost on various diets, we still maintain a reasonable weight, fluctuating halfway between our dream weight and our fear of obesity. But no one outruns the undertaker in every footrace, and so we are doing our best to live wise but free of fear.

Certainly there are two important questions anyone should have as they begin the final chapter of their memoirs. These are questions of real import.

First, what would you do differently if you could do it all again?

Second, what are you doing to be sure that you are a good steward of the years you have left? Let me launch into question one first.

What Would I Do Differently
If I Could Do It All Over Again?

I would put more emphasis on being a better husband and father. To the church or the university I would whip out a lot more noes, and a lot more yesses to my family. I would eradicate almost all of the "Daddy's-too-busies," and the "later, darlings," from my vocabulary. If the church suddenly came up with a critical meeting on circus night, I'd go to the circus.

I'd Celebrate My Mother in Her Presence

If I could live life all over again, I would celebrate my mother audibly and publicly much more than I did. She was a simple woman whose humility kept her from seeing just how great she was. This adherence to her modesty I would shatter with the sledgehammer of praise. How would I do this?

Her hands were so chapped in winter and her knuckles were so red. I would rush at the December winds. I would chop the wood, and I would carry the water. And she would be the queen of my intention. I would write her a check for all the times she struggled to keep our family together. I would stay up with her all through those nights she never slept because the pain of losing my brother Dickie stabbed at her well-being with empty, cold insomnia.

When she came home from the laundry, with her hair limp about her beautiful face from wringing hot clothes through steaming vats of bleach, I would kiss her home. And I would make sure she knew that the eleven dollars she made from her week of killing effort was stored as gold in the vaults of heaven. I would walk her to work in the morning and carry her lunch, and meet her when the day was over to tell her that I loved her. At the conclusion of each day, I would ask her if anyone had been mean to her that day. If anyone had maltreated her, I would get their address and visit them with an axe at midnight. I would be fiercely protective of her. For every time when I had made life hard for her, I would do seven years of penance.

Forgive me for assuming she is a part of the great cloud of witness in Hebrews 12. I often ask the Lord when he passes her at the corner of Gold Street and Platinum Boulevard to tell her how much I love her. I know my fellow scholars tell me that mothers don't really make it into that great cloud of witnesses; this is a more august gathering reserved for people like Moses and Jeremiah. I appreciate the Hebrew patriarchs, but my affection rests on an Oklahoma matriarch who taught me that humanity is the porch of divinity. I'm counting on Jesus to get the word through to her, until I get up there with her and can squander a millennium or two telling her just how great she was. Is.

One time when I was a boy, she gave me a dime and I walked to Kresses Five and Ten and bought her a little glass bowl and gave it to her. She got tears in her eyes and then she grew firm. "Son, that money was for you! I wanted you to spend it on yourself! Shame on you," she rebuked me. I remember her rebuke to this day. But could I live that day again, I would rebuke her right back, "No, shame on you! You've nothing of your own. I have received a million things from you. Take this crummy little gift; use it or shatter it, I care not. But my life will yield for you in years to come all that I can afford. Every day you object to my gifts will be as Christmas. There will be more gifts. For it is God's will that all who give must learn to receive. Your rebukes are as nothing to me, Mama."

I would be there all the more for the woman who was always there for me.

When I graduated from college, she was proud and she was there. The chandeliers in that pitiful graduation chapel envied the radiance of her face. When I got my master's degree, she was there, and she stood tall beside me for the photo I now treasure. When I got my doctor's degree, she was there, and I realize that she, who had no degrees, was the progenitor of all mine. At each of those occasions, had I the chance to do it all again, I would say, "Mama, it was not from my professors that I learned Dickens, it was from you. It was not from them that I learned to apply Scripture. These mentors came far too late to serve me well. It was you, you, you! They were as nothing to me. Mama, you were the teacher. Only you never knew it, 'cause I didn't tell you."

I can hardly wait for heaven! Boy, have I got some catching up to do!

I'd Build a Monument on Golgotha

Another thing I would do if I had it all to do over again is that I would build myself a replica of Golgotha, an Everest of a Calvary, so high that the empty cross at its summit would be hidden by the mists of sheer altitude. I would keep a shrine at the top of my giant Calvary, with no sugary idols where the dying was done. I'd have no icons there, for the living Jesus who has been the central icon of my life would meet me there. When he came at sunrise, I would be there with the bread. And when he came at dusk, I would be there with the wine. And I would reverse my prayer life. I wouldn't talk to him so much; I would listen more. I still wonder after a lifetime of chatty prayers, if I had not been so noisy in his presence, would he have told me more from his giant heart?

I would ask him why Saint Julian prayed to receive the three wounds. And if her reasons were valid, I would crave those wounds in my effort to be a clone of her Lord and mine. At the summit of my Calvary, I would ask the Lord why Padre Pio, in my teenage years, bled from his hands with the stigmata. I would want to know how it was that Saint Paul crucified himself, and why that was so all-important. And I would want to know why Frederick Faber said, "They love thee little if at all who do not fear thee much, If love is thine attraction Lord, Fear is thy very touch."

I would have a bold love, but it would be filled with terror.

I would rise each morning and ascend my private Calvary. I would ask my poverty-owning Savior why he paid so great a price for our friendship and it never cost me more. I would ask him what he really did that day when he took the pain from my life. I would ask him how atonement works! I would insist on knowing how he healed me of the hurt he could not avoid himself on that day he stood naked before Rome with a reed in his hand.

Who would not love such a Savior?

But who could not love him more? Who would not choose, if they could, to pay attention to every gift of sacrifice they might have given him? I would. Not so I could glory in my giving, but because only when I have given do I become fully human. Beneath my giant Calvary I would build a thousand little altars where I'd give like Jesus and not count the sacrifice.

I would build one of those altars on the railway platform in Agra, India. I was alone there one hot day, and all the days are hot in India. I approached an ice-cream vendor on the platform and purchased a six-ounce paper tub of strawberry ice cream. As I broke the cellophane seal on the cup, just the tiny, almost inaudible rush of air summoned fifty children to gather all about me.

It was an odd sensation.

These little ones looked up at me with a sea of wide, engulfing brown eyes. I stuck the wooden spoon in the ice cream and was all prepared to take a bite when, suddenly, I saw the wrongness of it all. Then I reached to hand one of them the untouched ice cream. But a flagging count of fifty little brown arms reached up to receive it. Since all of them wanted it, I stepped between my gift and the crowd, and handed it to one beautiful little brown boy. A beautiful little boy who might have been my own Indian grandson. He reached for the gift in a kind of wonder. It was as though he had won the Agra Lottery. He gave me a warm look of appreciation. But his look did not last long. Suddenly it looked as though the other children, who were as hungry as he, might tear it away from him. In but a moment, his look of gratitude turned to terror. Then with one giant surge of energy he leapt into his mother's filthy sari. He was safe. Then both his mother and he looked at me with a look I shall keep in the safety deposit bank of my memory for as long as I live.

I'd Babysit

Could I pass this way again I would take seriously a little girl in our church with whom I was hugging and laughing and having a great time, when suddenly she stopped my teasing her and asked point-blank, "Dr. Miller, do you ever do babysitting?" I told her I was too busy. But if I had it all to do over, I'd do more babysitting.

In general I'd take more time for children and perhaps less for deacons. I remember the funeral of a little girl in our church. Her father was in the military, and she was taken so suddenly from us. At her funeral I can remember a huge amount of consternation because there was so much military brass present. It was a terribly overwrought occasion. When the final passing-of-the-casket came, at the end of the service, I can remember two or three generals who approached the casket for the final moment of respect. I had been hugging most of the people who passed the form of the silent child in tears. As each of them passed, I reached out and touched them, or stood with my arm around them as they paid their last respects. But when the first of the air force generals passed, I was suddenly stiff. I didn't know whether or not it was proper to hug a general. Do you do that sort of thing?

In a moment of indecision, the general reached out and hugged me and held me as he wept. It wasn't just a hug he gave me. He gave me permission to hug all the military brass in the retinue. He gave me the license to hug every little girl I would ever meet. And so I did. And it was good and it was right. But I know now if I had it all to do over again, I would hug all generals with such exuberance they would eye me with homophobic suspicion.

But what of question number two?

What Am I Doing to Be Sure That I Am a Good Steward of the Years I Have Left?

First, I am determined that this question will not drive me. One thing I do not want for the years I have left is to be so preoccupied with an agenda that I will not have time for anything but the drive.

Years before John Piper addressed the subject, I wrote of "Christian Hedonism." Alas, he is far more famous, so I lost all credit for the quote. Still, I said it first, and I am determined that Christian hedonism will be the code of my life. I have written a good many books. The world must decide if they were worth the effort. What I have to decide is, "Was the drive that produced these books a strangling agenda that kept me from living life to the fullest, or should I have written less and lived more?"

I ask this because I believe that our intensity always produces a focus that destroys our perspective. Such a tight little squinting of the eyes gobbles up our peripheral vision. It steals the panorama of what we might have seen if we had laid down some of our busy agenda and looked around a bit.

I believe that is why many earnest Christians trouble me. There is a world of ideas and beautiful art they never see because they lock themselves into a furious "living for Jesus." I grudgingly admit that if you are determined to be one-dimensional, Jesus is the one dimension you should keep. But would a Savior who spent so much time healing other people's blindness be content to let Christians live with no appreciation of the art all around them? Is the God of lavish beauty pleased that we grow old and blind to art? Christianity is wonderful, but there are still the Grand Tetons, St. Petersburg during the white nights of June, the British Museum, Goya, Athens, Gogol, Harper Lee, scones and Cornish crème, Iona at midnight, the Black Wall in Arlington, the roar of Niagara, the villages of Nova Scotia, the rice terraces of Benaue, Oscar Wilde, fireworks over Cinderella's castle, and of course, Jesus. I do not list Jesus last because he is last, but because there exists among the fervent the idea that knowing him completely eradicates the first part of the list. It does not.

William James refused to become a Christian because of Christianity's one-dimensionalism. If you know the truth, the truth will set you free, said Jesus. But James could see that this great truth of Jesus did not set people free. For the most part it incarcerated them in little boxes of fervor, which became their cells of white-hot focus that destroyed the world outside their cell. It was too narrow a focus for James.

I noticed the tendency even in our church, where people would often "come forward" in tears of freedom and joy to "make their decision for Christ." But even during the invitation, a church clerk showed up, shoved a clipboard under their noses, and asked them to fill it out with the info it required. With "Just as I Am" still ringing in their ears, they were met with all the paperwork of the Social Security Administration. No sooner were they finished with the join-the-church paperwork, than they found themselves the targets of various people representing the various programs of the church. These minor lords and ladies were greeting them with invitations and literature to "encourage them" to become members of the men's group *or* the ladies' Bible study *or* the deeper life group *or* the church bowling league *or* the singles fellowship *or* the young married's department, *or* the . . . *or* the . . . *or* the. This odd clerical business of chronicling the work of the Holy Spirit I encapsulated in a little song.

Just as I am without one plea,
I've come to sign form one-oh-three

> That the church clerk just handed me,
> I understand the lunch is free,
> Oh Lamb of God I come.[25]

Oh we professional Christians do keep a narrow cell of wintry efficiency, do we not? And whether or not we like it, many people, like William James, still feel the church does not set us free but locks us into a very narrow dimension where nothing but our religious forms and fervor have any place.

I'll Stop Looking Ahead and Look Around More

I recently talked to a group who had just come back from a missionary trip to Russia. They had gone to liberate Russians who did not know Christ as their Savior. But what amazed me is that they somehow passed through Moscow and never saw Saint Basil's Cathedral or the architectural marvels of the Kremlin. We were perfect strangers when I tried to talk to them about Saint Michael's Cathedral. They couldn't believe that I saw it as anything of importance. I could not believe they passed so close to magnificence and cared so little about it.

Looking around more will be my focus in my final years. I will smell the roses of Versailles and count the scent as sweet as those on the altar of the church. I will bypass a great many Christian novels and go on reading Pulitzer Prize winners just as I have always done. And I will not be so bent on my writing that I have no time to look around. I will not type my manuscripted way into the grave, staying so busy that I cannot take a walk with my wife, work the *New York Times* acrostics, go to a movie, or see a play. And I am hoping that when I at last stand before the Lord, he will not say, "Why did you not lead more people to Christ? Why did you waste your time with *Dr. Zhivago*? A thousand years for you in purgatory, buster, for finding time for Pasternak and not loving the Penteteuch more."

I once did a watercolor for an evangelical friend of mine. When I gave it to him, I didn't want him to rave over the gift, but I always think a simple "thank you" is appropriate. But as he received the gift he said, "Thank you, but oh, my friend, how many people slipped into hell while you painted this picture?"

"I do not know the number," I said.

"Oh the attention we give to trivialities while the lost perish," he lamented.

"Do you want the picture or not?" I asked.

"Well, yes," he said, "but watercolors are so temporary, but hell, hell, hell is eternal."

"Well, hell," I said, "yes, hell."

I never painted him another picture.

I wish my intense friends would just release me from the grip of their neuroses. The intensity is terrible. There is a lot of money on the game of life. So much that it gets real hard to be human when the fever is high.

Pacing might help.

Heaven is the goal, and it is so important that many Christians seem furious to get there as soon as possible. The average Christian has a view of heaven I don't want to develop. I have never been much interested in gates of pearl or golden streets. I, like the best of those who love him, want to go to heaven to complete my union with Christ. I would like to stand with those I have brought

---

to faith in him, so the both of us may enjoy him together. But I think the issue of going to heaven often becomes the white-hot focus of one-dimensional Christians.

Worst of all, the heaven most Christians imagine is pretty terrestrial. It frightens me to think that I could live for eternity on a golden street between two cable evangelists, smug in their knowledge that people like me wasted a lot of time trying to do a decent watercolor or master Shakespeare. My only consolation for this fear is that—if they are right—the Bard himself will doubtless be either in hell for focusing so hard on his plays, or living on my block in a little house next to an evangelical luminary who clearly elected to ignore *Hamlet* while focusing on gospel cruises and tape ministries.

Looking around more means walking in a good direction but with an unhurried step. I would like to begin each day with God and then, coffee cup in hand, go out into the world. I don't want to try and dissect it. I don't want to figure it out. I just want to walk about in it. I also want to celebrate the simple things. In the eighteenth century a Methodist woman of no means wrote,

I do not know when I have had happier times in my soul than when I have been sitting at work with nothing before me but a candle and a white cloth, and hearing no sound but the sound of my own breath, with God in my soul and heaven in my eye. I rejoice in being exactly what I am—a creature capable of loving God and who, as long as God lives, must be happy. I get up and look for a while out the window and gaze at the moon and stars, the work of an almighty hand. I think of the grandeur of the universe, and then sit down, and I think myself one of the happiest beings in it.[26]

I don't know who this woman was, but she obviously looked around and lived a reflective life.

Looking around more, however, does not mean that I want to quit serving the Lord. Vance Havner said of his final years that he wanted God to be the Lord of what's left. So do I, of course. I want to die as I have lived: in his service. I pray that my mind will stay clear enough that I can speak his name from whatever pulpit is offered me. When I have finished my years, I want to say with the apostle Paul: "For I am now ready to be offered, and the time of my departure is at hand. I have fought a good fight, I have finished my course, I have kept the faith: Henceforth there is laid up for me a crown of righteousness, which the Lord, the righteous judge, shall give me at that day: and not to me only, but unto all those also that love his appearing" (2 Tim. 4:6–8 KJV).

I want to see and live for the world that's on the way, but I don't want to hurry those worlds or jam the one against the other. I want my crossing to be easy. I just want to lie down to nap on planet Earth and wake up in heaven. But if the scene should be more violent, I would like my friends behind to know that I still won't be cheated out of the "crossing" experience.

Maybe it will be even as I wrote in *The Singer* so long ago. The music that we long for will not be temporary.

> Like autumn leaves
> My final triumph is set to swirl upward into the sky.

And the song will come on forever.
And I will take possession of the distant real estate
I've always owned.
And I will live among the far pavilions I have always loved,
Where the parent stars themselves were tracked
By wounded feet.
And there standing free in golden light
I'll shake an unfamiliar hand and find it wounded.
And there I'll be reminded
This life I lived was never mine.[27]

Notes

1. Calvin Miller, "Perspective," Poem from *A Covenant for All Seasons* (Wheaton, IL: Harold Shaw Publishers, 1995), xvi.
2. Calvin Miller, "Two Lovers—One Will," Poem from *A Covenant for All Seasons* (Wheaton, IL: Harold Shaw Publishers, 1995), 18.
3. Edmond Rostand, *Cyrano De Bergerac* (London: Heinemann Educational Books LTD, 1953), Act 3, 97.
4. Calvin Miller, "Winter Love," Poem from *A Covenant for All Seasons* (Wheaton, IL: Harold Shaw Publishers, 1995), 52.
5. Calvin Miller, "A Soldier and a Maid," Poem from *A Covenant for All Seasons* (Wheaton, IL: Harold Shaw Publishers, 1995), 114.
6. Calvin Miller, "Two Diamonds Two Decades Apart," Poem from *A Covenant for All Seasons* (Wheaton, IL: Harold Shaw Publishers, 1995), 108.
7. Calvin Miller, *The Singer* (Downers Grove, IL: InterVarsity Press, 1975), 11.
8. Calvin Miller, "Not My Blood," Poem from *A Covenant for All Seasons* (Wheaton, IL: Harold Shaw Publishers, 1995), 124.
9. Calvin Miller, "Tombstone Shopping," Poem from *A Covenant for All Seasons* (Wheaton, IL: Harold Shaw Publishers, 1995), 150.
10. Calvin Miller, "If This Be Love," Poem from *A Covenant for All Seasons* (Wheaton, IL: Harold Shaw Publishers, 1995), viii.
11. Calvin Miller, *A Covenant for All Seasons* (Wheaton, IL: Harold Shaw Publishers, 1995), 161–163.

12. Parker Palmer, *The Courage to Teach* (San Francisco: Jossey Bass, 1998), 17.

13. May Sarton, *Now I Become Myself*, as quoted by Parker Palmer in *The Courage to Teach* (San Francisco: Jossey Bass, 1998), 9.

14. Parker Palmer, *The Courage to Teach* (San Francisco: Jossey Bass, 1998), 57.

15. Parker Palmer, *The Courage to Teach* (San Francisco: Jossey Bass, 1998), 110.

16. Dan Crawford and Calvin Miller, *Prayer Walking* (Chattanooga, TN: AMG Publishers, 2002), 134–135.

17. Robert Service, "The Law of the Yukon," Poem taken from *Collected Poems of Robert Service* (NY: Dodd, Mead & Company, 1907), 10.

18. James Hilton, *Good-bye, Mr. Chips* (NY: Bantam Books, 1934), 7.

19. James Hilton, *Good-bye, Mr. Chips* (NY: Bantam Books, 1934) p. 100.

20. James Rowe, "Love Lifted Me," 1912.

21. Priscilla J. Owens, "We Have and Anchor," 1882.

22. Charles Wesley, "Jesus, Lover of My Soul," 1740.

23. James Hilton, *Good-bye, Mr. Chips* (NY: Bantam Books, 1934), 89–91.

24. James Hilton, *Good-bye, Mr. Chips* (NY: Bantam Books, 1934), 113–114.

25. Calvin Miller, *Spirit, Word, and Story* (Dallas: Word Publishing, 1989), 189.

26. Eighteenth Century Woman, quoted by Mary Tileston in *Daily Strength of Daily Needs* (Springdale, PA: Whitaker House, 1997), 21.

27. Calvin Miller, *The Singer* (Downers Grove, IL: InterVarsity Press, 1975), 151.

About the Author

Dr. Calvin Miller recently retired as Professor of Preaching and Pastoral Studies at Samford University, Beeson Divinity School, in Birmingham, Alabama. The author of more than forty books of popular theology and inspiration, his work has appeared in various journals and magazines such as *Christianity Today, Campus Life, Leadership,* and *His,* and his book *Preaching: The Art of Narrative Exposition* was chosen 2007 Book of the Year by *Preaching* magazine. He and his wife, Barbara, live in Trussville, Alabama.